Who Will Make the Pies When I'm Gone?

Who Will Make the Pies When I'm Gone?

———•———

LIVING THE DARK SIDE OF CANCER
(NO SUGAR ADDED)

Jamie C. Schneider

iUniverse, Inc.
Bloomington

DEDICATION

For all those who have had to walk through life in a plane slightly parallel to the rest of the world, be it through cancer or some other devastating life course.

What people you've never heard of have to say about this book:

Terry Huston, who has had cancer since 2007:
"I can relate to many of the things you went through and are going through. I also get mad when nobody ever says, 'it must suck to be you' or 'why did you get this?' I guess I appreciate their good wishes, but I hate hearing 'You look great' when I feel like shit!"

Marilyn Davidson, whose mother and sister died of cancer:
"My sister always said, 'I just want my life back.' Your words helped me to get it. I keep waiting for the white knight to gallop in with the cure. Even though there is no white knight, there is a heroine, and she is you! Your story will make many laugh and cry, and it will remind us of our own mortality. Your words will inspire us not to take so much for granted."

Darlene Tolman, a friend:
"I am so appreciative of being able to observe your experience so close up. If I ever have to go through something like this, I will have your experience to give me perspective. Hopefully it can help me to understand others with similar experiences as well. It is a rare thing to get such a close look at someone else's journey."

Donna Belles, whose mother died of cancer:
"I was worried about the 'dark' part of the sub-title. I was afraid to get down in the trenches with you; that it might be too dark. But that wasn't the case; there are different shades of 'dark.' I found that the dark parts weren't black but were an integral part of the book, interspersed with humor, fond memories, and insight. It all worked together. The only thing my mother ever shared with me when she had cancer was how much it bothered her to see pity in other people's eyes. Reading this helped me understand what she went through. I wish she had shared more with me."

Mary Ronge, a friend:
"You have given us permission to cry, permission to acknowledge the severity of your health, and maybe to finally allow the frailty of life to sink in."

Michelle Daugherty, whose mother died of cancer:
"I can relate to the highs and lows and the hope, but I never truly understood how it feels. I wish I had read this before caring for my mother and father. My mother was sixty when she was diagnosed with breast cancer and then colon cancer."

Contents

When there is no turning back, we should concern ourselves only with the best way of going forward.
—Paulo Coelho, *Life: Selected Quotations*

Introduction

THE LIVING DEATH

I find that having cancer has put me in a strange place. Maybe it's the fact that it is stage IV ovarian cancer, which means that I'm definitely not in Kansas anymore. And, sadly, it ain't the other side of the rainbow either. From the moment I found out about the cancer, I have been separated somehow from the rest of the world. I'm not really part of the living anymore, but I'm not quite dead yet.

This kind of thinking may sound rather morose, but it is a fact. I remember what it was like in that other world. I used to live there, and not so very long ago. It is the place where we hurriedly go about our daily business. We're a lot like the little field mouse; we generally are only aware of what is right in front of our nose. We don't really have to think about anything but what we're dealing with at any particular moment, because there is always tomorrow—or the next day, or the next week—to think about the rest.

I can't do that anymore. Each and every thing I do has to be thought of in a new way. Every time I do something, I am aware that it could be the last time I do it. On the way to my sister Therese's house for Easter about two months after the news, I looked out the window as my husband was driving. I hoped he wouldn't see my tears, but generally, there's no hiding from him. As he reached over and covered my hand with his, Bill asked, "What's wrong, Jamie?"

"I was just thinking, this could be the last Easter I get to see … get to spend with my family. It could be the last time I get to see the spring flowers." I watched as the forsythias, in full bloom, sped by. They were in their glory this year—sprays of deep golden splendor, glowing in the sun. They came in all shapes and sizes. Some had been carefully cut into little circles or neat little boxes. Others, my favorites, had been left to their own devices and stood in huge clumps that rose fifteen to twenty feet into the air, each sprig stylishly weeping over at the top. Still others, left a little too long on their own, or to the harshness of life, had huge sections of dieback, only broken up here and there with a touch of yellow. It was just enough to provide a reminder of what they had looked like in their heyday. Maybe I was the most like that last bunch. My body had areas of dieback—areas as good as dead. Surely nothing good could grow in *those* spots. Maybe, though, I had enough sparks of life left in me to remind those around me of the days of my glory. Maybe when they looked at me, trying to find some visible sign of my cancer, trying to see just *how* I had changed, they would still see enough of the old me somewhere in there to make them smile.

"Tsk!" He didn't say any more, but he shook his head, and I saw the tears rolling down his cheeks.

"I'm sorry," I said. "I can't help it; it's just what I think. I'm sorry." I hadn't even thought, when I made the comment, how it would affect him. He's the one who really has the hard part. I'm not afraid of dying. By the same token, I really wasn't quite ready for it yet. Still, once I'm dead, it's over for me. He is the one who has to go on alone, or at least without me. He is the one who will have to think about all the things we had planned to do when we "got old"—things that will now never happen. I think about it now, but he'll have a lot longer to think about it than I will. *I'll have to be more thoughtful about what I say,* I tell myself.

No, nothing can be done without that grim reminder that my days are numbered. As I walk through this strange, shadowy world, somewhere between being alive and being dead, I am nothing but envious of those who are still alive. I wonder how long I can go on like this. I think back to people I have known who have had cancer. I remember seeing them a week or so before they died—at the pool for water workout, or at the little league field, where we sat and tried to act excited as our little boys dragged out a six-inning game for hours. Had I not known they had cancer, I would not have been able to tell. Yes, I did it too. I looked at them when they weren't looking. I wanted to see what cancer looked like on them. But I couldn't tell. Now I know why. I was looking in the wrong place. It was their soul that had changed. They had been doing what I am only now learning to do—pretend.

People like it better if you look just like them. They like it if you seem okay. They beg you to say you are okay, because they don't know what to do if you're not. I was at a Christmas party ten months after my diagnosis, and a friend of mine was there who had recently lost her dear, longtime friend to cancer. The deceased friend's struggle with cancer had been fairly brief. As in a lot of cases, and like mine, her friend hadn't found out about it until it had progressed to the fourth stage. My friend had been drinking, and I'm sure her words and actions were heavily fueled by alcohol.

"You're still alive, and my friend is dead. You have to be happy that you're at least still alive," she said, slurring her words, on the verge of tears and incoherence.

"Well, I *am* glad I'm still alive, so far. But, you know, it's really hard to accept and adjust to life like this. I feel crappy all the time. I can't do any of the things I used to do." I knew she was drunk, but still I resisted her desperate urges to make me be grateful. It was useless, I knew. Because of her intoxicated state, this wasn't a real conversation. I knew that, but I still wouldn't let her force me to say the words she longed to hear.

She went on, becoming more desperate. "I want to hear you say it. Say you're happy that you're alive! My friend is dead, and here you are. Please say it."

Others in the room were starting to tune in to our conversation, and it was becoming more uncomfortable. I just wanted to get away from her. The hostess of the party stopped and tuned in long enough to hear what was going on. "I can understand how you feel," she said to me. "I don't think I would want to say it either."

I moved away from the small group of women, all of whom were drinking but me. I had, for the most part, given up alcohol. When you know your liver is damaged, it makes you reluctant to cause it any more stress than absolutely necessary. Occasions like this party reinforced that my decision was a good one, for more reasons than one.

My friend followed me, not ready to give up on her quest to make me admit I was grateful to be alive. My own desperation to be understood possibly equaled her desperate, inebriated state, and we remained at a standoff. She continued to beg me to be grateful, and I continued to resist saying the words she so badly wanted to hear. I knew she was pained at the loss of her friend, but I was feeling my own pain right then, and I let that take precedence. My husband came to my rescue. "Ready to go, Jame?" Over the past several years, certain family members, and a small group of friends, had taken to calling me "Jame"—pronounced like James without the *s*. Bill and I quickly wished everyone happy holidays and made our exit. I was no sooner out the door that the tears started. It was situations exactly like this one that made me reluctant to go out in social situations. I never had been any good at pretending, and now all I could see in my future were situations where I would have to pretend to be okay and happy, regardless of how I felt.

Generally, though, because I can't stand that uncomfortable feeling either, I go along with people. I read the signs in their eyes and their words, and I acquiesce. It's easier for everyone. But when I'm alone, or when I find that rare soul who really wants to know what it's like or how I'm doing, I am suddenly pulled from the depths of despair. Just when I thought I was running out of breath, someone has rescued me. And the freedom is indescribable. They don't cringe if I tell them that I feel crappy. They don't fling a platitude at me ("You've got to stay positive!" or "Hang in there!") and hurry on their way. They ask me questions because they want to understand what it feels like. They don't tell me how I should feel, act, or think. They might be afraid, or uncomfortable, but they do it anyway. These people have such courage; they're willing to get in there with me, walk around with me for a little while, and see where I really am. And they watch for signs—signs of little things they might be able to do for me. *For me!* These are things that will mean something to me, not things that will make them feel better. This usually means that in the end, we both feel better.

Don't get me wrong. I've been that person. I understand that helpless feeling. And I don't hold it against people. But there has to be a better way. I have read several cancer books. And most of them are in the literary category of "inspirational." They are all about staying positive—not really a bad thing, but it's just not enough. Maybe it's time we broke the silence. Maybe we can't all be good little cancer patients who smile politely and say our prayers of gratitude every morning. "Sure is good to be alive! Thanks, God." Maybe it's time we talked about the dark side of cancer.

I'm just an ordinary sixty-year-old woman—nothing special about me. I have a good life; I love my husband and my children more than anything. My world begins and ends with them. I love my home. I love life. I have been fortunate enough to do most of what I have wanted to do in life. No, I never jumped from a plane, never climbed Mt. Everest, never went deep-sea diving. Like I said, I'm ordinary. But I did spend twenty years as a therapist in a drug and alcohol treatment facility, and in that time, I had the honor of touching many lives; I hope I contributed to the clients' opportunities to find something better. And while I was helping them to examine their own selves and their lives, I took advantage of the opportunity to do the same thing for myself. Our consultant used to say to us, "Never ask a client to do something you're not willing to do yourself." I took that to heart.

I learned to line dance. I love gardening, and seeing new growth every spring is one of the most spectacular things I have had the joy of witnessing—year after year. I still want to start a book club; I hope I'm around long enough to do that. Watching my boys grow into men and become wonderful additions to the world around them has been a privilege. Spending day in and day out with a man who loves me, and whom I love, has settled me into a good, secure, wonderful, and adventurous place in this world.

The idea that this could all change in a heartbeat is not something you get used to overnight, or even in a week, a month—or maybe ever. This kind of living on the edge is not exciting. I must be reading a book about someone else's life. This can't be the way it all ends. I always thought I'd just plain wear out. Most of us hope to die peacefully, in our sleep. But when you have multiple daily reminders that you will likely be dead soon, you have lots of opportunities to think about what that will be like and what it might be like afterward. You realize that along with your very existence, your death will most likely cause only the tiniest, if any, ripple in the overall scheme of things. And that ripple will be gone before it comes close to reaching the edge of the pond. I have never cared for being in the limelight; I have preferred to spend my time more in the background. If I make any ripple at all, I want it to be one that leaves things a little better than they were before I was here. Since I found out I have cancer, my life as I knew it has been over. One of the most difficult things has been figuring out what the point of this new limited version of life is. Now I think it is writing this book. By writing about the dark side of cancer with complete candor, maybe I can make things a bit better for someone else who has to walk this same shadowy world.

Chapter One

THE BUILDING OF OMENS

I don't really believe in omens, unless you consider an omen to be the extra thought sometimes given after the fact to events that had no special significance at the time they occurred. Of course, when I look back, I can see that surely I should have caught on to the idea that something big was brewing. I have always been a detail person. "Life is in the details"—my kids have heard me say that many times. It's not like I ignored the details. I commented on some of them. I told my doctor about some of them. I went to the quick clinic about some of them. I just never expected them to add up to cancer. I guess people usually don't.

One of the amazing things about many cancers is that you generally don't know you have it until it has progressed to the point that it is hard to treat. Unless there is a specific test for it, when cancer is caught early, it is usually found accidentally.

I am unlike most of my family. I actually believe in modern medical science. I know doctors are not God and they make mistakes. Many of them have lousy communications skills and horrendous bedside manners, but the important thing is that they know what they are doing. I have always believed that, surely, after all those years in school and residencies, for the most part, doctors had a pretty good handle on the human body and what might go wrong with it. So I began many years ago going for routine checkups. I had my yearly female exam, and I always believed I was okay. Once, sometime in 1974, after my annual PAP smear, I was told I had abnormal cells. There was really nothing to be done, I was told. It was just something to keep an eye on. People who had these abnormal cells were more likely to end up with cancer later on. At the time, I was devastated. But as the years went by and all my tests came back normal, that little scare became a faded memory.

In September 2009, I had my yearly gynie exam, and in December I had my boobs squished. All okay! I was good to go for another year! I barely batted an eye. I was so used to hearing this that it barely caused the tiniest of ripples in the pond of my life. It was what I expected to hear—what I already knew I would hear.

When I was told five months later that I had stage IV ovarian cancer, my first comment was, "I don't understand. I just had my exam five months ago, and everything was fine. How could this happen in such a short time?"

"Well, it's a very aggressive cancer. It can grow very rapidly."

You'll never convince me it grew that rapidly. What you mean to say is that nobody found any evidence of it earlier. Maybe the gynecologist who did my exam really didn't notice that my ovaries were so big. After all, how many ovaries does he press on in a day? Don't they all start to feel pretty close to the same after a while? For sure, he couldn't remember what *my* ovaries were like when he pressed on them the *previous* year to have a basis of comparison. Or maybe he was just "in the zone" that day, and unless they were as big as cantaloupes, he would not have noticed. Or maybe under all that extra padding I have, it was virtually impossible to feel my ovaries, regardless of their size. Whatever the case may be, in the end, he declared me in fine shape for another year.

Everything they say about ovarian cancer is true. The symptoms, which I only began to notice in the last four months before I was diagnosed, can all easily be explained with other, much more benign, answers. And then, in my case, I was doing a "liver cleanse" up to within a couple weeks of my diagnosis, so that really masked the symptoms. Still, I look back on that time in wonder, amazed that I could have been that sick and not even known it. How could I have been that close to death and not have heard her breathing down my neck? How could I not have noticed that dark shadow following me around everywhere I went?

Cancer is insidious. It is a thing of wonder, really. Cells gone wild. You could think of them as juvenile delinquents, or eccentric old women who refuse to be bound by the same societal norms as most of us. They go where they want, not being the least bit concerned about whether or not they are violating the boundaries of another. They do what they want and take what they need to get by from those around them, and they don't worry about any devastation they might leave in their wake. The price for the life of those cells is high, generally costing the host his or her life. Yes, cells gone wild.

The Crow

In January 2009, my husband and I had a special vacation planned. I had never been to California, and here was my chance to go, at a very low cost. Bill belonged to a group called Insurance Agents and Brokers. Each year, they had a convention in some nice place, and spouses were invited to attend at a nominal fee. In addition, our son and his girlfriend were living in Colorado while our son attended graduate school at the University of Denver and his girlfriend taught elementary school. So we concocted a plan that would combine the convention with a visit with our son, Patrick, and his girlfriend, Carrie. We would drive to Colorado, fly to California and back to Colorado, and then Bill would fly home and I would stay and visit the kids for a few weeks longer. Never afraid of traveling alone, I would then drive home from Colorado by myself. For the occasion, we purchased a GPS device. I was confident that I could get from Colorado back to our home in Kittanning, Pennsylvania, without any major problems.

The time in California was wonderfully relaxing, but the four days flew by. After a few days back in Colorado, I felt the need for an adventure. I looked at the map and decided that Arches National Park was just what I was looking for. It appeared to be just over the state line into Utah. My family always got scared when I looked at a map, because they knew that for me, it was like reading a foreign language. But I had my trusty new GPS device, so I wasn't afraid of getting lost. Still, it took me the better part of the day to get there. Driving through the Rocky Mountains helps you get a realistic perspective on just how insignificant you are. I had to stop a few times along the way just to soak up the spirit that lives in those magnificent formations. When I arrived in Utah, it was near closing time in the park. I decided I needed to spend the night so I would have an entire day to see this wonder of nature at a leisurely pace.

As a couple, and then as a family, our favorite vacations were to the national parks. Working sixty to eighty hours a week on a regular basis can be very exhausting, and I always found the visits to the national parks a good way to rejuvenate. Just being there gave me a chance to step back, and I could feel my soul coming back to life. As I settled into my motel room for the night, I was already envisioning the sights of Arches National Park, and I was feeling the energy of this magical place. I got up early the next day, and after spending an hour in a wonderful gift shop in Moab, Utah (where I purchased some jewelry, an authentic Navajo vase, and two new lamps for our living room), I headed for the park.

It was mid-January, but the temperature was in the high fifties and the sky was the kind of deep blue that by itself gives you an inner peace you rarely experience in the business of your day-to-day life. As I slowly meandered my way through the park, I got out for a deeper exploration several times. The place was something out of a fairy tale, with its world-famous natural arches of many shapes and sizes spanning across the landscape. The deep reddish-orange color of the rocks, lying in jumbled piles or crafted by nature into all sorts of odd shapes and configurations, seemed to have absorbed centuries of calmness, and I could feel the ancient spirits coming to life within me. But even with all that, or maybe in combination with it, the most stunning part of my visit was the silence and the stillness. The air was still, and there were no extraneous sounds: No droning of insects you might hear in the summertime. No steady purr of automobiles snaking their way around the park. No tourist noises. No people talking. No cell phones. There was just the quiet and beauty of nature in surround sound.

The first time I heard the noise, my reaction was to look for someone with a computer. Of course, nobody was there but me. In fact, in the six hours I was there, I saw perhaps a handful of cars drive through. So what was that noise, and where had it come from? My best description is a fairly high-pitched musical/electronic sound. It was quite unlike anything I could put my finger on. Finding no likely source, I continued on my hike. As I moved through the park, I heard the noise three more times. The last time, I was determined to find the source. I stood in the utter and complete silence, when I saw a crow fly from a distance ahead and land in a pine tree directly in front of me. He sat at the top, in a section of dieback, so I had a good view of him. I watched as he tilted his head up, exposing his neck, and I observed the gurgling motion of his throat muscles moving in conjunction with that same melodious sound I had heard earlier.

"Well, you're a particularly dense one," he seemed to be saying to me, "so I guess I have to get right on top of you for you to get the message."

I looked up at him, silhouetted against that deep, sea-blue sky, and just stared. The silence surrounding us echoed into my soul, and I couldn't take my eyes off of him.

Later, after I found out I had cancer, I became interested in power animals. I was looking for help from any direction. I knew this was not a battle I could fight on my own. I learned that "although few think of the crow as a songbird, there have been [unsubstantiated] claims over the years that when it is alone, it will sing in a soft musical voice." How was I privileged enough to have that experience?

It was only in the upcoming months that I realized what his message for me was. I read several books about power animals, trying to determine what my own personal power animal was, and then to be aware of him and make accurate interpretations of his message. *Animal Speak* by Ted Andrews was my favorite. Through my research, I decided that either the crow or raven was my primary power animal; and in looking back, I interpreted the message that crow sent to me while I was in Arches National Park to be "Things are not always what they seem to be." Yes, this is after the fact, but it is no less poignant. With the benefit of hindsight, I had a sense of panic as I replayed that last year, with all the symptoms I had experienced. Had I understood the message earlier, would it have made a difference? Was it too late? Time would tell the tale.

Zeus Could Smell It

On a typical afternoon, on any given day in late spring, or through the summer and fall, I would be out and about for a variety of reasons. I might be shopping for baking supplies, spending the afternoon picking berries, visiting a friend, or stopping at the local greenhouse to replace flowers that didn't make it through the transplant phase. I was a woman on the go, and if I wasn't home baking, I was out on an errand.

I retired in 1997, after twenty years of being a therapist in the drug and alcohol field, and my goal was to do less in more time. I wanted to slow down. My normal work week probably had averaged at least sixty hours, and that didn't include my time being on call for emergencies. I had had enough of that life. I wanted to take things slower, to have some time to relax, to enjoy life. When I started selling baked goods at the Kittanning Farmers Market, I thought that since I would only be doing that twice a week, I would be able to enjoy a more leisurely lifestyle. It didn't work that way. Although it was not evenly dispersed, I was still working fifty to sixty hours a week. I guess it was just not my nature to have a leisurely lifestyle.

When I returned home after being gone for a couple hours, my dog was there to greet me as usual. Zeus was a Bernese mountain dog. He lived up to his name in every way; he was the king, and he knew it. Although he only weighed 109 pounds, most people thought he weighed at least 150 pounds, which gave him a commanding presence. With his thick, wavy black fur, punctuated by the white and golden brown outlining his face and the bottom of his legs, he made people take notice when they drove by. I always said he listened about 80 percent of the time, which was better than most kids, so I was happy with that. We had enjoyed eight years of his company.

When he was a puppy, we had an electric fence installed both for his protection and for our peace of mind. He went through the training program like a pro and respected the boundaries laid out for him. He literally could not be dragged outside the line. I was able to leave him outside when I left the house and be completely confident that he would not leave the yard. So, as soon as I pulled in, he would lope from his spot under the front porch, or from the little hole he had dug in the gravel along the retaining wall, and let me know how happy he was to see me.

There was one small difference that summer before I found out I had cancer. He would follow me the whole way up the sidewalk and through the front door, sniffing all the way. He just couldn't seem to stop smelling me. I would walk down the hallway to the computer room and sit at the desk to check my messages, and he would still be sniffing at me. Finally, I would yell at him: "Stop smelling me!" At this, he would turn and leave the room.

After this occurred a few times, I started to feel creepy about it. I commented to Michele, one of my sisters, "Zeus won't stop smelling me when I come home. I must have some bad disease." I said the same thing to some of my friends. We would laugh about it, but it wasn't completely humorous to me. I was left with a feeling of unease, which I tried to dismiss as being silly. Still, I had heard stories of dogs that were able to sniff out diseases in their owners. What would I do, go to my doctor and tell him about the sniffing? What would he check me for?

In November 2010, Zeus died of cancer. For months after, I would look for him to greet me when I pulled in the driveway, only to remember that he was gone. In the time before he died, I wondered which of us would lose the battle first, and at times, I couldn't bear to look him in the eyes. During his last couple months of life, though, I watched him closely, wondering how much my journey would parallel his when I got that close to the end. I thought about how nice it would be for somebody who loved me to be able to look at me and know it was time, and take me to the clinic for a peaceful exit. Unfortunately, it doesn't work that way for people. I was jealous of him.

HERNIATED DISCS

In the summer of 2009, the last summer before I found out I had ovarian cancer, the physical intensity of performing tasks related to baking finally became too much for me. After eleven years of selling baked goods at the Kittanning Farmers Market, I was forced to slow down when I found out I had two herniated thoracic discs. Whether I was picking berries for four to six hours in the hot sun or standing over my table, kneading dough or rolling out pie crusts, I spent an inordinate amount of time with my head slightly bent and my shoulders curved forward.

Most people don't realize what it takes to be a vendor at a farmers market. Since it's only two days a week, it doesn't really seem like that much work. My product was baked goods. The Saturday sales were usually double the midweek sales, and that meant more baking. I would generally start in the kitchen around 6:30 a.m. on Friday, and in the beginning, I would bake until I got a quick shower and headed up to the market on Saturday morning—around 8:30 a.m.

I took pride in always having fresh baked goods, and my sales showed it. That's why everything had to be made the day before. In my heyday, I would arrive at the Market with thirty-two dozen cinnamon rolls, eight to ten fruit pies, one to two dozen loaves of different breads, coffee cakes, zucchini and banana breads, pumpkin rolls, and other items in season. On the off days, I would make jams and jellies from fresh fruits and berries that were picked by my husband, my friend Betty, and me. Patrick and his girlfriend Carrie always picked the strawberries, since strawberry jam was his favorite. When he was in college, as a joke, I made him a two-quart jar of strawberry jam for Christmas. I think it took him about two months to finish it off.

My only helper with my baking was my husband. After a long day at work, he was always willing to pitch in when he got home, doing what he called "grunt work." This included doing things like washing my baking pans, cleaning up the kitchen, peeling peaches or apples, bringing up supplies from the basement, and going to the store for those items I had unexpectedly run out of (or forgotten to buy in the first place!).

The cycle of baking, picking berries, and making jams and jellies was physically grueling. I had gradually begun to cut back on my baking time and allow for at least a few hours of rest between baking and going to market. This was hard to do; since I had less baked goods, I ended up feeling like I was letting my customers down. So I developed a plan to run in-home baking classes. I was excited. I always felt passionate about teaching. No, I had never formally taught, but the idea of helping people learn things that they really wanted to be able to do was exciting. If I couldn't bake it myself, I would teach others to do it for themselves! I would have the best of both worlds—baking and teaching.

In the spring of 2009, during the time I was seeing my doctor for knee problems, I developed a strange pain above my right breast. At first I noticed it only when I went to bed and was in a supine position. It grew in intensity, and I had more and more difficulty finding a comfortable position to lie in, and therefore more and more difficulty getting to sleep. When I mentioned it to my doctor, he poked me a couple times and then said, "I wouldn't worry about it."

Dismayed, I said, "But I can't sleep!"

"Oh, well, then we better check it out." His response was half-hearted. He sent me for a chest X-ray, which showed nothing abnormal. I knew I had to do something; or rather, I knew he needed to do more. The question was how to get him motivated. I had worked hard to develop a relationship with this doctor. Most of my visits with him were fairly routine, so he never had to think outside the box. Now, though, was the time when I needed him to do just that. He was ready to dismiss my complaints, since his first, rather generic, response showed that I didn't really have anything wrong with me. Once again, I would take the responsibility for the problem.

"I'm sorry," I whined, both out of my own desperation and as a way to placate him. "I'm not very good at describing what is going on. I'm trying to think of a good way to help you understand what I'm experiencing." I was pretty sure that as long as he didn't feel challenged, he would be more responsive. Now that I had acknowledged that the fault here was mine, we could proceed. I thought that if I could at least get him to actually listen to what I had to say, maybe I could get him to tap into that unused part of his brain that surely had been active when he decided he wanted to be a doctor. I hadn't studied him for ten years for nothing!

"No, that's okay." I seemed to have his attention now. "Do you think it's your gall bladder?" Was he seriously asking me to draw a conclusion like that? Based on what? How would I know? Still, he was engaged!

"I don't think so," I replied, drawing upon my vast store of medical knowledge. "I don't notice anything changing when I eat, or eat different things. It seems to be more positional."

"Well, there is something going on. What about your back? Do you feel anything there?"

"Truthfully, it's hard to tell. It seems to go from the front to the back, but it's all inside, and I can't really tell where it starts sometimes."

"Maybe we better get a scan." Yes! I had his attention now! We were finally getting somewhere.

The scan revealed two herniated thoracic discs. Ever the consummate investigator, I did my research. I learned that herniation of thoracic discs was very uncommon and that when they were found, they were usually found incidentally. In addition, they rarely caused pain. Rare or not, I was in pain. I had to return three days early from a visit to Washington, DC, because the pain was involving the bottom of my rib cage on the right side. I would later find out this was the same place I had cancer nodules, involving my liver.

I met with an orthopedic surgeon. He educated me about the rarity of surgery being done on herniated thoracic discs. Since the surgery was extremely risky because it was so close to the lungs, it was only done when patients lost control of their bowels and had severe sciatic pain, leaving them unable to walk. Options I had were steroid injections into the herniated area, and physical therapy. There was a limit of three injections annually. Within three months, I had had two injections, and the relief had only lasted for about two weeks for each one. This option did not seem like it was going to help me much. I experienced a small amount of relief from the physical therapy.

In an effort to do everything I could for my back problems, I enrolled in a clinic. This move was one of desperation. I had heard an advertisement about a clinic that offered an innovative approach to chronic pain issues. What did I have to lose? Only about $10,000! With this investment, I became educated about how people in desperation spend their life savings on cures that the average person can easily see are bogus. Of course this wasn't my life savings, but it was still a sizable investment. If a friend had told me he or she were doing something like this, I would immediately have begun thinking about how desperate he or she must feel, to be so gullible. I couldn't see that in myself; I was too desperate.

This clinic had several alternative approaches to helping people. Although the body of the program consisted of chiropractic maneuvers, there were several other atypical treatments. I used to tease the girls who soaked my feet in the ionic solution that was supposed to detox my whole body. I told them it looked an awful lot like the drops I was taking to cleanse my liver. I told them I knew they had a secret little room where they funneled the results of the foot detox into little bottles and then turned around and sold it as a liver cleanse. Sadly, I was only half joking. Still, what did I know? Often, new and effective ideas are scoffed at by the experts of the time. Perhaps there really was something to the things they were doing. I would follow instructions. I would do as I was told. Nobody could say I didn't give it my best. In spite of experiencing very little relief, I stuck with the program.

UTI

In the beginning of November, I was sure I had a urinary tract infection. In between my treatments at the clinic, I decided to run to the Take Care Clinic at the local Walgreens. Surely, this would only take a few minutes. They would check my urine, give me the results, and I would be back at the clinic in time for my next treatment.

Things never seem to go as you expect them to, especially if you're pressed for time. After waiting an hour (I had already called the clinic to say I would not be back in time for my next treatment), I was finally escorted to the exam room. The physician's assistant, in between coughing fits, did a very thorough exam. Initially I was impressed with the time she took to get the details. After the first half hour, I became impatient.

Jesus Christ! I came here to get a quickie check of my urine, not a full-fledged physical exam! Of course, I kept this to myself and reluctantly continued to answer her questions. I explained about the relatively mild pain I was having in my lower right quadrant, which seemed to move to the left with bowel movements. Nobody had ever asked enough questions to get far enough to reveal this information before. And it didn't seem that important. I was just recently beginning to notice it, but I was sure it was related to the UTI. Finally, she did the dipstick test.

"Well, nothing is showing up here, but that doesn't mean there is nothing going on. I'll send this sample in, and they will run a more thorough test. Someone will call you within two days with the results. We usually give a script for UTIs right away, but with your other symptoms, I don't want to do that. I want you to see your PCP right away about this."

By the time I saw my PCP, the results had come back, and they showed I did indeed have a urinary tract infection. *So much for the "quick clinic,"* I thought. I dreaded going back to my PCP. I already knew what he would do. He would say it was no big deal, and for once, I might agree with him. Eleven years earlier, I had undergone surgery for a prolapsed bladder and a prolapsed rectum. I had experienced relief for several months following but then had reverted back to the same issues with bladder incontinence. I had tried a couple of the newer medications for urinary incontinence with no relief, so I thought maybe it was time to visit the urologist again to see if there was anything more she could do. I called right away. Unfortunately, I was unable to get an appointment until February 18, 2010. Oh well, I had waited all these years; a few more months would not really hurt anything—or so I thought.

I was able to get an appointment with my PCP within four days. Things went as I had expected. He looked at the report given to me by the PA at Walgreens, and said, "This sample is contaminated. That's all. We'll just run it again. You know PAs; what can you expect." I explained that I had scheduled an appointment with the urologist. I left with a prescription for an antibiotic. I never understood why, when you tell a doctor you think you have a UTI, you are given an antibiotic before you even have any test results. Apparently this is standard protocol. At any rate, a couple days later, I received the call from the nurse in his office, telling me there was no UTI, so there was no need to finish the antibiotic. I stashed it in the back of my drawer.

About a year after I found out about my cancer, I stopped at that Walgreens clinic, and the same PA was working. I wanted to thank her for being so thorough with me, and told her my story. She was astounded at the turn of events, and appreciative that I had thought enough of her to stop and talk with her. I thought she deserved to know, and I wanted her to keep doing what she had done with me. Perhaps although she might annoy others, she might save their lives. She hadn't let years of practice dull her sense of responsibility, and she still did a thorough examination. And she hadn't let the word *quick* drive her behavior or change her attitude. Good for her.

The Cleanse

As I finished up my treatments for my back at the clinic, the chiropractor reviewed the results of the urine test that showed I still had heavy metals in my body. This was a test that was not sanctioned by modern medical science, so I was a little leery about it. My liver was not processing things as it should, he said, and he recommended I do a liver cleanse. (Of course, having cancer in your liver would also make it not process things as it should, but I didn't know I had cancer at this time.) Once again, as soon as I got home, I perused the Internet for information about liver cleansing. It sure sounded like a nasty business to me. At my next appointment, I expressed my concern about the liver cleanse.

"Oh, no, this is not that kind of cleanse. I've done it myself, and I really like it. It has no impact on your bowel movements. It's not like a colon cleanse, where you have to run to the bathroom all the time." He proceeded to explain to me how this particular cleanse he was recommending actually worked. It consisted of two protein shakes and one full meal a day, along with daily drinking of a supplemental beverage. One day a week, I was to eat nothing and drink an additional supplemental beverage. It was beginning to sound an awful lot like diets I had seen advertised on TV.

Still, I needed to lose weight anyway. I had continued in my path of total commitment to this program. It was important to me that I would know that I had given the program 100 percent. My husband and I had been planning a post-holiday trip to Florida. The first part was a convention hosted by the Independent Insurance Agents and Brokers of America, for which he was the director for the state of Pennsylvania. We would drive down together, attend the convention, and then drive back up to Fort Lauderdale, where we would stay with my brother and his wife. At the end of the week, my husband would fly back home, and I would continue with an extended visit. It was at this time that I would start my liver cleanse

The first day of the cleanse, I was prepared. As I poured the called-for portion of the supplemental drink, I knew I was in trouble. I could barely stand the smell, gagging as I looked at the four ounces of something that was surely akin to toxic waste. Still, I forced it down and set about making my protein shake, adding a piece of fresh fruit to make it more palatable. I soon learned that it would take a lot more than a piece of fresh fruit to accomplish that! But I persevered, telling myself I could do anything for four weeks.

My perspective had always been that you go to Florida for sunshine. Even though it had been an unseasonably cold spring for the Sunshine State, I dragged my chair to the beach most days. I found a relatively isolated spot in the sun, and while I relaxed, I read books and just spent time contemplating. For whatever reason, one day my thoughts drifted to my family, and I found myself wondering which of my eight siblings and I would be the first to die. We had all been relatively lucky in the health department, with nobody experiencing any devastating health concerns. Our father had died at the age of forty-two of colon cancer, but our mother, most of our grandparents, and most of our aunts and uncles had lived good, long lives. Our ages ranged from forty-five to sixty-two, I being fifty-eight. There was no easy pick. Nobody had any kind of health issue that seemed likely to end in an early death. We all had a tendency toward severe arthritis, and several of us had high blood pressure. But aside from the aches and pains associated with arthritis, and a tendency toward being overweight, it looked like nobody was going to be leaving anytime soon.

I used to joke about how I imagined that I would be just like my mother. I'd end up an old lady, with one of those broken-down Polish bodies that nothing worked right on anymore but just wouldn't quit. It seemed to be the way things went in my mother's family. In that case, I sure wasn't going to be the first to go. Well, it seemed like there was still plenty of time to think about this, so I drifted off to sleep, luxuriating in the warmth of the Florida sunshine. I didn't realize that this would be the last time I luxuriated in the sunshine anywhere.

Within the first three days of the cleanse, I had lost six pounds, and I was encouraged that I would at least have some success in that aspect of the experience. By the end of the first week, however, I was beginning to notice that I was having trouble finishing that single meal each day. I told myself that my stomach was shrinking and that that was a good thing, as I always ate too much anyway. At five feet, six inches, and 210 pounds, I was no Slim Jim. On one of my shopping trips, I noticed myself feeling a little shaky as I tripped up onto the sidewalk. Still, all these "little" things could easily be attributed to my cleansing project, so I wasn't worried. I didn't know that bloating after eating was one of the most telling symptoms of ovarian cancer. My anxiety was turned up a few notches when I had to make a trip to the local emergency room. That morning in the shower, I noticed what seemed to be something hanging out of my rectum. After multiple phone calls to decide the appropriate course of action, I finally went to the ER.

"Is this what you're talking about?" the doctor in the emergency room asked me as he felt the slight bulge at the base of my rectum. As I lay on my side in a lovely blue hospital gown, I was, of course, embarrassed that I needed to have *that* area of my body looked at so closely. In the upcoming months, this would be small potatoes compared to the frequent poking, prodding, feeling, pressing, and general abuse of even more private parts of my body.

"I think so," I replied hesitantly.

"Well," he stated pleasantly and reassuringly, "you have a pretty good size hemorrhoid there."

He recommended I see a colorectal surgeon, and since I had just been to the ER, I was able to get an appointment within two days. I knew that if I waited until I returned home, it would take a lot longer for me to get an appointment, so I decided to go. Unfortunately, I left that appointment feeling even more confused. This doctor, I decided, was in the right profession—an asshole looking at assholes! After his exam, he relayed his diagnosis that I had a fissure.

"What about the hemorrhoid that the ER doctor told me about?" I asked him.

"I don't know about any hemorrhoid, but you do have a fissure."

To myself, I said, *What do you mean you don't know about any hemorrhoid? You just looked up my ass; did you see one or didn't you?* Still feeling confused, and now with another thing to worry about, I kept this comment to myself. He made no treatment recommendation, other than to hand me a pamphlet that would educate me about adding more fiber to my diet. I guessed that the assumption was that I had developed the fissure as a result of straining with my bowel movements because of constipation that was due to there not being enough fiber in my diet. The simple truth was that I had no constipation, but he never bothered to ask if that was an issue. (I had, however, been experiencing some difficulty with my bowel movements, and some obscure, ill-defined pain.) In addition, he recommended I have a colonoscopy, since it had been almost six years since my original one. This was scheduled for February second, a couple days after I would get home from Florida. I'd experienced no problem with my first colonoscopy, so I wasn't worried about having a second one.

It took me two and one-half days to drive home from Florida, because of a highly unseasonal southern snow and ice storm that stretched from South Carolina to the southern tip of Pennsylvania. I sure was grateful that I had decided against my frugal nature and gotten the new tires on my car. As I drove home drinking water and eating the four approved almonds a day as a snack—instead of my usual half box of Cheez-Its and several cans of Wild Cherry Diet Pepsi—I had plenty of time to think.

While I visited with my brother, Judson, and his wife, Peggy, we did a lot of reminiscing, as usual. As I drove home, I thought back to the stories we had been entertaining each other with. Our childhoods had been a little on the crazy side. Growing up in a family of nine children had its moments. As adults, we had many opportunities to make fun of each other and our mother. She had died in March 2007, leaving behind a rich depository of stories, and there seemed to be nothing sacred. Some of the anecdotes would have made her laugh too, but others would have hurt her. At any family gathering, these stories would emerge, and they always provided a great deal of entertainment.

As an adult, and especially as a mother, I had developed a better understanding of what she may have experienced. She was a city girl through and through, having grown up in the row houses of the Polish section of Pittsburgh. When she got married, she moved onto seven and one-half acres of land that lay in the outskirts of Altoona, in the foothills of the Allegheny Mountains. While the rest of her family had stayed close to each other, all living within a few blocks of the ancestral home, she was virtually alone in the middle of nowhere. That by itself would have been stressful enough, but with nine kids in the mix, it was a life that would have been hard for even the most seasoned woman. We never went hungry and always had decent hand-me-downs on our backs, but there was little left over for extras.

I was suddenly engulfed with a sense of embarrassment and shame. Who was I to poke fun at my mother? All in all, she had done a good job raising her family, under some rather dire circumstances. When my father died at age forty-two, my youngest sister was three years old. This meant my mother was left to take care of nine children between the ages of three and twenty. Initially, her only sources of income were social security and, since my father's death was determined to be service-connected, a small income from the Veterans Administration. After she received her master's degree, she worked until retirement age. And in spite of all these drawbacks, her children all became educated, responsible, independent adults.

I began to think about my own days as a young mother. I had worked hard to be the best mother I could, but I knew there were things I could have done better. There always are. My mind darted around to instances of things I had done with my sons—things that, in spite of my best intentions, were not stellar moments. As I got closer to home, I felt a sense of urgency. One of the first things I wanted to do was apologize to them for these things.

I made an opportunity to talk with each of my sons. I knew they had grown up with a fine appreciation for the skill of poking fun at others—only in a good-natured way, I hoped. I knew they would have lots of funny stories to tell about me as they went through life, and I wanted them to be free to do that. But I told them I wanted them to know that I hadn't always been the best mother and that I was sorry. I had examples ready to refresh their memories. I appreciated the fact that each of them, in turn, looked at me like I was strange, asking what I was talking about. This was reassuring to me, but it didn't really assuage my guilt.

Isn't this what people do before they die? They want to wipe the slate clean; they want to be forgiven by those they have wronged. Indeed, I was developing a growing sense of unease about my health. There just seemed to be too many symptoms at one time, even when most of them seemed to have reasonable explanations. Somewhere inside, I must have known that I was skating close to the edge.

My husband, who had done just fine on his own while I lay around in the Florida sunshine, met me at the garage as I got out of the car. We were happy to see each other, but I was exhausted. He told me to go upstairs and relax as he emptied out my car. I grabbed what I could carry in one trip and dragged myself up the stairs. It was a struggle.

As I entered the hallway and looked around, I saw that Bill had done some serious cleaning. Everything looked great: dusted, swept, wiped up, dishes done, bed made. My husband and I had an atypical division of labor. Bill was not afraid to do housework, and I loved being outside, digging, planting, cleaning up. He was also a good cook, probably having made more meals as our two sons grew up than I did. Unlike some of my friends, who would feel obligated to prepare meals ahead for their husbands, I knew that wasn't necessary with mine. Bill would never expect it from me. He could take care of himself quite well on his own. We easily moved in and out of the usual man/woman setup, doing each other's chores without even thinking about it.

He asked me what I wanted for dinner, and I reminded him I was still doing my cleanse for two more weeks and that this was the "eat nothing" day. "Oh, I forgot," he said with some disappointment. He was realizing that a big part of his welcome home plan had just been annihilated.

It was only early afternoon, but I was already exhausted. Since there were candles lit in the bedroom, it was not hard for me to grasp what Bill had on his mind. It had been about three weeks since we had seen each other, and therefore, that same amount of time since we had had sex. I was too tired to think about it, but I knew Bill wasn't. As we lay in bed watching television, we gradually eased into a more romantic interlude. Within a short period of time, we both knew the timing wasn't quite right, so we decided to postpone this activity until later. Neither of us knew this would be the last such interlude for a long time to come. The next day, I had to begin my colon cleanse for the colonoscopy, and things would go downhill quickly from there.

THE COLONOSCOPY

After my first colonoscopy, six years earlier, I was left wondering what the big deal was. I breezed through the colon cleanse with no problem, other than the inconvenience of needing to be near a toilet most of the day. The procedure itself had been completely unremarkable. Upon awakening, and after leaving the prescribed amount of gas behind, I went home and had a day like any other day. So I went into this procedure with no concern about the procedure itself, or the outcome.

Things change in six years. As I was wheeled into the procedure room, the doctor reviewed the concerns that had brought me here: a very small amount of bleeding, a fissure, and a hemorrhoid. The next thing I knew, I was awakening in my little curtained-off recovery cubicle with stomach-cramping the likes of which I hadn't felt since I was in labor with my second son. I had ended up having a C-section after eighteen hours of labor and delivered an eleven-pound, six-ounce baby. I knew there would be no such reward for these pains.

The pains came in waves, again akin to labor pains. In a blur, I heard my husband speaking with the doctor and asking him questions. Even in my semi-alert state, I could hear the annoyance in the doctor's voice as he answered the questions while inching his way across the threshold of my recovery space. In between pains, I learned that there had been some difficulty getting the scope around the bend in my sigmoid colon and that he had had to switch to a pediatric scope. Other than that, my scope was declared a success. Nothing was found in the travels through my intestines, and the need to switch to a pediatric scope was not of concern to the doctor. "I really don't have time to talk right now," he said, impatiently. "If you want to talk about this, you can call my office to schedule an appointment." I knew I would never see this doctor again. An asshole dealing with assholes. Not only was he unconcerned about the difficulty getting through the sigmoid colon, but he also made no recommendations about the bleeding, the hemorrhoid, or the fissure. It's not until you have to ask questions that you find out what kind of person your doctor is, and he had failed miserably. The report I would receive a few weeks later would declare me healthy and in good shape for another five years. Hmm. Maybe, doc, it's time for you to start thinking outside the box. Maybe when you can't get the scope through, there's a reason for it—like stage IV ovarian cancer.

I spent the next week in severe pain, with the intermittent cramping fading over the next three days. After that, I still had severe pain, but as long as I moved very carefully, I managed to get through it. I sure was glad that there had been no problems with my colonoscopy. In my panic over not getting any answers to the problems that had led to the colonoscopy in the first place, I had cried to the nurse in the recovery area. She was kind enough to give me the name of the doctor they all went to. He came highly recommended for his thoroughness and his ability to make a good diagnosis. Unfortunately, when I called his office to schedule an appointment, the first one available was one month away. In the end, I wouldn't need this appointment anyway, even though at the time I was beginning to wonder if I would be alive when that date came.

The Urologist

Time seemed to be stuck in slow motion. After I finished the liver cleanse, I had a tremendous amount of difficulty going back to eating three meals a day. I experienced cramping and diarrhea, and in general I felt as though I had a bad stomach flu. I cursed the chiropractor who had recommended it to me. I cursed the company who made the cleanse. I sent them scathing e-mails about their product and assured them that if I had my way, nobody would ever purchase their liver cleanse again.

As time crawled by like a one-hundred-year-old tortoise, my sense of urgency increased. As it turned out, scheduling the appointment with the urologist had not only been a good decision, but it had also saved my life. This was a good doctor. Dr. Sagan was very thorough, as was her office staff. They asked detailed questions, getting all the information down. It's funny how you get so used to being ignored that when someone actually is attentive, it's a little scary. Why were they taking so much time with me? What could this mean?

"I think we need to get a scan of everything in there; let's just check it all out, see what is going on. We'll do the abdominal area, the pelvic region, the works."

"Okay," I said, relieved to finally get to the bottom of things. *Too bad I couldn't have gotten a sooner appointment*, I thought. *This lady knows how to take care of business.*

This appointment was on a Thursday; my scans were on the following Monday afternoon. The satellite where I had my scan was about thirty minutes from where I lived, and when I was about halfway home, my phone rang.

"Mrs. Schneider? I just got a call from the lab, and there are some concerns with your scan. Your ovaries are much enlarged, and there is a shadow on your liver. You need to see your gynecologist right away." Dr. Sagan was clearly concerned.

"Well, it's pretty late today; I'd have to wait till tomorrow," I said, perhaps trying to ignore, or pretend I didn't notice, the urgency in her voice.

"Well, call first thing in the morning, and if you have any trouble getting in, you call me right away, and I'll take care of it."

"Okay. Thank you."

It took me about fifteen minutes to finish the trip home, and I sat in a chair, not really thinking, just stunned and dazed. I decided not to call my husband; another hour was not going to make any difference. Besides, he had decided to go for a massage after work. I'd been trying to talk him into doing this for over a year, and there was no sense in ruining his first experience at Backrubs and Bodyworks. He'd never go again. As he walked in the door, I tried to paste a normal expression on my face.

"Well, how was your massage?" I asked.

He had half a grin on his face. "Pretty good," he said. "I'm pretty sore, but it was great." I reminded him that I had been sore for a week after my first one, but after that, I could definitely feel an improvement. And with each subsequent massage, there was less soreness afterward. He was glad he'd decided to do it, and he would definitely go back again.

"Well, I got some not-so-good news today." I just didn't know how to tell him. I think I knew that I had cancer, but there was no sense jumping the gun. I explained about the scan and the call from the urologist.

He just sat and looked at me, searching my eyes and my expression to see what all this really meant. "Okay," he finally said. "Do you want me to take you?"

"No, I think I can take care of it myself. I'll have to call in the morning and see when they can see me; no sense in you missing work." Bill had learned a long time ago that I liked my independence; I liked to take care of things myself. So he didn't argue.

We went about our business that evening, trying to act as though it was like any other night. But there was that sense of tiptoeing around something that we both knew was there. For sure, it must have been a sleepless night. I kept trying to imagine my way through the appointment, but I always came to a blank page when I got to the part about the outcome. Maybe I just didn't want to think about what I already knew it would be. What exactly was I going to find out? I tossed and turned my way through the night and finally dragged myself out of bed, looking for the number of my gynecologist.

When the receptionist answered the phone, I explained my situation. "Well, your doctor is out of the office for this whole week," she said.

In a panic, I cried, "I can't wait that long. I could be dead by then!"

"Don't worry," she said, reassuringly. "We'll get you in this morning; you'll just have to see one of the other doctors."

"Okay. I don't care who I see, just so I see someone." We worked out the details. I would have to go to one of their other offices, about an hour and a half away. This didn't give me much time. As I began to get myself ready, I realized how shaky I was. I honestly didn't think I could drive myself in that condition.

I called my husband at work and explained the situation to him. He left for home immediately. We drove in silence, I with my eyes on the speedometer. Since Bill drove about one hundred miles round-trip to work each day, he had learned early on that it didn't pay to speed. He just settled into the zone, and that was that. I wanted him to go faster, but I knew it would not change anything.

My one and only visit to this office of my gynecologist's practice is nothing but a blur. I remember a brief exam, followed by a brief consultation, with the explanation of "likely cancer" ringing in the air. We sat with anticipation in the waiting room while calls were made so that we could go directly to an appointment with an oncologist at Magee-Womens Hospital. We sat mostly in silence, except for my episodes of tears. Bill somehow managed to hold himself together. I was vaguely aware of others in the waiting room furtively stealing glances our way. I remember thinking that surely someone should have had the foresight to set aside a little room for people in our situation. I may as well have been naked; the raw and painful intimacy of the moment hung over us like a shroud wrapping a corpse.

"I haven't even had a chance to see or hold a grandchild yet." This was the first painful realization that flooded over me. As we waited, little vignettes played through my mind. How would I tell my sons? How could I dare to cause them such pain, to disrupt their busy lives this way? What would it be like for Bill and me from this point on, getting from one day to the next? A tremendous sense of my own failure ate at me like tiny ticks sucking my lifeblood from my body. I felt weak. How could I ever get up again? I was a failure at life. The devastation of the betrayal of my own body was more than I could bear.

Getting from the South Side of Pittsburgh to the other side of the city is a monumental task, no matter what the time of day. The late-morning traffic was unbearable. Magee is located in Oakland, a mecca of universities and hospitals just east of downtown Pittsburgh. Fortunately, it is at the end of the busiest section of Oakland, with a more modern, user-friendly parking area. The hospital itself is much easier to navigate than some of the more archaic, multilayered structures.

As we drove to the oncologist's office, I called both of my sons. In a stroke of luck—I guess, depending on how you look at it—they both answered their cell phones. I gave them the news and promised to call them as soon as we knew more. I told them I was sorry to have to put them through this. My love for them pulsed through my body, and the pain of thinking about how they felt after I talked to them was more than I could bear. Bill quietly drove through the traffic, taking us on the next leg of the adventure, which would preoccupy our lives from this point on.

Chapter Two

---◆---

The Earthquake

If I think back on all the moments in my life when I thought *This is the worst day/time/whatever of my life,* nothing comes remotely close to the moment when I found out I had cancer—and not just cancer, but stage IV ovarian cancer. It settled in like the aftershock of a devastating earthquake, one ripple at a time. And just like in an earthquake, where people slowly pick up the pieces of their lives and try to begin again, I knew things would never be the same. Occasionally some sign of hope is pulled from the rubble, and there begins to grow the notion that maybe life can be salvaged from this wreckage. Soon, though, that small spark is lost in the never-ending ripples of the disease that eats away at what is left of life.

When I broke my ankle in 1975, I was devastated. I was not allowed to put any weight on it for six weeks, and I was not handy with crutches. Since I was a waitress at the time, that meant I was unemployed. Having just lost a good thirty pounds, I definitely did not want to regain any of it. I was at an all-time lowest clothing size and at my fittest. All that work would *not* go down the drain. I was determined not to let that happen. So I ate little and agonized by walking around on my crutches as much as I could tolerate. Riding a bus into downtown Pittsburgh and walking for blocks and blocks while carrying bags left me sweating, shaky, and completely exhausted. But, with this exercise, and with the help of strep throat, I was able to lose another ten pounds. My size-ten clothes hung like bags, and my right leg was a good inch and a half smaller than my left one. The weight of the cast, combined with the atrophy in its muscles, left that leg nearly useless. For the first three weeks, I struggled to get through the painful burning that went with the rush of blood to the toes of my injured foot every time I stood up.

But even more difficult than all of this was the feeling of having no control over myself or my life. I was unable to drive—at least not with my doctor's approval. Since I was renting a small attic on the third floor of a large house at the time, I was unable to manage the steps that I needed to use, sometimes multiple times a day. As much as I hated the idea, I had to move back in with my family. This was a place I never wanted to have to go back to, at least not on a full-time basis. I loved them all dearly, but the craziness was more than I could handle. Sometimes visits were hard enough to manage.

Fortunately, as time went on and my ankle healed, I gradually regained that sense of control. As I became braver, and stronger, I began to drive. I did more things and felt better about myself. Finally, at the end of the prescribed six weeks, the cast came off, and in another two weeks, I was back at work. It was brutal at first, but eventually my broken ankle, and all the physical and mental anguish that went with it, was a faded memory. I was back into life in full swing.

As bad as I thought that time was, it was nothing like how I felt when I found out I had cancer. The news sent me reeling, as I realized how little control I had over what was happening to me. For someone who believed strongly in the idea of taking charge of life, this was difficult, if not impossible, to accept. How could something like this happen to *me*? My life came abruptly to a halt, my routines no longer fitting nicely with my day-to-day activities. I was a stranger in an unfamiliar land. I would need more than a tourist's handbook to get me through this journey.

The Defining Moment

We arrived at the hospital where the oncologist's office was located within about forty-five minutes. After another short wait, we were escorted back to the exam room. The medical assistant took care of the basics, and a physician's assistant came in and did a cursory pelvic exam. Shortly, the door was opened and the doctor entered, a friendly smile on his face. Since I was an "add-on," I knew that I had just added a significant amount of time to his already hectic day. I had worked in a drug and alcohol rehab clinic for twenty years, and we dealt with emergencies all the time, often leading to ten- or twelve-hour workdays. But his manner betrayed nothing. He appeared fresh and full of energy, as though he was just starting what was promising to be a wonderful day.

"Hi, Mrs. Schneider, my name is Paniti Sukumvanich, but you can call me Paniti, 'cause that's my name." I liked him immediately. His down-to-earth manner soothed me, even under these stressful circumstances. Small in stature, with the hint of some accent, he spoke clearly in a straightforward manner. After my third pelvic exam of the day, he told me to get dressed while he went and reviewed my scan. Upon returning to the room, he gave me the news that would change my life forever.

"When we see a scan like this, the most likely explanation is cancer. It is likely ovarian cancer, but it could also be peritoneal, although they are very similar. I talked with the lab, and I just traded the life of my firstborn child for a slot for you to have a biopsy done right now. I'll call you by Friday, possibly Thursday, with the results; but I'm ninety-nine percent sure it's cancer. Generally, we do surgery, but because of the liver involvement, that is not an option right now. We'll do three cycles of chemotherapy, then evaluate. Depending on how things go, we'll either do surgery then, or three more cycles."

As he finished speaking, he was already putting a reminder into his phone to call me when the biopsy results came in. As he was on his way out the door, I mentioned one more issue.

"I can't eat." Gradually I had come to accept that my difficulty eating had to do with more than that horrendous liver cleanse I had done.

"Is it because you feel bloated, full?"

"Yes," I replied.

"Try drinking some of those protein shakes. You'll start to feel better after you begin treatment." With that, he was gone.

Slowly, I got dressed. I gathered my things together, and as I entered the hallway, Dr. Sukumvanich was standing there.

"Hang in there," he commented. I searched his face for some sign of hope, some reason to feel positive. I desperately wanted someone to tell me it was going to be all right. But there was no more encouragement forthcoming.

I knew I was in trouble if that was the best he could come up with. I was in real trouble.

We left the office and headed up to the third floor for the biopsy. After signing in, I went into the hallway to make a few phone calls. I called my two sons to give them the update. They too looked for something hopeful to hang their hats on, but I was unable to help them. I was to have met three old college friends for dinner that night. I called one of them to give her the news, and I asked her to call the others and tell them what was going on. It struck me as odd that I had waited this long to cancel the dinner plans. Did I seriously still think I might go? I relayed the information of the day to my friend, Elaine.

"But you don't know for sure yet, right?" This almost made me laugh. I guess that I wasn't the only one who was having trouble accepting this news. I already knew, though. I didn't need a scan to confirm it. Everything from the last few months had started to fall into place. It all made sense now. Things I had barely noticed, or maybe had tried to pretend I didn't notice, had an explanation. There is a fine line between being a whiner—or maybe the medical term is hypochondriac—and being attentive to your body. I was ever mindful not to cross over that line. So I had learned to "suck it up," ignore things that didn't seem important, and recognize that aging brought an ever-so-gradual breakdown of bodily functions. One had to accept these things and just get on with life, I learned to tell myself. My thinking was that everyone experienced these things and there was nothing to be done about them. *Just set them aside and get about the business of living,* I would think. Maybe I had set too many things aside.

When I was young, I had a book about martyrs and saints of the Roman Catholic Church. I read that little blue book so many times that I had it memorized. While other kids dreamed of being nuns, nurses and such, I dreamed of being a martyr. I had images of being persecuted for my faith, in the old style. As an adult, sharing this childhood dream always produced a good laugh. I laughed too. I thought it *was* humorous in a dark sort of way, but personally, it was a very distasteful memory. As I came to see the Catholic Church in a very different light, it was just one more thing to create the distance I made sure I kept between it and myself. Maybe a bit of that martyrdom had slipped through unnoticed, and maybe I had taken the whole "suck it up" adage a bit too far. Maybe.

The biopsy was anticlimactic. Since there was some bleeding at the site of the biopsy, I had to lie flat on the table for an extra hour. Again I was an add-on, so the nurse who was already on overtime had to extend her stay even longer. I listened as she called her family to explain why she was late and as she tried to keep the irritation out of her voice. Maybe when she heard me telling my husband that my heart was broken and that I wanted to go home and take a couple of those old pain pills because I didn't know if I could bear all this, she felt sorry for me. The pain in my heart was so much worse than the back pain I had been given the pills for a year before. I was still dealing with the frequent coughing, which was from the fluid in my lungs, as opposed to the bronchitis I thought it came from. That probably didn't help stop the bleeding. Maybe then she took pity on me, and asked if I would like a piece of hard candy to suck on.

We drove home in a state of shock. "Well, I never saw that coming," my husband commented. I knew he was trying to process it all, just like me. But he didn't have the benefit of having lived with the symptoms, as I had for the previous few months. I was a far cry from the prolapsed bladder and rectum I had thought were causing all this trouble.

"What do you want to do about dinner?" Bill asked, interrupting my reverie. Dinner was the last thing on my mind, since I couldn't eat much anyway. However, Bill probably hadn't eaten all day. He had a habit of skipping breakfast, and sometimes even lunch. Because he had been with me since around 10:30 in the morning and I hadn't seen him eat, I was sure he was quite hungry. It was then about 7:30 in the evening. We decided to stop at Panera and get some soup.

This would become the staple of my diet in the upcoming months: soup from Panera, soup from Valley Dairy, soup from good friends and family who were thrilled to find a way to be helpful. My sister Joan alone could have kept me in soup for breakfast, lunch, and dinner for months. And I ate it all, a little bit at a time. With my oversized coffee mug, I would sit in the old recliner, wrapped in a blanket, eating my homemade soup with a few Ritz Chips several times a day.

Oh, How the Walls Crumbled

When the call came two days later (February 25, 2010, to be exact), it was simply a matter of putting the official stamp on something we already knew. My husband had insisted on staying home with me for those first few days; he wanted to be there for me literally as well as figuratively. Since our second phone wasn't working, I took the call by myself while my husband listened in the background.

"Mrs. Schneider, this is Dr. Sukumvanich. I got the results of your biopsy, and it looks like it is ovarian cancer. We can be pretty sure that is what is in your liver too, although the only way to be one hundred percent sure of that would be to biopsy your liver. There isn't really any point in doing that."

"So, what stage is it in?" I had done my research, and I already knew it was stage IV, but I needed to get the official word.

"Well, stage IV, because of the liver involvement," he said, confirming my conclusion.

"That's pretty bad, right?" I asked him. I already knew the answer to this, too. I had read that on average, women diagnosed with stage IV ovarian cancer live for twelve months after they are diagnosed. Only about 18 percent were still alive five years after they were diagnosed, depending on severity levels. Of course, I planned to be in that small percentage. Still, you never know. I was fast learning that it was not all up to me, that I didn't have control of everything, as I thought I did.

From his spot on the futon, my husband mouthed for me to ask about prognosis. Both as a reply to him, and as a question to the doctor, I said, "He can't really tell us that. My husband said to ask you about a prognosis."

"There is really no way of telling," he said carefully. "It all has to do with how you respond to the treatment. Some people may be in stage

I but do poorly because they don't respond to the treatment, while others may be in stage IV but do very well because they respond well to the treatment."

I already planned on being in that second group. I would respond well to the treatment. Dr. Sukumvanich outlined the next steps I would go through. I would receive a call from the oncology nurse, Chris, and she would schedule my appointment. She would then review the treatment and get me started on the chemo. After calculating to himself, he commented that he thought she might be able to call me the next day, a Friday, to get me started. I was grateful for his manner. He was thoughtful, yet he presented the facts without embellishment. "Just the facts, ma'am"—just like on *Dragnet.* This was what I wanted, needed. No pretending, no false hopes; I wanted to know exactly where I was so I could accurately plan my escape route from this land of the living dead.

I awoke the next morning feeling alive and full of energy. As I lay in bed, slowly becoming aware of where I was, the whole cancer thing slowly worked its way into my conscious mind. *Maybe it had all been a bad dream,* I thought. Maybe I didn't have cancer. I mean, I felt relatively normal. As I worked my way out of bed, the reality slowly settled in. No, it wasn't a dream; it was real. I had stage IV ovarian cancer. I was very sick.

Even though I was disappointed that the oncology nurse didn't call that day, I controlled myself. I didn't call. I would agonize my way through the weekend. But when I still hadn't heard from her halfway through Monday, I could wait no longer. I made what was the first call to her—the first in a long history of calls. I protested loudly when she tried to schedule me for the following week.

"But I could be dead by then," I cried in consternation.

"No, you will not," she replied in a firm voice. Still, she managed to squeeze me in the next morning, bright and early.

I know that at a later point, in conversation, this same nurse told me that when she met with me to get me started on chemo, my anxiety level looked to be about ninety-nine on a scale of one to ten. Surely this couldn't have been unusual. While concentrating on her voice and the information she was imparting, my mind wandered off to various thoughts and images, all of them painful. Somewhere in the mist, I heard her say, "Our goal is to have you around long enough to become an old woman." A nice thing to say, but it barely registered before I dismissed it as the party-line pep talk that surely all cancer patients received in their orientation. I knew the chances of me being around long enough to become an old woman were slim to none. My life as I knew it was over. And I had yet to learn in exactly how many ways it was over.

THE NEWS SETTLED IN

Perhaps one of the benefits of growing up Catholic is obedience. I seemed to have learned this well. Whatever the treatment regimen, I could be counted on to do exactly as I was told. I knew these people were the experts, and I wanted to stay alive. There would never be a problem with me cancelling or forgetting appointments, or coming up with lame excuses for missing my treatments. The only question was, would it be enough; would it keep me alive?

Right before I had that fateful scan, I had gone to one of the quick clinics in town for what I was sure was bronchitis. Indeed, this was the diagnosis I received, along with a Z-pak of antibiotics. For good measure, a chest X-ray was ordered to be sure I didn't have pneumonia. The PA thought he heard something in the left lobe of my lungs. After finding out I had cancer, the coughing didn't seem to be getting any better. I had finished the antibiotics, along with a whole bottle of Mucinex, with no relief.

"I just want to stop coughing," I cried to the PA on my return visit. "My ribs and abs are so sore from coughing, I can't stand it anymore." I was ordered another round of antibiotics, and a bottle of cough medicine with codeine, to quiet the cough. It wasn't until I got my own copy of the scan report that I saw the description of "moderate left-sided effusion." This meant I had fluid in my lungs, on the left side. I knew I could take all the antibiotics in the world and it would not stop my symptoms. This was another symptom of stage IV ovarian cancer.

I would start each day coughing. I had the feeling that I desperately needed to cough something up, but I rarely did so. Efforts to take a deep breath left me on the verge of panic. It took all my reserves to keep me from falling over the edge and just giving in to it. I would force myself to take smaller breaths and not think about the fact that I felt as though I were drowning. On the rare occasion when I would cough something up, for a few minutes I was in pure heaven. Yes! I could breathe again. It felt wonderful, but within a short time, I was once again left feeling breathless and weak.

I spent that first month after starting chemotherapy mostly sitting in the old, crooked recliner. Some days I couldn't even walk out to pick up the mail and the daily newspaper. It was a staggering round trip of at least 250 feet. If all I had to do was heat up some soup or scramble an egg, I was okay; but I was unable to do much more without a rest. My husband learned to have dinner on his own, fixing meals for himself that I was either unable to eat or couldn't bear to smell. Mealtimes, previously always a pleasant time for us, became a chore. I ate because I knew I needed to eat. With the bloating (caused by ascites, an abnormal accumulation of fluid both in my pelvis and abdomen), I would feel very full after eating just a small amount. Multiple small meals worked better, so my eating schedule rarely coincided with our old dinnertime routine.

This was just the beginning of a never-ending series of changes that would require our adjustment. But, with my eye on the prize, I looked toward brighter days. If I could just get better enough to have the surgery, I would be okay. It was only three to six months—a small chunk out of my life. I could do anything for three to six months. This was becoming one of my catch phrases: "I can do anything for [a period of time]." So what if I had to sit in a chair for the next six months? I knew it would be worth it in the end.

And so I settled in for the battle of my life—or for my life. My world became smaller and smaller. My focus became more and more narrow. All the things I would normally be doing in early spring became a distant memory. I stood on the porch and looked out at my perennial garden, wondering about the 250 bulbs Bill and I had planted the previous fall. Would I get to see them come into bloom? My monthly massages fell by the wayside. Lunches with my son became a thing of the past. Social outings were not even considered. For sure, physically, I barely had the energy to get up and get going each day.

But, even worse, mentally and emotionally, I was still trying to process the whole thing. How could this happen to me? I had control of my life. Other people got cancer, not me. Things like this just didn't happen to people like me. I read the books sent to me by family and friends. I was always a big proponent of considering the psychological aspect of what went on in a person's life. Now, being confronted with this devastating turn of events, I had to begin thinking about how this applied to me.

One of the theories about how and why people get cancer is that people who are depressed, unhappy, or live unfulfilled lives are the ones who are unable to fight off the cancer cells we all have in us. I refused to see this applying to me. I had done what I wanted to do with my life. I had so many things that I felt intensely about, that I found wonderful, that I was thrilled to do. Of course, like everyone, I had my share of disappointments and disillusionments with life, and maybe I was a little slow in processing them at times. Eventually I got things figured out, and I never let them stop me from getting on with my life.

There were many other theories, and combinations of theories, about how and why people get cancer. I read them all and thought about how they might apply to me. Some of them offended me; some of them made sense. In the end, what I learned was that there were no clear-cut answers. Yes, I was overweight and out of shape, but so were millions of other people who never got cancer. Yes, I ate a lot of processed food and drank diet drinks, but so did millions of other people who never got cancer. Yes, I probably ovulated a lot of times in my life (one theory is that people who ovulate more have a greater chance of getting ovarian cancer), but surely there were millions of women who ovulated more than I did and never got cancer. In the end, I had no better idea why I got cancer than I did before all my reading.

For about thirty-five years, Bill and I had been having our cars fixed by a man named Jim. He is a good mechanic and has a very laid-back garage. While he performed routine maintenance work, I would hang out and talk with him. Most of the time, we would joke and tease each other. But when his wife had breast cancer, things changed. He talked about the difficulty in trying to understand cancer. "You go on, thinking you're doing things right in life. We go to church, my wife is a good Christian, and she is a good woman. It seems like that should count for something. But you find out it doesn't."

At that time, I had nothing to say back to him. I was aware of how painfully irrational what he was saying was, but I could understand that kind of thinking. Looking for an explanation when there is none can lead the most rational of us into being so desperate for answers that we go to some mighty strange places.

After my diagnosis, I found myself at that very same place. I wanted to understand why I had gotten cancer. In my mind, I went over and over how I had lived my life. I knew there were many things I could have done better. I just couldn't add it all up to cancer.

I have come to the conclusion that having cancer is like *The Perfect Storm*. Most of us have seen this movie, which portrays a team of seasoned fishermen who happen to get caught up in a grand convergence of weather systems that results in an unlikely, but extreme, weather condition. Even with all their knowledge and experience, they are unable to weather the storm, both literally and figuratively. Cancer, then, is the unlikely convergence of just the right factors in just the right time frame that results in a particular person ending up with some form of cancer. They say we all have cancer cells in our bodies. The people who don't end up with cancer seem to have the ability to keep the cells from going wild. Some of us, though, are unable to weather the storm. When conditions are right, the cells do go wild, and we do end up with the disease.

Having cancer has been one of the most humbling experiences of my life. For a person who is used to being in charge and independent, there is no worse fate than to have to rely on others to perform simple daily tasks. With my activities pared down to a bare minimum, I was able to take care of myself, get up, get cleaned and dressed each day, and eat, as long as the preparation wasn't too involved. But I could do little else. My husband, ever the Helpful Henry, soon learned to ask before doing things. He knew that if at all possible, I would do it myself. In spite of my appreciation of all his help, I became highly offended if he assumed without asking that I couldn't do something for myself. What a no-win situation for him to be caught in. But he perseveres, always wishing that he could do more. He would do anything to make me feel better.

Always short on time, like most young parents today are, Bill and I learned to be efficient. We were practical. We couldn't waste time dwelling on problems. We quickly took care of things and moved on. Besides, it was the message we wanted our kids to hear: "Life is full of problems; you take care of them and keep on going." It is perhaps this attitude that enabled me to refuse to be daunted by the turn my life had taken. Six months in a chair? I don't like it, but one six-month period out of my life isn't that bad.

Don't get me wrong. I cried a lot. I talked about dying. I thought about all the things I'd never get to do. My sons were just getting started with their adult lives. I cried for the wonderful men I was sure they would become, whose lives I would not get to share. I cried for their women—one son's wife and the other's girlfriend. Marc and Pat were lucky enough to be happily in relationships that were wonderful. They both believed they had found the women of their dreams. I loved these girls like the daughters I never had. These were four young people who were bound to do good things for each other and for whatever part of the world they touched. And I cried that I would not get the pleasure of seeing all this happen. I cried for the grandchild I would never hold, never get to teach to pick berries, never get to walk and pick wildflowers with, and never get to help with homework. I would never get to experience with that grandchild the wonder and joy of a young, innocent perspective of the world. I cried quietly to myself. I wept out loud when I was home alone. At night, in bed, I cried quietly against Bill's back. In the evening, we would stand or sit, arms wrapped around each other, and cry for the golden years we would never have together. Or we would just cry because of the hand fate had dealt us. No words were needed then. We just cried.

Still I didn't give up. Within the first two weeks, my husband and I together developed a guided imagery that I used to help heal myself. I imagined the sun, with all its healing warmth, drying up the cancer cells, and a gentle breeze blowing them away. In the beginning, my husband would read this to me, but gradually, I became able to do it on my own. If I didn't do it first thing in the morning, I always fit it in somewhere in the day. I believed firmly in my own power to heal myself, along with whatever modern medical science had to offer. What a team!

Around the bouts of tears, Bill did everything he could to keep our life as normal as possible. He would offer to take me shopping. This had always been my thing. Bill, being a typical man, treated shopping like a job to be done as quickly as possible so he could get on to more fun or important things in life. I carried on the family tradition passed down from my mother: always being on the lookout for the outstanding bargains. To take advantage of these bargains required a never-ending vigilance—in other words, frequent shopping. But after my diagnosis, we actually went clothing and grocery shopping together. And, even more strangely, we honestly seemed to have fun. With Bill along, I could take pain pills and not have to worry about driving; that way I could enjoy the shopping and last longer.

At the same time that Bill was trying to keep our life normal, I was also making every effort to ensure that Bill's life didn't revolve around my cancer. I insisted he get out and play golf. As soon as the weather cooperated, I pushed him out the door for an afternoon of golfing. This had always been his favorite pastime, and there was no reason for that to change. Gradually, we seemed to have created new routines that accommodated all the devastation left in the wake of the cancer. Bill's second-favorite nice-weather activity was gardening. We discussed whether he felt like gardening in the upcoming growing season. He made the decision not to garden, since he didn't really know what to expect now that I had cancer. For the first time in the twenty-two years in our log home, we didn't have a vegetable garden. When we looked out the kitchen window, it was sad to see that area populated by nothing but weeds.

As we gradually acclimated to this new adventure in our lives, there was one thing that nagged at me. Bill had a tendency to want to keep everything nice. Probably our biggest source of conflict through the years was that I liked to rant about things occasionally, especially things I felt very strongly about. Bill, on the other hand, liked to keep everything smooth. When this new leg of our life together started, he had the attitude that we would beat this thing. Although I, too, wanted more than anything to beat this disease, I had to think about what might happen if it didn't work out that way. I needed to know that Bill had thought about this, that he would be all right if I died. I needed to know he had at least considered this possibility.

Things came to a head one evening, and as we both cried, we talked about what would happen if I didn't make it. Initially, the focus was on practical things like funeral arrangements. My desire was to be cremated. I didn't want people looking at me when I was dead, standing around saying things like, "Doesn't she look good? She looks just like herself; she looks so peaceful." I have always wondered why people say such trite things at a funeral home, because they are rarely true. I guess they are looking for something nice to say. But I would have none of it. Still, when it was so painfully close to me, I realized that it was more about the people still alive and that since I would be dead, it really would not matter much to me. This is—as far as I knew, at least, and as far as I guess any of us knows—what will happen when we're dead. It's what we have to work with.

"Are you okay with this?" I asked Bill. "You are the one who will have to deal with this. How do you feel about it?"

"I'm okay with it," he replied. "If it's what you want, then I'm okay with it."

"I think you should have a big party out at St. Jude Golf Club. Make sure there is lots of good food, lots of beer and wine. I want people to have a good time. Hopefully they will have lots of stories to tell about me, including some of the dumb things I've done."

"I'm not having a party for you at St. Jude!" he protested loudly.

"Why not?" I asked, perplexed.

"Because you don't like golfing! I'm not having a party like that at St. Jude when you don't even golf!"

"Well, what are you going to do," I asked him, on the verge of laughter, "have a party for me at Toys Landscaping?" Toys was the greenhouse/nursery where I bought most of my flowers, trees, and shrubs. "Maybe you could lease a TJ Maxx or Marshalls store for a few hours and have my party there!" These were the stores I shopped at most frequently.

This brought the comic relief the situation desperately needed. We then thought up multiple silly scenarios for where Bill would have my funeral wake. I realized I'd have to leave explicit instructions for how to prepare, or it would never come close to what I envisioned. Yes, I would have to plan ahead. In later months, I would come back to this discussion, as it provided the birthplace for the May Day Party I would have the next year.

We now at least had brought it out in the open and could build on what we had already discussed. Just verbalizing some of these thoughts was a start. Now Bill could allow himself to consider the possibility that I might die soon. The idea wouldn't be a stranger to him.

And so we settled into our new routines. We adjusted to life with never-ending unexpected twists and turns. We learned to make do. We took advantage of those moments when I felt something close to what I called normal. They were few and far between and could change in a heartbeat, but we learned to see them with a newfound appreciation. On the spur of the moment, we might call a few friends and suggest we get together someplace for dinner. We might go out for a bite, just the two of us. We might take our kids out to dinner. We might go visiting. And in between these little gems of life, I sat in my chair and waited to see what life was going to bring me—life or death.

WHAT'S GOD GOT TO DO WITH IT?

As a child, I had the stereotypic vision of God with a long, flowing white robe and equally long, flowing white hair and beard. He had a rather stern look on his face, unlike the tender and gentle look ascribed to his son, Jesus. I envisioned God as someone who was always watching, catching me in private moments committing mostly venial sins. He knew how bad I really was, regardless of what other people thought.

Growing up Catholic, I knew the answers to the Baltimore Catechism questions, which I committed to memory by rote. They had no significance for me other than that they enabled me to get As on my tests. I derived no comfort from any notions I had about God, Jesus, or the Holy Spirit. The disconnect was solid, and the idea that Jesus loves me didn't make me feel special. I was not interested in exclusive membership in the "one true faith" club, a concept espoused by Catholics that separates them from the masses and puts them just a little bit closer to God.

As I moved into independent adulthood, so my beliefs about God and spirituality moved into a different sphere. I was unable to reconcile the traditional ideas with the world I lived in. I began to develop my own ideas, none of which seemed to fit into the tidy little categories of the concepts I had memorized as a child. Maybe I used too much reason and logic in relation to my spiritual beliefs, where I should have let faith take precedence.

To say that I don't believe in God would be inaccurate, but I do, perhaps, have unorthodox views of God. I don't attend any church, and I don't follow any structured religious practices, yet I do consider myself to be a very spiritual person. I believe strongly in respecting the soul of all living things. While I realize I don't have control of everything in my life, I do believe strongly in taking responsibility for the choices I make and the direction my life takes. In this light, I have always been able to understand how I've ended up where I've been. People, things, and events just are; they happen, and you deal with them. To label things as evil or use energy hating them is a waste. I believe it is malicious intent that makes things evil.

Maybe cancer is insidious, but it lacks malicious intent; only people can have that. So, in my mind, God did not make cancer as an evil for us to deal with. Cancer is a life form that is simply trying to survive, like all other life forms. And therefore, how could I hate God for creating cancer or hold him responsible for my having cancer? Would I ever believe that God has malicious intent toward Jamie Schneider? No. Do I believe there is a God who directs the course of human destiny, in that he plans for what happens to each of us individually? No. Was God just sitting around up there, and one day he said to himself, "Hmm. I think I'll give Jamie Schneider ovarian cancer today"? I don't believe that. Am I being punished for any evil deeds I may have committed in my life? No, I don't believe that either. Perhaps that's what is so maddening about cancer; there really isn't anybody to blame. Perhaps that's what makes God such an easy culprit. Why not blame him? You can get as angry as you want with him. But you can't beat him up, you can't sue him, you can't kill him. Even if you could, in the end, you would still have cancer.

This all leads me to conclude that my having cancer has nothing to do with God. So where did cancer come from? What went into its development? We have yet to determine that. We do know that it's been around for a long time, since it's been found in dinosaur fossils. There are many theories about how cancer develops, and many of them make much sense, except none of them conclusively explains all the facets of cancer. When I worked in the drug and alcohol clinic, we had a consultant. If I did an intake with a particularly difficult client, our consultant would say, "Difficult clients require a complex conceptualization. The solution in the end might be simple, but the conceptualization has to be complex." Cancer is like a difficult client. It requires a complex conceptualization. I don't believe we have figured out completely what that is yet. When we do, we might be surprised at how simple the solution is. Until we do, we will have to struggle doing the best we can with what we have.

Chapter Three

TELLING EVERYONE

Nothing fits the description of "baring your soul" like having to tell people you have cancer. No matter who they are or what the nature of your relationship to them is, there is something about letting them in on such a personal, intimate detail of your life that makes you feel as though you're running through the streets naked. I have always found it annoying that as a society, we are so interested in the intimate details of other people's lives. Famous people have it really rough in that respect. If they end up with something like cancer, the whole world somehow feels it has the right to go through it with them. There is nothing sacred for them. I am certainly not a famous person, but in my little town of Kittanning, Pennsylvania, I really don't want everyone knowing this intimate detail about my life. Unfortunately, I have no control over this. Once you tell people, or once the word gets around, things change. People treat you differently. There is a strange mixture of pity, encouragement, avoidance, and curiosity, with a very occasional pinch of honesty thrown in.

In the beginning, you get enough cards to fill baskets, vases of flowers, little quilts all prettily decorated with positive affirmations and quotes from the Bible. Well wishes come in a large variety of forms. The cards are wonderful, the flowers are beautiful, and the quilts are cheerful. Many offer help, and a few actually give it—some even in the form of very practical things: house cleaning, rides, company, food, even a few visits. Many people, if you happen to see them out and about, will say, "I was going to call you, or stop and see you, but I didn't know if you were up for that." What they really mean to say is, "I don't have a fucking clue what to say to you, or if I can handle my own feelings, so it's just easier to send a card, or stay away." This is okay. I understand this. I've done it many times myself. I think it comes down to what level of risk people are willing to take and how far outside their own comfort zone they are willing to step.

Outside of family, and a handful of others, I didn't want to tell anyone. Those I did tell had to promise me they would keep it to themselves. I'm sure they did their best to keep that promise. Not telling people meant I couldn't be around them either. How could I be with them and have that huge secret? Since I didn't feel much like being out anyway, it made it easy to keep to myself. In my mind, I would play out the scene where I would tell them, and I couldn't bear the look I imagined would be on their faces: devastation, shock, pity, confusion. "Oh," I imagined them thinking. "So you're one of them—one of the people who get cancer." They would then have to rethink what they knew about me. "What was it about you that made you get cancer? Poor thing." After that they know you in a more personal, more intimate way. Even people whom you never really wanted to be a part of your life become intimately connected to you, whether you like it or not.

No matter how I played it out, it was an unbearable situation, so I avoided it. Gradually, however, reality set in, and I came to accept that I could not go on like that forever. In a small town—and Kittanning is a small town—news travels fast, be it good or bad. Finally, I contacted the friends whom I had told, and said it was okay to tell others. This was likely redundant, because most people I encountered already knew. In fact, I would react with surprise when I had the rare experience of running into someone who didn't know.

If you're one of the fortunate ones, where they "caught it in time" and you hang on for a while, people eventually just go on about their lives and let you go on about yours. They give you the inevitable "You look good" when you see them, as well as "Hang in there" and "Stay positive." The cards stop, the calls fade, and people assume you are okay, just getting on with your life too. "They got it in time" means you didn't die right away. It says nothing about the quality of your life, about how you feel, about what you can do. And besides, you should be happy just to be alive. Don't be greedy, now. You should be grateful just with the fact that you are still here. The fact that you spend most of your time sitting in a chair is irrelevant.

These are the details most would rather not know about. It's just plain too uncomfortable. I suppose this is another reason I wanted to put off telling people for as long as I could—not only my own feelings of being put on display, but also the discomfort it would cause others. But, in the end, the word gets out, whether you want it to or not. When I finally told my friend Sandy, she looked at me with a mixture of something that looked like sadness and betrayal and said, "Why didn't you tell me?"

I didn't have a good answer to that. All I could say was, "I couldn't. You don't know what it's like. I just couldn't." As I left her house, I was overcome with hurt and guilt, trying to put myself in her shoes and imagine how I would have felt if the situation had been reversed. I would have been devastated. To think of my good friend having to go through all that physical and emotional pain would have made me unbearably sad. Maybe I would have wondered why she felt she couldn't tell me, and believed it was somehow a fault of mine. Shortly after I arrived home, she was at my front door with a vase of beautiful flowers. She handed them to me and quickly left. We were both crying.

THE KIDS

Both of my sons already knew about my cancer. They knew right after I did. Marc and Pat were used to a family where we shared important things. I knew they would want to know. They would have been devastated if I had kept this from them. Our history was to work through the difficult things together, and this was no different. Still, I could never recall anything this earthshattering.

Marc was just about two years into his first job out of law school. I knew he was busy. I guess we all are. When he was little, he could become upset about the smallest changes. He had developed solid ideas of what things were supposed to be like, to look like, and he didn't take kindly to having a monkey wrench thrown into the works. Since we were not sticklers for routines, I'm not sure where this trait came from. I flew by the seat of my pants, always trying to cram more into a single day than could ever possibly be done. But there it was.

As an adult, Marc is highly motivated, if not tremendously organized, and he is loyal to his ideals and to the people in his life. His sense of family has never wavered; he has always viewed it as a priority. He is still close friends with people he became friends with in his early childhood.

I knew that Marc needed to be a part of my cancer experience; the thought of not telling him would never have occurred to me. When he came to visit shortly after we got the news, I looked expectantly behind him as he came through the front door. He was alone.

"Nikki said she just couldn't come yet," he said apologetically. "She just doesn't know what to say to you."

"That's okay. I can understand that; I don't know what to say either. You tell her that whenever she's ready is the right time for her to come." Marc's wife, Nikki, is a very bright and intense young woman who grabs life by the horns and makes things happen. I had no trouble at all seeing how she and Marc ended up together. Dealing with something so antilife would be hard for her. I didn't mind at all. I appreciated the honesty more than anything.

Marc, standing almost six feet tall with his reddish blond hair, came over, and we hugged. I cried against him, saying over and over that I was so sorry to have to put him through this. We sat, I in my crooked recliner and he at the corner of the couch closest to me. I filled him in on the details of what was going on, of how everything had added up to cancer for me. He looked at me somewhat wistfully and said, "I always imagined you'd be around for a long time, till you were an old lady."

"Yeah, me too," I said forlornly. And it was true. I had pictured myself in my mother's old, broken-down body. I was only fifty-eight, not nearly ready to call it quits. It was true that I had lost the ability to do as many things as I wanted to do; I couldn't fly around the floor anymore when I went line dancing, I couldn't spend an entire afternoon outside digging and planting, and I couldn't bake for twenty-four hours straight anymore. Still, doing these things in smaller pieces was good enough.

Marc had the inquisitive mind of a good attorney from the time he could talk. He was curious about everything and asked questions constantly. I was pleased by this because I wanted to be sure my kids didn't grow up being fearful of going out into the world, as I had been as a child. I watched him make connections between cause and effect, and develop mental constructs on a regular basis. This process enabled him to be excited about school and to look forward to new experiences.

He is no different now. He asked me questions about my diagnosis, about things the doctor had said, listening carefully to what I had to say. He asked me about my imagery and made sure I was doing it regularly. He wanted to understand everything I was going through and to be sure I was getting all the information I needed to deal with this new journey of my life. His presence was reassuring to me, and we spent the afternoon just catching up.

When he can't make it for a visit, Marc calls me to see how I am. We have a standing joke: anytime he calls, as the phone is ringing, I already know it's him. I am right about 98 percent of the time. This kind of connection goes far beyond a card or a basket of flowers. Cards are wonderful, and I love flowers, for sure. But this is a deeper connection. When he was born, I can still remember the expression on his face as he looked deep into my eyes as if saying, "So this is who I've been getting to know for the last nine months ... Well, aren't you gonna feed me?" We have had this connection ever since. I can recall when he was in second grade and his teacher said to me, "It's so nice to see a kid who actually really likes his mother!" I took this as the highest form of compliment.

Patrick was just finishing his last semester at Denver University. Two years earlier, in a flurry of excitement, he had taken off for Colorado with Carrie, his girlfriend of four years. It had been such a joy to watch the two of them getting ready, carefully planning out every part of their trip. As a mother, one of the greatest joys is to see your children grown up, taking charge of their lives and being able to carve out a good, secure place for themselves in the world. He and Carrie were a great team. She was a young woman who was excited about getting started with her adult life, and already had a teaching job lined up before they arrived in Colorado. She had so many ideas, I knew her students would be lucky to have her as a teacher. The two years of Patrick's master's degree program in sport and performance psychology was coming to a close. It was hard to believe he was almost done. Shortly before I found out I had cancer, he told me of an opportunity he had to take a trip to Las Vegas with a fellow student. Now, instead, he was planning to come home to see me. Of course, I was thrilled that I would get to see him, but it was also another thing to feel guilty about. He reassured me that the trip wasn't that big of a deal and that he would have other chances for such a thing. This was probably not true, but I appreciated his effort to make me feel okay about his decision.

Patrick had always been a very happy child; it seemed he spread sunshine wherever he went and always left people smiling behind him. Early on, he had demonstrated a particular sensitivity to people's feelings. The third year since we put up a bluebird box for my older son, Marc, was a particularly good year, and five baby bluebirds had lived to get out of the box and explore the world of our backyard. One morning, I went out to the backyard and found one of the baby bluebirds dead. This was very upsetting to me, and I came back in the house, saddened and tearful that the bird hadn't survived.

It was the first Saturday in July, and we would be traveling to my sister Joan's house for her annual family picnic. We had planned to stop on the way to visit a longtime friend who had just had a baby a couple weeks earlier. As I sat and cried, Patrick came into the kitchen and saw me. He approached me hesitantly, asking what was wrong. I told him about the baby bluebird. With all the wisdom of a bright, especially sensitive five-year-old boy, he said, "Don't cry, Mum. You'll feel better soon."

"When?" I asked him curiously.

He paused for only a second or two and then said, "When you see Marcie's baby."

How could he have known that? Somehow he had made the connection that for every ending of life, another was beginning, and that though the endings were sad, if we put our energy into the beginnings, life would go on. He was right; I immediately began to feel better.

Marc picked Patrick up at the airport when Patrick came home during his school break. As I awaited their arrival, I could feel myself becoming more anxious by the minute. How could I face him? How could I ever look at him again after what I was doing to him? I knew this was irrational, yet I couldn't get away from this feeling. I went to my bedroom and lay down to do some imagery to relax myself. It was hard to concentrate.

When he finally got here, I hugged him and immediately apologized for doing this to him. He laughed at me, saying I was not doing anything to him. He made it very clear that my having cancer was not something of my doing. That was his way. Both of my boys were like that. They wouldn't let that sort of irrationality fly, and they would have no qualms about straightening me out right from the start.

Patrick spent a week visiting. He bought a five-hundred-piece puzzle. Putting big puzzles together had been an enjoyable cold-month family activity for us through the years. He also bought the game Boggle. While I didn't have the stamina to sit at the table for more than a few minutes to work on the puzzle, we played Boggle many times every day. He almost always beat me. His presence was comforting to me, and we talked of many things during that week.

He accompanied me to my chemo treatment that week, just sitting there, letting me talk. He quietly took things in, getting the lay of the land. I knew the week was fast coming to a close, and it would be hard for me to say good-bye to him. Even though he didn't say anything, I knew he was rearranging whatever postgraduate plans he had begun to make. Had it not been for my cancer, I think he would have stayed in Colorado. He and Carrie loved it there. They were an adventurous couple and had made many new friends and done lots of hiking. The Colorado lifestyle suited them well. And here I was, interrupting their plans, throwing a monkey wrench into the works.

Would I spend the rest of my life apologizing to people for causing them pain? I guess all I could do was make it as easy on them as I possibly could. I made extra effort to be sensitive to others, to be aware of how they felt about my having cancer. I wanted to be sure I would not contribute to anyone having regrets in relation to me. I would accept any form of help, well wishes, and prayer that others were inclined to give me. What mattered was not the form it came in, but the intent of the giver. This was where I put my focus.

FAMILY

Coming from a large family has its pros and cons. At that point, the thought of having to talk with eight siblings was more than I could even think about. As my two sons grew up, I watched computers, via e-mail and IM, replace human interaction, and I wondered what kind of long-term effect this artificial method of communication would have on relationships. Now I was thankful for it, as it gave me a way to communicate something very painful, yet keep a little distance. In spite of our constant fighting as children, we had as adults, for the most part, developed manageable relationships with each other. Now I was thankful that I could send an e-mail to my siblings and their families to let them know about my cancer. As a follow up, I could talk with them individually and allow them to have whatever time *they* needed to process the information.

The decision to even tell my brothers and sisters was one I had to give thought to. Seven out of nine of us live within about a fifty-mile radius, and although we share major holidays and have occasional other contacts throughout the year, we don't have contact on a regular basis. I was truly unsure of what kind of response I would get.

Within a short time, I did hear from each of my siblings. Each in his or her own way expressed concern and let me know he or she would be thinking of me, praying for me. I was offered help in many different ways. When you have something like cancer, you can never get enough well wishes, prayers, and good thoughts. They are all good regardless of what form they come in. Again, it goes back to intent.

All of my brothers called me to ask about my cancer and to wish me well. My oldest brother, Jerome, called first, and I was surprised at the depth of feeling I detected in his voice. He is not one who often lets any emotion show. This made his call more meaningful to me. His wife, Mary Ann, has become a wonderful e-mail companion. We have extensive chats this way, and she is a large part of my support group. She helped organize a visit last summer so that I could see Longwood Gardens, a place that had been on my to-do list for years. My cousin Kathy and I drove to New Jersey and had a great few days visiting.

My other three brothers are all younger than I am. When my brother Judson, from Florida, called, he said, "What's going on up there?" It made me laugh right off the bat. But, since I had been visiting him and his wife shortly before I found out about the cancer, I couldn't help wondering how they might feel. If I were them, I would have been thinking back on the visit and trying to see if anything stood out that might have been a clue to the storm that was brewing. I felt some guilt for putting them in such a spot. Irrational, I know.

My brother Joe—the youngest of my brothers, and easily the quietest person in our otherwise rather loud-mouthed group—called and offered his support. Since he doesn't have a home computer, our contacts all have to be by phone. I call him, he calls me; we stay in touch, and I appreciate his concern. When we get together for family gatherings, he always seeks me out to find out the latest scoop.

My sister-in-law Kathy offered to set up a meeting with a priest she knew who had been helpful to her when she was dealing with breast cancer. She also offered me holy water. I declined these offers, thanking her for her concern and thoughtfulness. While they were not the kind of things that had special significance to me, I knew that her offer was heartfelt and came from her desire to do something meaningful. I was grateful that she wanted to do something special. She also mentioned to me that her husband, my brother Jeffrey, wanted to do something; he just couldn't figure out what. He had recently sent me an e-mail that made me laugh out loud for minutes. I suggested he could keep those kinds of e-mails coming. It's always a pleasure to read them.

My sister Joan called and said, "I have soup; is this a good time?" and in a short time, there she was, at the door. She brought her daughter, Cassie, whom I've always enjoyed and loved. Joan gave me a little time in the beginning to tell her how the cancer all came about, and then she took charge. She and Cassie worked as a team, and before I knew it, we were telling stories about my boys and Cassie, from when they were all little. We were laughing, having a great time. I don't really know if she consciously thought this out, if it just came naturally for her, or if it was what she was comfortable with. It doesn't matter. The point is that she came, she was herself, and she was thoughtful and concerned. That was the important part. There is no script. It's a come-as-you-are, in all your purity. That is all you have to offer anyone.

Two of my other sisters, Therese and Michele, came together. It's always easier if you're not alone; this is true for most things in life. And they brought food; what could be better? They called to see what I was hungry for. We sat and ate, I talked about my cancer, and we cried a little together (okay, I cried more than they did). I could feel their pain.

If the tables had been reversed, and one of them had told me she had cancer, what would I have done? I don't know how I could bear to hear something like that. There would have been no end to my weeping. I loved them for their anguish. Sitting together, the three of us eating, talking, crying, laughing—this was all I needed.

My oldest sister Janice called me from Florida. I don't know which of us cried more. Neither of us really knew what to say, so we just cried on the phone for a few minutes. I mentioned that I was sad that I hadn't gotten to hold a grandchild yet, and she offered to share hers. She has three, and I can tell she loves them more than anything. It's a joy to see her with them.

Friends

Friendships come in many forms, levels, and depths. I have found it easy to go through life being friendly with people. This, however, has nothing to do with friendship. I have always marveled at people's friendships. Some are amazing. When someone has a friend who plans a surprise fiftieth birthday party for him or her, I find this amazing. I can't think of any friend I have who would do such a thing for me. Some people seem to have so many friends that they just don't know what to do with them all. Others don't seem to have any. I guess I am somewhere in between. I have only a few people whom I would call very good friends. There are also very few people whom I dislike intensely. Most people I know fall somewhere in between. The few whom I consider very good friends are the ones I told about my cancer first. I never wanted the ones I dislike intensely to know about my cancer and the ones in between would gradually find out, one way or the other.

I found myself at times reflecting back to when I had found out that friends of mine had cancer. With my new, firsthand experience with cancer, I became aware of how completely inadequate my responses to them had been. I suppose when it comes right down to it, just about any response is inadequate. Still, I had done the best I could, as people were doing with me. It all comes back to intent. At least I knew my intentions were good. I smile at this because so many times in my younger years I heard the old adage, "The road to hell is paved with good intentions." Probably not.

I've decided that a handful of very good friends are enough. That is not to say that there isn't always room for one more. My son Marc talked with me about someone he had met, and he explained how they had become fast friends. As he described the situation to me, he said, "It worked out perfectly; we both had an open spot." This was an interesting way to put it, and upon further reflection, I decided this is a perfect description. I wondered how many times I had missed the opportunity to make a new "very good" friend because I had been so busy in my life that I didn't have an opening. I wondered how many times someone had offered himself or herself to me and I had been so caught up in my own life that I didn't even recognize it. Maybe this is one of the things that having cancer has done. Maybe it has opened me up, and now, because I myself am starving for someone to be willing to hear and see me while I am on this lonely journey, I can better recognize the offering when it is made to me. Maybe now, when I likely have so little time left and I want to make the most of every moment and every experience, I have an unlimited supply of open spots.

Sometimes I wonder how it took Donna and me so long to become the good friends we are today. After the first few times we talked, as I left her I had the feeling that she had really been there with me. I liked that feeling. Aside from getting together every now and then, we have an e-mail relationship that goes far beyond forwarding the cute, funny, clever e-mails that make the circuit and are often the only contact I have with some people.

Donna is a person who doesn't know the depth of her own spirit. When we spend an afternoon together, we connect on many levels. Our time almost always includes eating and, generally, shopping. We both enjoy the thrill of the hunt—that is, looking for that special bargain. Our conversations range far and wide, but wherever they roam, they are always real. She is always interested in the details of my cancer battle, and although it's never the only thing we talk about, she is never afraid of going there with me.

Diane and I share a love of line dancing. She has given me rides when I haven't been able to drive because I've taken pain medication so that I can enjoy myself and shuffle around the floor a little bit. En route, we talk about our kids, ourselves, life in general. Somehow, I usually end up having poop stories for her, related to my colostomy. She never minds talking about poop. This says a lot about a person. I look so forward to Thursday nights not only for the line dancing but also for Diane's company.

I love stopping at Sandy's house; she always has little kids running around. Watching her with them is joyful; she sure has earned the title of "Mom" that many of them bestow upon her. There is always iced tea, and more often than not, I leave her house with a container of one of her delicious homemade soups.

Mary, the teacher in my tai chi class, has listened to me many times. I can see in her the true desire to hear me and to see things from my perspective. I can see her listening, and when I send e-mail updates, her responses are always very meaningful, and I know she has given thought before answering me. I don't think she knows what this means to me.

Outside of a handful of people, I let the grapevine take care of telling everyone else. As time went on and early summer approached, I began to get calls from my regular customers at the farmers market. These customers were looking for pies, cinnamon rolls, or perhaps some jars of jam or jelly. I would have to explain to them that I was no longer baking, because I had cancer. For the most part, I wanted to keep it short and sweet, so I thanked them for their prayers and quickly ended the conversations. Some shared stories about someone they knew who had cancer and beat it, as they were sure I would. They all told me to stay positive.

This triggered memories of some of my customers who had themselves died of cancer in the previous few years. I recalled how sad I had felt at their passings, and how, at the time, it had struck me that with them gone, I had lost a little piece of the joy I found in being a vendor at the Kittanning Farmers Market. I began to think about who would fill my old spot at the market and whether the customers would line up and wait for them as they had for me. I was sure that, gradually, I and my baked goods would become nothing more than a faded memory and the market would go on. That is the way of life. I remembered my husband, on a Saturday evening one fall, saying, "I wonder how many people in Kittanning are just finishing up their dinner, getting ready to cut into one of Jamie Schneider's famous apple pies?" At the time he said this, it gave me a wonderful feeling. But thinking back on this moment, it made me sad, and I cried, thinking of all the joy I had gotten from baking but would have no longer.

Enemies

I am at an oldies party with friends. It is early evening. We are here to laugh, dance, eat, and generally have a good time. I will do my best to make it this way, but I will never forget that big *C* badge I wear. I try to pretend that I am like everyone else, but I know I am not. As I walk across the floor with Donna, I paste a friendly smile on my face. It doesn't have any connection to the thoughts that bounce around in my mind. I am busy imagining all the cancer-related thoughts I am sure people are having about me. Donna and I go to check out the food table. She sees some people she knows and introduces me. She asks if I know one particular woman, who has been at St. Jude Golf Club, along with a number of others at the party. I say I've probably seen her.

The woman looks at me, and says, "Oh yeah, how are you doing?" We both know she is asking about my cancer. We both know "Oh yeah" means "Oh, you're the one who has cancer." And we both know "How are you doing?" means "I want the whole scuttlebutt so I can talk all about it when I get together with my friends."

I sort of shrug and say "Okay." Not the kind of thing I really want to go into detail about—first of all at a party, and secondly with someone I barely (if at all) know. But she persists and asks about my chemo treatments, and she then continues by telling me the details of someone she knows that has cancer. I mumble something and say I'm going to go sit down. I am angry and embarrassed. What could possibly have made her think that was a good way to go? Here is a good example of how intent guides my response. Clearly, her intent was to gather gossip, with little concern for how I might feel about her intrusion into the personal details of my cancer treatment.

Somehow, people seem to feel a need to let me know that they know what it's all about. If I go out with just a hat on, and no wig, I can see people looking at my lack of hair. Some note it and just continue on as they would in any case. Others seem to feel they have to let me know that, yes, they got it. They see, they know I have cancer, and they know what it's all about because they know someone who has, or had, cancer. I especially love it when they tell me a story about someone who died from cancer! Those are always very inspiring! These "enemies" are energy suckers—enemies to my well-being. These are people in the category of "disliking intensely"; people with whom I would never, under any circumstances, want to share any intimate details of my life. And yet I have no choice. What a feeling of powerlessness! And yes, resentment. Fortunately, this is a very small group. I don't want anything from them, especially pity.

I only have control over my response to this kind of invasion to my privacy. I can choose to limit the part these people play in my life—at least to the degree I am able to do that. When I do see them, I give them cursory responses and quickly move on. I am happy to pretend with them. The best I can do is take them at face value and accept their well wishes as sincere—at least as sincere as they are capable of being. I certainly have more important things to worry about.

Lunches, Lunches, and More Lunches

Whenever something bad happens in your life, you are expected to make the best of it. Of course, this makes sense, and it is what we should do. I've always thought of tough times as opportunities. They usually come around more than once, so if you miss out the first time around, you'll likely get another shot. Unfortunately, really big opportunities are rarer in occurrence. I thought having a baby was a really tough experience. Labor is the right name for it. I think if I could have had, say, four opportunities, I would have been pretty good at it by the time number five rolled around. Alas, I only had two chances, and labor was still labor at the end of the second experience.

I'm thinking cancer is an experience that one should only endure once; and I'm hoping that is the case for me. It looks more likely than not that I will get my wish, because so far my first experience is never-ending. As I work my way through this yo-yo existence and do what I can to make the best of it, I look back to see what good might have come from it. The only thing that stands out for me is that I have developed some deeper relationships with a few people that, without my having cancer, would likely have remained superficial. In response to cards, flowers, phone calls, or some impromptu contact, we started going out to lunch occasionally.

Generally, such situations involved just me and one other person. The other people were women whom I knew, perhaps as a result of our kids playing the same sport, or as a result of our belonging to the same organization. After a brief contact of some sort, we became interested in getting together again. Lunch seemed like a natural way to do this. When you know you are likely to die soon, it is easier to get right to the big stuff with people that are sincere. You don't feel a need to skate around the edges or get caught up in being worried that maybe you are approaching a subject that is too personal. What can be more personal than dying? At our annual pig roast, I caught up with Darlene, whom I had known for years. Our sons had played soccer and hockey together, and she and I had together run the soccer boosters program for a year. After hearing me make jokes about hair loss while waiting in line at the food table, she approached me to find out what that was all about. So I told her about my cancer. She looked flabbergasted, and the first question she asked me was, "How's your faith?"

I appreciated how she had put this question to me. There was no judgment, no preaching; she didn't try to tell me what I should be doing, thinking, or believing in relation to God. It was more along the line of "How are you dealing with all this? How deeply has it impacted you?" We talked for a long time. A couple weeks later, she called me to see if I wanted to get together to talk or have lunch or something. At that point, I didn't know if she was just doing her Christian duty by helping someone in distress or if she was interested in me personally. It didn't matter. I sensed her uncertainty in asking me, and that made me want to spend time with her. She was just offering herself—nothing fancy, nothing pretentious, just herself. It has been a wonderful experience getting to know her. Yes, there is life beyond being a soccer/hockey mom!

There are others. Lynn, an old college friend, always manages to pop in with something tasty, such as a wonderful homemade quiche. We love to talk about our kids. Amazingly, we have known each other since college, yet is seems as though we are just getting to know each other. Carolyn and I have had many lunches and talked about many things. I am amazed at what a good person she is, and I am more amazed that she doesn't even know it. My cousin Kathy always seems to call or e-mail to set up a lunch date just when I need her company. Her mother was my favorite aunt, and I can see the same qualities that demonstrate thoughtfulness of others in Kathy. My Aunt Mary was a fantastic baker, and even as children, my siblings and I named some of our favorites after her: Aunt Mary bread and Aunt Mary cookies. What a rare treat when Kathy shows up with her Aunt Mary bread (now made by Kathy, since my Aunt Mary died several years ago), chipped ham off-the-bone, and fresh tomatoes! The only way she can top that is by also bringing some of her home-made, chocolate-covered, double-stuff Oreo cookies!

Like two blasts from the past, Betty and Lisa came back into my life after years of not seeing them. Betty and I had reconnected in the year before my diagnosis, after the death of a mutual friend. Her wit is like her mind: sharp. We worked together at Arc Manor for several years, running group therapy as a team. Somehow, the connection we developed then survived through the long separation, and we picked up right where we left off. Like a breath of fresh air, having lunch with Betty is always rejuvenating. I always end up having multiple good belly-laughs while we eat. She listens better than anyone I know. She has a way of summing things up so that I know she has been attentive, and she always seems to add a fresh perspective. I walk away feeling like I have a much clearer idea of what I'm dealing with than before we spoke.

And Lisa is so down-to-earth that after I speak with her, I feel like I have just walked through a meadow of wildflowers where I have been touched by their gentle spirit. I know she doesn't see herself that way; but then maybe most of us don't really know how we are perceived by others. All topics are open to discussion with Lisa, a prescription that is just what the doctor ordered for me, especially on this journey. We seem to discover one connection after another, and I can't imagine ever running out of things to talk about with her.

Then there are those who give me rides home from my chemo treatments. I always treat them to lunch; it is a small way I can show my appreciation for their company, as well as the ride home. My sisters Therese and Michele, and my good friend Elaine, have put up with my motormouth, which I always seem to have a bad case of, after chemo. I have come to know these sisters as two wonderful women instead of just my younger sisters. They are both strong and independent, and they have made good lives for themselves. It's funny how long it sometimes takes to see our family members as people who have lives outside the family.

Elaine and I have had many discussions about God, spirituality, and the like. While not all of our ideas are the same, we are the same in that we each have ideas that are rather different from the norm. These discussions are good, because as I approach moving into the spirit world, I am fascinated by all the possibilities of what that world might be like.

In spite of my hesitation in telling people about my cancer, in the end there have been good things that have come from it. I know of people who have kept themselves isolated through the process of dealing with their cancer. What a lonely place that must have been. Just having cancer creates a separation. The moments I get to spend with someone who lets me bring him or her into my world are the moments I live for. While these moments are huge in spirit, they are grains of sand in the hourglass of time. It is enough. I have to make it enough. Even though there only seem to be a handful of people who are interested in coming with me for that moment in time, I am forever grateful for those who have the willingness to take that journey. I can only hope that in some small way, I might have given something of value back.

Chapter Four

THE LOSSES

In the beginning, when I knew I was very sick and I knew that many people at this level of sickness don't live much longer, I was happy just to be alive. The longer I could stretch it out, the better I felt. I became more hopeful, thinking I just might be one of those select few who beat the odds. As I dragged my tired body through those first six months of chemotherapy, I was anxious to get back to my old life. "Okay," I'd say to myself, "All you have to do is live for six months. You just have to deal with this chemo for now. Once you get to the point where you're ready for surgery, things will get better. Then, maybe you can get your old life back."

But that moment never came. My life moved in a downward spiral. Just when I began to think I was approaching something that looked like life before cancer and the yo-yo was flying high, I was once again plummeted to the bottom, left there bouncing and jerking, and I knew for sure that I would be there for a while. Recovery from each major fall required a whole new rewind and a new start. I felt tired just thinking about it. If you read the *fine print*, it does say that with ovarian cancer there is generally an initial positive response to treatment, but it almost always comes back.

The best way to describe living with cancer is that it is a never-ending series of losses. Some of them are direct side effects of the chemotherapy treatments, and others are more insidious. Individually, they seem trite, and I imagine that if I complained about them singly, I would sound quite whiny. It is the sheer number of them that makes them significant. As a normal part of life, we are all called upon to incorporate changes—some convenient, some not—into our everyday lives. I had always prided myself on not sweating the small stuff. "Just deal with it, and get on about the business of living your life" was my philosophy.

Jim, the mechanic who lost his wife to breast cancer, told me a story of an experience he had about a year after she died. He was cutting the grass at his little camp along the river. Suddenly, his lawn mower stopped. He sat down in the yard to see what the problem was. As he took it apart, he dropped a screw he had taken out, and it rolled away. After a minute of looking for it, he just sat down and cried and cried. He said that his only thought was "I just can't bear to lose one more thing."

Halfway through spring, my husband finally removed our Harry Lauder's walking stick tree. This tree was one of my all-time favorites. We'd had him for at least twenty years. Harry was a twisted, gnarly mass of branches, and I'd always found him much more attractive in the winter, when there were no leaves to cover his bones. While he seemed to barely survive in the first spot we put him in, he really settled in and grew in the second spot. Sadly, three years ago, he developed a disease, and our treatments did little to help him get healthy again. When he rode into spring with only a handful of leaves, we knew it was time to say good-bye. He had lost his battle.

I was unable to stop myself from comparing his struggle with mine. I did the same thing when our three-year-old forest pansy redbud tree (given to me by four friends after my mother passed away in March 2007) died during the spring of 2010, even after many buds showed the promise of a good, healthy year. I tried not to look at these losses as omens. Perhaps they were opportunities to prepare myself for the loss of my own life. Both trees were replaced, and the new ones showed every sign of being around for a long time. Perhaps the message I was to be getting was that life goes on. Patrick told me this when he was five years old, when the baby bluebird died and he reminded me that a new baby had just been born.

Bill probably gets the best firsthand experience of seeing all the losses cancer has brought to my life and our life together. He is around me more than anyone else, and often, he is with me when I have the first experience of each new loss. We could be in the middle of doing something we've done repeatedly in our thirty-four years together, and he gets to see my frustration and hear my comments as I try to do something simple—something that I've done so often that I don't even have to think about it—yet I no longer have the stamina to get it done.

One weekend, he spent most of Saturday working in our blueberry plot. While we have actually had to provide very little special care to the bushes themselves over the years, keeping their plot looking good and keeping the birds away has been a much bigger job. Just weeding took him several hours. The oldest bushes are about twenty years old, and in that time, we have developed what we consider a pretty good method of keeping the birds away. This involves putting up a fence around all thirteen bushes. A 7' × 100' piece of deer netting serves that purpose beautifully. Then, for the "roof," a piece of 24' × 35' netting covers everything in our 20' × 20' plot. But wait, we're not done yet. Since the bunnies like to chew through the netting on the bottom, to get in and eat the bark off the bottom of the blueberry canes, it's necessary to put an 18" roll of chicken wire around the bottom. Done yet? Nope. Now the roof has to be woven to the sides with something like plastic weed-wacker string, and the same needs to be done to attach the chicken wire to the side netting. In spite of all this, it is likely that more than once per season, I will look out the window above the sink and see a bird inside the netting, flapping away like crazy, knocking blueberries all over the place.

This is a job we had always done together, with Bill acting as director and me doing the grunt work. When he was close to done covering the bushes that Saturday, Bill asked me to come up and inspect his handiwork. It was noon, and I was still in my jammies. I made the hundred-foot trek to where the blueberries were growing, and I was amazed at all the work he had done.

"Wow! It looks great!" I said with all sincerity. "How about those pink lemonade blueberries? Any berries on them this year?" We had just planted them last year, and they appeared to have survived their first winter well. Just something different—and fun.

"No. But the bushes are growing well. Maybe next year," he said. I wondered if I would be around to see those pink lemonades. I hoped so.

Within a few minutes, I could feel the heat of the sun, a forbidden pleasure for me in my condition. I could already begin to feel my body getting shaky, not only because of the sun but also because of the chemo settling in to work on destroying my body—some of the good along with the bad. Saturday is one of the worst days after a Wednesday chemo treatment.

"I have to go in. Too hot for me."

"Do you need me to help you?" he asked.

"No, I'm okay. I just need to go in." He stayed outside to continue his work, while I made my way back to the house.

When we decided to take a short trip to Florida in the spring of 2012, I was a little leery about it. A trip to Florida had always meant fun in the sun to me. So, on my last appointment at the cancer clinic before we took off for the Sunshine State, I asked the PA to review why it was that I had to stay out of the sun while I was undergoing chemotherapy.

"It's because you could get badly burnt. Chemo is hard on the skin cells."

I just sat looking at her while she waited for me to say something. I could feel myself getting angry. "We're going to Florida, and I just wanted to be sure I understood why this is important." My anger was already beginning to segue into sadness.

"Well," she said, with a helpful tone of voice, "You can put a real good sunscreen on, wear clothing to cover as much as you can, and get yourself a nice, big hat …"

I stopped listening to her. Was she serious? Was that really supposed to make me feel better? "That's *not* being in the sun," I replied, beginning to feel angry with *her*. And all she was trying to do was help.

Every time I wake up and can see that the sun is out and it's going to be a beautiful day, I just want to roll over and stay in bed all day long. I resist my urge, but it is my first reaction to seeing a sunny day, knowing that I can now enjoy it only from a distance. That wonderful feeling of the heat of the sun on my bare skin is now something I can enjoy only in tiny doses, or in my mind.

Later in the weekend, after the blueberries were all secured inside their cage, Bill and I lounged in the shade on the front porch, on our beach recliners, pretending we were listening to the waves, and pretending we were feeling the sun on our middle-aged, overweight bodies.

This sense of loss is something that I experience on a daily basis. Even I am amazed at the simple things that trigger it.

My husband; my son, Patrick; and I are going out to dinner. On the way to The Villa, the conversation turned to Carrie, Patrick's fiancée. I commented that she was an amazing teacher and that I loved to hear her tell stories about her students. It is so obvious that she loves her job, and she takes it very seriously. I said her students were lucky to have her. My son agreed. Then I commented that the boys he works with were lucky to have him. He works with young autistic boys, helping them to adjust, to fit in, and to cope with their feelings. He gave a small chuckle. I began to feel sad. I felt cheated that I would likely have such a short time to enjoy seeing these two young people make a difference in their world. I forced myself to begin thinking about something else; I didn't want to put a damper on a nice evening out. Later, from the psychologist I started seeing, I found out that this is called mindfulness—a new psychology buzzword.

I think this is the biggest thing that people don't understand. It is all these losses that have taken my life from me, that have left me dangling, wondering what I'm supposed to do now. In the movie *A Few Good Men*, Harold is one of two marines being charged with the murder of a fellow marine, and Tom Cruise plays military lawyer Lieutenant Daniel Kaffee. Kaffee tells Harold that he can get him out in six months, and that he should take the plea. Harold looks at Kaffee and says, "We'll be dishonorably discharged, right?" Kaffee confirms this, and Harold says, "And what do we do then, sir?" Of course Kaffee doesn't get it, because he is only thinking in terms of how great he is for getting his client such a short sentence.

I feel like Harold. I feel as though I've been dishonorably discharged from life. I have been given more time to live, but there is much less that I can actually do in that time than I would have been able to do before I had cancer. So I want to say to my doctor, "And what do I do now, doc?" There is no part of my life that is normal. Everything has to be done with special accommodations. This is one of the many parts of having cancer that people don't see. They see the finished product—the me that I have prepared for them to see so that they will think I am normal, just like them. How ironic that I then complain that people don't really see me.

CHEMOTHERAPY

While chemotherapy is not the only course of treatment for cancer, it is the one I chose. I have friends who have told me that if they had cancer, they wouldn't do chemo. They are into alternative medicine or alternative treatments. When I first found out I had cancer, and after I began telling people, I got an endless stream of e-mails offering to sell me different cures for cancer. There seemed to be no end to the possibilities. Although I say the e-mails offered to sell me cures, to be honest a few weren't selling something. A couple of my favorites recommended four tablespoons of pureed canned asparagus a day, and yawning. I cast my lot with the doctors right off the bat. While I also did things like acupuncture, Reiki, healing imagery, I knew that if I was going to have any chance to get better, it would be through modern medical science. Interestingly, those friends who wouldn't do chemo if they had cancer had all turned to modern medical science when they had something major go wrong with their bodies. For me, the risk was too great to be experimenting with potions or natural healing.

There is a huge difference between having an intellectual discussion about what you would do theoretically and being faced with the actual situation. I have learned that lesson many times and have had to eat my words because what I thought in the abstract meant nothing when I was actually confronted with the reality. I had never really thought about what I would do if I got cancer, because, of course, I was not a person who would get cancer. Humility is a marvelous thing. It's astonishing how big we can let our egos get, until we are confronted with something.

When you hear about all the nasty, negative side effects of

chemotherapy, it might seem hard to understand why people would put themselves through all that. Perhaps it's our "no pain, no gain" mentality. Or perhaps it's more basic than that. Perhaps it's a desire to hang on to life at all costs. I have chosen the course that I think gives me the best chance of survival. My commitment is 100 percent. It is all I can do.

My husband insisted on accompanying me for my first chemotherapy treatment, to be sure I got started off on the right foot. I was up at 5:30 a.m. to get ready. The trip from our home in Kittanning to the hospital in Oakland was an hour, if everything went smoothly. We left with an extra half hour, to accommodate traffic, parking, elevator waits, etc. Unfortunately, just because we were on time didn't mean we would start as scheduled.

After an hour wait, we were escorted back to the treatment rooms. Each reclining chair had its own little curtained-off cubicle, complete with a chair for the one allowed visitor, a small television, and the various pieces of medical equipment needed to complete the treatment. I began my treatment with the golden standard: a combination of two "old time" chemicals.

We settled in for the duration as Barb, the chemo nurse, approached with a big, friendly, welcoming smile. She would be my regular nurse. She explained all the "premeds" right before she administered them. I had already taken five steroid pills the night before, and five more that morning before leaving home. In addition, I would receive an injection of more steroids. This was to help counteract the side effects of the chemo, as well as help fight the nausea. I also received a separate anti-nausea medication, and an antihistamine to counteract any potential allergic reaction to the chemicals. Since I had never taken the antihistamine before, I had no idea how it would impact me.

About five minutes after it was administered, I began to feel very woozy. My speech was slurred, and I found it difficult to concentrate, let alone carry on a conversation. Barb assured me this was a typical reaction. I dozed off several times in the middle of conversation with Bill. We made it through the morning, though, without a hitch, and when we stopped for lunch (soup at Panera), I still felt groggy from the antihistamine. I might compare this to how I felt after having two or three beers, not an unpleasant feeling. I had yet to feel anything from the chemo itself.

For the next six months of my chemo, I developed a rotation with two of my sisters, Michele and Therese, and my good friend Elaine taking turns bringing me home. While the side effects of the antihistamine did diminish with each consecutive treatment, I was still not in a good condition to drive myself. Aside from this, I needed the company. Once a month, I had an appointment with either a PA or the doctor before my chemo. Just having to talk about the finer details of life with cancer was brutalizing, in a way that is hard to explain. I could remember a day when I would go to the doctor with some small complaint, and he would prescribe me some medication that would take care of whatever was ailing me. For example, I knew that when the antibiotic had run its course, so would have my bronchitis; or after finishing the steroids, my poison ivy would be all dried up.

Now I knew there was really no cure for what ailed me. Recommendations for dealing with the side effects of the chemo, I soon learned, would always fall short of the mark. Still, I would follow them, if for no other reason than to feel like I had some control over what was happening to me. Besides, I didn't want to come across as being difficult, or perhaps argumentative. All of these people were dedicated to their job and went out of their way to be helpful and understanding, in their own way. Perhaps, at times, I felt resentful that their help wasn't more helpful. I wanted to feel better. Each time I left that office, the idea was more strongly reinforced that I would never feel better.

I was generally a basket case by the end of my appointments; every nerve felt raw, exposed. I would have loved to have just crawled into a cave somewhere. But what I had to do was put on a pleasant face, go up to the fourth floor, and go through two to four hours (including the inevitable wait time) of treatment. The nurses went out of their way to be cheerful, but sometimes I was unable to be friendly back. I'm sure their approach is generally the best approach for a situation like that; what else would they do? Sometimes I just couldn't respond in kind. If I cried or looked sad, they would say, with a surprised look on their faces, "What's wrong?"

What could it possibly be? Surely not that I have stage IV ovarian cancer! When the nurses were giving me my chemotherapy, if I said sad things, they would quickly change the subject. I found it easier around them to just act as if I were fine. I did my best to look cheerful when I went to the cancer center. I rarely ever saw any other patients crying, so

I think probably I was one of the most unpleasant ones. The first time Barb was not my chemo nurse, I worried that she had asked someone else to deal with me because I was too difficult.

I felt bad for whoever accompanied me on any given day. As long as I was talking, I was awake, but if I paused for a few seconds to listen to one of my sisters, or my friend, I would usually fall asleep. And they had to sit on the hard chair next to me. Perhaps they should have had the recliner. I was entirely focused on myself. When I was tearful, and started talking about all the things in life I wouldn't get to do or experience, there was really nothing they could say to make me feel better. They never complained; they just listened—the best thing in that case. I will be forever grateful for their company. I could never have gotten through those first six months without them.

The side effects of chemotherapy are numerous. Each type of chemo has its own particular set, although there are some side effects that are common to most forms. I had already experienced the biggest and most devastating losses—the loss of confidence in life, and the feeling of betrayal by my body. The first and biggest loss I could attribute directly to chemo was the loss of my hair. Being a very practical and realistic person, I had the idea that this would not be a big deal. After all, living bald was very much preferable to being dead with hair. This, though, was just the beginning, and it was not nearly as easy as I thought it would be.

Each day, at least two or three times, I would run my hands through my hair and make a little pile with what came out in my hand. I would save it up on the counter in the bathroom for my husband to see when he came home from work. Maybe it was a concrete way for him to understand what I felt like. At the end of each day, he or I would flush it down the toilet. Within a few weeks, my hair was so thin that there was no denying my ensuing baldness. I had my wig ordered, and it arrived just in time. Two of my sisters, Therese and Michele, were kind enough to go with me to help me get through the shaving experience. It helped that they didn't fall over in shock or disgust, or laugh hysterically once my hair was gone, although I was sure they were just being nice when they said I didn't look too bad as a bald person.

Until it's gone, you don't realize how many imperfections a good head of hair can conceal. I had no idea of the actual shape of my head. It was a lot smaller than I thought it would be under all that hair. And that flat spot right at the crown was a lot flatter than it was when covered by my hair. There is nothing obvious that tells you that you are a woman when you are bald, if you look at yourself only from the neck up. For the first two weeks, I could not bear the idea of my husband seeing my bald head. When I did not have my wig on, I wore a cotton cap.

I was also surprised at how much colder my head was without hair. My light blue cap was designated for sleeping. Gradually, I realized that it would be virtually impossible to get through the rest of my life without my husband ever seeing me bald. So, after going to bed wearing my little blue cap, I waited until he fell asleep. Then, once he was snoring, I removed the cap. Since he always woke up before I did, I knew he would see me while I was still asleep and have time to prepare himself for that moment of reckoning. Then he could try to look at me as if I didn't look any different. The next morning, a Saturday, I lay in bed awake, trying to prepare myself to go out and "be seen" by my husband, who was already in the living room.

In 2010, we celebrated our thirty-two-year anniversary. Ours has been an easy relationship because Bill is so easygoing. He rarely gets his feathers ruffled. I, on the other hand, am the one who is known to get intense about things—sometimes seemingly unimportant things. Bill is "steady as she goes." I could go into a rant over something completely unexpected. Even after all these years, I think he just doesn't really know how to respond, so he generally lets me go on until my rant has run its course before he might venture to add something. For some reason, this worked for us. Perhaps we are different sides of the same coin. We have settled into a comfortable state of ebb and flow.

"Good morning," he said, as if it were any other normal day. "That doesn't look so bad."

Of course he would say that. What else could he say? "Wow! That looks a lot worse than I thought it would!" "God! I don't know if I'll be able to stand looking at you anymore!" "Your head has a very weird shape," or "Boy, I sure hope I don't look that bad when I go bald!" These, of course, are all things I thought, and so I figured he surely must have been thinking them too. But he truthfully didn't seem to care, and so we adjusted. I became comfortable enough to sit around the house wigless. Wigs are a wonderful thing, but you never forget that you have one on, and they never become easy to wear.

That was the beginning. Since my cancer was already stage IV when I was diagnosed, my chemotherapy regimen was what the oncology nurse called "a hefty dose." Mostly, the only side effect the layperson is familiar with is nausea and vomiting. That's the only one I had ever heard about until I had to deal with it myself. Since I never experienced that one, people assumed I was feeling pretty good. But in fact, there is an extensive list of side effects, and I had most of the other ones. Side effects vary according to which particular variety of chemo you are receiving and to the dosage you receive. There is a reason they give you the mega doses initially. This is because early on, your body has more stamina and is therefore more likely to tolerate the devastation caused by the chemotherapy. For every cancer cell it kills, it also kills healthy cells. So for every little bit better you feel due to there being less cancer in your body, you feel a little bit worse because you have less body to feel good in. Still, it is preferable to being dead.

By the end of the first cycle of chemotherapy, I noticed a dramatic improvement in the way I felt. I remembered Dr. Sukumvanich telling me at the end of my first visit with him that I would start to feel better once I started treatment. He was right. I guess the chemo had enough impact on the cancer to reduce its effect on me. Perhaps the ascites began to diminish and the fluid in my lungs began to dry up; all of this would leave less pressure in my pelvic and abdominal areas. I could breathe again.

One cycle lasted four weeks, with chemotherapy once a week for three weeks, and then one week off. The first week, I was treated with two drugs, and then, on weeks two and three, only one. In my case, the first time I had to skip that third week because my white blood cells were practically nonexistent. I remember when Chris, the oncology nurse, called to tell me this. My reaction was to say, "I might be dead in two weeks!" Round we went with her reassuring me that no, I would not be dead, and me insisting I would be. I didn't believe her, but there was nothing I could do about it. Chris was matter-of-fact, and I learned I could count on her to be direct, albeit not unsympathetic. While she didn't sugarcoat things, she had no qualms about letting me know when I was being ridiculous. It was what I needed, the no-sugar-added version of what to expect in life with cancer.

In spite of my having received only two treatments that first cycle, I had more energy, felt less shaky, and had my first deadly bout of hope. Within this first cycle of chemo, I also had my initial education about the CA-125. This is a very official-sounding term, and just as it sounds, it represents experiment number 125, related to a cancer antigen. In simple terms, this is a protein that can become elevated in the blood as a result of ovarian cancer. It can, though, become elevated for a variety of other reasons that have nothing to do with cancer, so it is not a good screening vehicle for ovarian cancer. However, it is reliable enough that in some cases (like mine, my doctor thought), it can be a good indication of tumor growth or reduction. It gives a fairly good indication of whether tumors are shrinking or growing. This is a valuable piece of nonsurgical, non-scan information.

For a normal person—that is, someone who is cancer-free—this number should be below 35. Imagine my reaction when I found out that my initial number was 15,780! I marveled that I was still alive. Fortunately, at the same time I got this information, it was at the end of my first cycle of chemotherapy, at which time I found out that my number was down to 7,230. And, so began my life by numbers. This was probably my first smooth ride to the top of the yo-yo. I was doing well. I was kicking my cancer's ass!

My excitement was short-lived. By the second cycle, my initial good results became clouded over by overwhelming feelings of fatigue and weakness. As I continued my chemo treatments, these feelings increased. I only passed out one time, and fortunately Bill was home then. I woke up on the floor in the bathroom, and he was able to help me to the bedroom. This was sometime in the third or fourth month of chemo. Gradually, I learned to pace myself. "Pace yourself" is a phrase frequently used as a solution to those feelings of tiredness and fatigue experienced by cancer patients. These are side effects that seem to be common to all chemotherapy treatments, to one degree or another.

Here's how pacing worked for me: After getting my shower, I would quickly dry off and then lie down for fifteen minutes or so. Then I would get up and finish with the body lotions, moisturizers, eye drops, etc. Since skin cells are fast-dividing cells, the chemotherapy does a good job of destroying them too. The consequence is severe drying out of your skin. So, after each shower, complete body moisturizing is the best route. Another rest of fifteen minutes or so, and I would be ready to get dressed. After one more bed rest, I would come out to the kitchen and sit down while I decided what to make for breakfast. On a given day, I might decide on a bowl of cereal. Since I generally added fresh fruit and raisins, this would usually require one or two rest periods to prepare, and then I could sit down and take my time eating. There was no hurry anyway, because I would likely be spending the rest of the day in "my chair." I designated it as mine, because I spent so much time there, and it was always left available for my use.

This fatigue and weakness were closely related to bone marrow suppression. I experienced it all. My white blood cell counts were low enough that my chemotherapy was postponed. All in all, as a result of unsatisfactory blood count levels, I missed five of the eighteen scheduled chemotherapy treatments in that first six months. That probably was why I was unable to be on my feet for more than fifteen to twenty minutes at a time. After that, the shaking and weakness would start; then would follow a heavy feeling, as if my body had somehow gotten an extra three hundred pounds attached to it. These were all things others could not see when they looked at me. So when I went out to run an errand, such as picking up my meds or running to the bank, and I saw someone I knew, of course that person would tell me that I looked great, that it was good to see me out, and that he or she was glad I was feeling okay. How nice!

My eyes and nasal passages dried up like little mud puddles on a hot summer day. Blinking became a process that happened in slow motion, and my dry eyes struggled to close and open again, with lids that were parched and eyeballs that seemed to suction themselves to the lids. It was the same feeling I used to get when I spent the day in the sun at the beach, fighting with the waves. By the end of that day, the combination of sand, sun, and saltwater was enough to make me just want to close my eyes and leave them that way. Now, with cancer, this was a normal, everyday feeling. My eye doctor recommended drops—one steroid drop a day and over-the-counter drops up to eight times a day, just for the moisturizing quality. This helped, but shortly after I applied the drops, my eyes sucked up the moisture and would be begging for more.

Unfortunately, there was no treatment that helped my sinuses. I constantly had bleeding sores in my nose and a dryness that would at times suction my nostrils to the inside of my nose. Strangely, despite all that dryness, if I bent over, clear mucous would at times just drip from my nose. None of the sprays I used seemed to change any of these symptoms.

Other common side effects of my initial chemo treatments included peripheral neuropathy, with such symptoms as numbness, tingling, pain, or decreased sensation in your fingers and toes. This could result in clumsiness in doing things like buttoning your clothes, and changes in your walking ability. My case of neuropathy was mild enough to only be annoying. Then there were mouth sores, redness, and irritation of my gums and throat, and taste changes. My dentist prescribed a rinse solution, made for chemotherapy patients, that helped tremendously with the mouth sores. I only had sores after my first cycle of chemotherapy; once I started using the rinse, my mouth, gums, and tongue would be irritated, but I never had any more sores.

Within the first few months, food had little taste to me. I complained that Bill wasn't putting any salt in the food he made. Finally, I realized that no matter how much salt I put on it, the food just didn't have any taste. It wasn't Bill's cooking. It was my lost taste buds. On top of all this were stomach issues like diarrhea and constipation, which I only experienced at mild to moderate levels, depending on which chemo I was receiving.

Sexual problems included the possibility of permanent inability to have children. Since I had already gone through menopause, I fortunately would not have to worry about that one. Of course, who could think about having sex at a time like this anyway! I hated my body. It had betrayed me. It had refused to do what it was supposed to do; it had basically fallen down on the job. How could I ever have any good feeling connected with it again? Not to mention that my insides had dried up and become shriveled and tight. This had already begun before I had cancer, but it had been at a manageable level. Now that smooth feeling of pleasure that used to come when my husband's penis slid inside was replaced with a harsh, painful scraping that was beyond unpleasant.

Then there was the general category of flu-like symptoms: fever, headache, joint and muscle pain, and fatigue. To complicate matters, these flu-like symptoms could be the result of withdrawal from pain medication. I was in a constant state of worry about whether I was taking too much, and I would go as long as I possibly could before taking another dose. Twenty years of working in a drug and alcohol rehab clinic was not lost on me! Were the symptoms caused by the chemo, the low blood count, or the pain medications? I drove myself crazy trying to figure this out. I think it came down to control; I wanted it to be under my control.

Finally, Bill said, "I don't think you should worry about that now. When you get off the chemo, you'll find out what it is and deal with it then." He was right, of course; it was the same thing Chris told me. I think it was then that I realized the nurse probably wasn't worried because she knew how unlikely it was that I'd ever be off the chemo. So my standing joke was "When I get off the chemo, if I'm hooked on the pain meds, I'll just go to rehab." I was only half-joking. I still couldn't bring myself to accept that I would likely never be done with chemo.

My Body

When I look at myself in the mirror, I see my mother. She was eighty-four when she died. I am fifty-nine. I see the skin hanging from my neck—a wattle, I think it's called, on birds. The skin on my arms has taken on that fine, translucent look of the aged. Before I apply body moisturizers, the skin on the back of my hands looks somewhat like a five-thousand-piece piece jigsaw puzzle, with tiny lines crisscrossing each other repeatedly. Since I have been significantly overweight for about half of my adult life, I know that has been a contributing factor. But it is the chemotherapy that has sped up the process so tremendously. I noticed the gradual loss of elasticity over the last few years, but within the last year, I seem to have aged about ten years.

I have suffered from osteoarthritis for several years—not surprising, as I have a family history of joint problems. This has led to a gradual decline in my ability to do things. I remember watching my mother struggle to get up from a seated position and thinking that I would work hard to be in better shape. I did that. I worked hard at this and took pride in the fact that I could do it well. Now, though, just getting up and down, or walking short distances, has become a chore.

Now when I see my reflection in a window, I see a somewhat hunched-over figure of an old woman who walks with a limp, who has sagging skin that wobbles as she walks. There is no definition at my neck. I even see sagging skin on the calves of my legs. My body is no longer my friend.

I have been line dancing for about ten years, and I love it. The woman who got me started, Jeanine, ran an exercise class at the local YMCA. She was about fifteen years older than I, but she was a fitness buff and in better shape. About three years ago, she developed colon cancer. I remember when she came line dancing after several months of absence. Everyone was excited to see her and told her how great she looked. She looked awful. Her body was skeletal. She had always been on the thin side, without an ounce of body fat, but she was now emaciated. I was unable to bring myself to approach her for quite some time. She got up once to dance, and that lasted for about thirty seconds. As the evening progressed, I approached her. I gave her a hug and told her that she was my hero and that I hoped that if I were in her situation, I could even be half as brave as she was. We cried a little bit together, and she thanked me for that comment. She left shortly after. I was unable to stop crying for the rest of the evening.

Two months later, I found out I had stage IV ovarian cancer. I have always said that God gives us many opportunities to prepare for what comes at us in life. I think most of the time we ignore them or don't realize that they are opportunities. When I look back on that night when Jeanine last went line dancing, I feel stunned. It was like God heard what I said to her and then said to himself, "Well, let's just see how brave you will be." I know this is irrational, but it's hard to keep my thoughts from going there.

I sent her a little note, telling her about my illness and commenting on how strange fate is sometimes. She called me, and we talked for a little while. Always a very proud woman, she asked me if I cried a lot. I had to tell her yes, and then we cried together on the phone. She told me that her medical team wanted to try a new form of chemotherapy on her, as her cancer had spread to her liver. She said, "I'll probably call you again." Two weeks later, she was gone. She had insisted that her family go to the store to get a few things, and when they returned, she was dead.

At one point I noticed that when I told people I still went line dancing, I seemed negative. I had to think about why I still went. The only answer is that I told Jeanine I wished I could be half as brave as she was in the same situation. It felt like a promise I made to her, but it was really a promise to myself. I go because I can. It is something I can do, and since what I can do is so limited, I don't dare leave anything out. I think about her most nights when I go line dancing, and I thank her quietly for her inspiration.

At times, I wish I had started line dancing much sooner. It is sad to think that I could have been having that fun much for a longer period of time. But at least I had these ten years. The faster and the wilder the dances were, the better I liked them. I would taunt some of the other dancers to get them to pick up the pace. Now when I go line dancing, I do more of a light shuffle around the floor. I always get pleasant greetings from the other dancers; they are trying to be positive and encouraging to me: "You look great!" "It's good to see you out." "Doesn't it make you feel good to be able to come here?" No, not really. I am still mourning the loss of my previous dancing abilities.

There was one dance that several of us wanted to bring back. It was one we had done a few years before, and we all really liked it. It was a fast one, to the song "Jambalaya" by Joel Sonnier and Eddie Raven. It took a while, but finally we figured out how to do it. Jackie and Ernie, our teachers and my good friends, were ever patient with our requests. I practiced it at home in my kitchen. When the big day came that we were going to do it in dancing class, I was unfortunately unable to keep the pace. After less than a minute, I had to sit down—too fast for me. So I keep to the more simple routines, and even when I do those, I shuffle. While I used to take up a large space, I now confine myself to about two square feet.

I still go to tai chi classes when I can. I had already been going to them for about six years. It has been a wonderful form of exercise, tremendously improving my sense of balance and body control. I have never been very well coordinated, but with practice doing tai chi, I have much more confidence. Now when I get in an elevator, I relish being able to stand in the middle. I can feel my body adjusting to the movements in the elevator, and that old feeling of panic I used to get is a distant memory. I have always said it's the little things in life that really make a difference.

Now when I go to tai chi, I can do most of the forms, with slight movements. But for anything that requires being on one foot, I make an adjustment that will leave both feet planted firmly on the floor. As long as I am moving, I am okay, but if the teacher stops to talk or explain something, I have to sit. It gets harder and harder for me to get up early enough to get to the tai chi class. It is a twenty-five minute drive, and the class starts at 8:00 a.m. When my stomach isn't great in the morning, that means I have to get up around 6:00 a.m. to accommodate everything I need to do. I need to eat slowly, so it is a tedious process if I need to be somewhere early. The old fly-by-the-seat-of-my-pants routine just doesn't work anymore.

When undergoing chemotherapy treatment for cancer, nothing else can be dealt with. Any other physical ailments must be left untreated. I desperately need a knee replacement, and I would love to deal with my varicose veins, which are painful more often than not. This started after the surgery I had after my first six months of chemo. I already had cataracts, but they have progressed at an alarming rate in the last year. I can't even get my teeth cleaned. Doing any of these things would require that I take a break from the chemo treatments, and then there would be the recovery time after the procedure. There is a risk that the healing process may be impaired as a result of low blood counts. And the risk in taking that break is that the cancer will progress at a faster rate. So all these problems are left untreated.

MY LIFE'S WORK

I consider myself to be fortunate enough to be in the perhaps small group of people who have more than once figured out what they want to do with their lives. My first time around, I spent twenty years doing therapy with drug and alcohol clients. I loved this work. I can remember some people as if I worked with them yesterday. It didn't matter if it was the old homeless man who was stinky, dressed in well-worn clothes, and talked with tears in his eyes about when the love went out of his life; or the professional businessman who felt trapped behind a façade of happiness—a face he put on to impress family and friends with how well he was doing in life. Underneath, their pain was the same, and they had turned to alcohol and other drugs to soothe themselves. This line of work showed me people who had reached an unimaginable depth of despair, and I was lucky enough to help some of them climb back up and begin life again. While the doctors and related medical personnel who are helping me now have that same opportunity related to physical ailments, I dealt with it on a mental, psychological, and emotional level. I can honestly say that within those twenty years, I saw some amazing recoveries, while at the same time, I also saw some painful failures.

To think that I may have played some small part in those recoveries is rewarding beyond what words can describe. This was my small gift to the world. It was the best I had to offer at that time.

When I decided it was time to leave that profession, I had no idea what my retirement would be like. The only thing I knew was that I wanted to do less in more time. I felt a need to slow down. However, within the first year, I had had enough of the slow life. I was ready to get moving again. This was the summer of 1999. It was a banner year for berry picking, one of my favorite pastimes. There were so many blackberries that I had already frozen forty quarts, and that had hardly made a dent in the crop. My favorite, black raspberries, were not quite as plentiful. Twenty-eight quarts of these gems (I call them black gold) already filled a shelf and a half in our freezer. The fact that they were there was reason enough to pick them.

I was a regular customer at the local farmers market, so one day I decided to talk with one of the vendors. She told me that there was a $150 fee per year to join the market. Since berries are very seasonal, this would not have been worth my while. She told me they did need someone to sell baked goods. This interested me, because I have always enjoyed baking, as well as making my own jams and jellies. Within the next month, I had gotten my certification as a home baker and was ready to go. My baked goods practically flew off the table. I was so excited that I didn't know what to do with myself. One of the other vendors bought one of my nine-inch pies, for which I charged $4.00. It was made with black raspberries. The next market day, as soon as I arrived, he came over to me and said, "You need to charge more for your pies. At our bake shop, we charge $4.00 for a four-inch pie." That day, my price went up to $6.00.

My baking business took off like a cheetah in a heated run for his dinner. It seemed like no matter what I made, it was a good seller. Before I knew it, I was once again cramming my days and working like a dog. Since the ripening times of the different berries all had a slight overlap, once I started, I was in berry picking mode for most of the summer. Between picking berries and baking, I was back into living a very busy life. But I *loved* this life. The idea that my baked goods gave people some small pleasure was more than enough reward. I'm not sure how people who do things like this make a living, but I know I would never have been able to support myself this way. Fortunately, my husband worked hard enough, and made enough money, that it was enough for my work to provide discretionary income.

This was my new gift to the world. Even though I had slowed down in my baking because of back problems, I was unable to imagine life without baking. Once I found out I had cancer and started chemotherapy, I was sometimes unable to make a simple meal for myself, let alone do baking for a business. What I considered to be my life's work, I was unable to do anymore. In spite of being grateful to be alive, I had the audacity to actually want my life to continue to have some value. I wanted to be able to keep doing something meaningful. This didn't seem like too much to ask. And once it finally sunk in that I would not be going back to anything remotely like my old life, I became angry—very angry. Exactly what was I supposed to do with myself? People offered me suggestions like "What about crocheting?" I was not looking for a fucking hobby or a way to pass the time. Time was the one thing I had plenty of. I was looking for something I could feel had value to me and to the rest of the world. Crocheting, something I could never master anyway, was not what I needed.

I was unable to even do things that I used to squeeze in around the edges of my busy life. As I struggled with this, I was perceived by the medical team as depressed. Of course, the first solution to that is medication. I was not interested in medication. I did not want a pill to make me feel better. I wanted to feel better because I was doing something worthwhile. To me, this is where real self-confidence comes from. It comes from doing something good and meaningful, not from telling yourself you're a good person. It certainly doesn't come from a pill. It would take me some time to find a replacement for my baking.

Gardening or Spare Time Interests

The Master Gardeners Program was developed in the mid-1950s, in an effort to recruit a corps of volunteers to help the horticultural agencies (county extension offices) fulfill their mission. In Pennsylvania, Pennsylvania State University was responsible for providing services to horticultural consumers, helping them with information about how to grow things, identifying insects and diseases on their plants, and recommending treatments when necessary. To become a master gardener, the Extension Office would provide thirty hours of initial training, while members donated fifty hours of volunteer service toward the goals of the Extension Office. At the end of the first year, they would give you the designation of master gardener. Each year, an additional eight hours of training and twenty hours of volunteer service would maintain the designation.

I began my training in 2004, and from the very beginning I was enthralled with the program. Like most other things I got involved in, I was unable to do the Master Gardener Program in a small way. My first year, I racked up 170 hours of volunteer service, and I loved every minute of it. However, since this mostly took place during the same time of year that I was doing my berry picking and baking, I was a very busy woman. In addition, I found time to tend to my own six flower gardens and make twenty baskets and six boxes to hang on the porch, deck, and side of the house. I lived for this time of year.

During the first spring/summer after I found out I had cancer all that changed. The fall before, I had purchased about 250 bulbs, and that October, Bill and I had spent hours planting them, and all the while I pictured them flowering the next spring. *Now,* I thought to myself, *I might not even get to see them bloom.* I would stand on the porch, looking longingly out at my big corner garden of perennials, afraid to get too close to it at first. Besides, I was not allowed to be in the sun anymore. I was only supposed to be in the sun for fifteen minutes at a time, and that was with my skin covered and sunscreen on. This nearly broke my heart. Probably since my skin tanned very easily, I had somehow resisted the trend of worrying about sun exposure, and every year, I would sport a fantastic gardener's/berry picker's tan. How could I get through the season with pale skin? It was too much to think about. It wasn't just the idea of having tan skin; I *loved* being in the sun. now, I would just look out and cry while I sent encouraging thoughts to my flowers to grow!

Most days, I would force myself to walk out to get the mail. Gradually, I got the courage to segue to the corner garden to check on my babies. Each time I visited my flowers, I would pull a small pile of weeds. This would always leave me feeling spent and shaky, but I didn't care. If I had to do fifteen-minute trips all day long, I would garden. I would do it any way I could. My resolve was slow to actualize, however. After coming back into the house, I would have to rest, sometimes even nap. Sometimes I didn't make it back outside in the afternoon.

Something that had always given me such energy, and such a feeling of accomplishment, was now such a chore that I could barely manage to eke out fifteen minutes of work.

Throughout the piles and piles of cards came offers to help. Some of my gardening friends offered to come out and tend to my gardens. I greatly appreciated these offers, but the fact was that flower gardens that someone else took care of were not mine. This would be like having children but hiring a nanny to take care of them. I never could see the pleasure or the responsibility in that. How could you call them your own, in that case? Gradually, though, I accepted that if I were going to have flowers that year, I would have to allow others to help me. I asked those whom I knew really had the appreciation for gardening and would want to help as much for their own pleasure as for helping me. I wanted nothing but positive energy to go into the plantings. I sent out an invitation/request for help, for a morning of gardening, followed by an early lunch on the front porch.

This small group of about ten people was here bright and early, got right to work, and finished within a couple of hours. My son, Patrick, had helped me position the plants where I wanted them in the seventy-foot retaining wall. All that was needed was to pop them out of their pots and stick them in the ground. I had grouped the plants for each basket and box. My husband had filled the cart on his tractor with last year's soil and added a large amount of compost, so it was easy to fill the baskets and boxes and then just pop the plants right in. We had a sort of assembly line going with all these jobs. Then each was watered and hung where it belonged, ready to decorate our porch, deck, and the corners of our house for the rest of the summer.

They got done so quickly that they all moved to my big perennial garden and pulled weeds, cleaning it out and disposing of the weeds. By 11:00 a.m., we were ready for lunch. Our front porch extends the length of the front of our house, with a 16' × 20' "room" along the far end. It was a perfect place to relax in the shade while we ate our lunch and just talked about gardens. There was such a feeling of camaraderie that I almost forgot that I had cancer and needed the others' help.

Gardening was what I considered a hobby, or spare-time interest. In reality, I guess I don't know how to do anything small enough to be considered a hobby. As the summer wore on, my energy dissipated and I was able to do less and less. By the fall of that first year, I sent in my letter to resign from the Master Gardeners Program. I couldn't even take care of my own gardens, let alone do volunteer work. How ironic that I now have all the time in the world but have difficulty filling it.

EKING OUT A LIFE

As my first six months as a cancer patient came to a close, in spite of all the losses, I was still positive. I was still operating under the illusion that I would at some point get my old life back. Perhaps this false hope, more than anything, made it possible to cope with the emptiness of my days.

Yes, I have a family that loves me. My husband would do anything to help me and to make me feel better. My sons are a regular part of my life. I have visits from them, along with Marc's wife, Nikki, and Patrick's girlfriend, Carrie. My siblings keep regular contact with me and help me in various ways. I have friends who are concerned and check up on me. I have my lunches. Jackie, one of the PAs I see for my appointments at the end of each chemotherapy cycle, tells me that my family values me. I tell her that is not the same as my life having value.

I rarely make any meals; my husband has taken over that job. He also does most of the house cleaning. Before I even get out of bed on a Saturday or Sunday, he has already been up, done the dishes, washed the kitchen floor, and started the laundry. Once I do get up, it usually takes me about three hours to have some breakfast and get cleaned up and dressed for the day. Then I'm usually ready for a nap. When I awake from my nap, it's time for lunch. Occasionally, I will be ready and able before noon to go grocery shopping with my husband. If I don't fall asleep on the way home, I will be ready for my chair and an afternoon nap once I get back.

My friend Betty that I pick black raspberries with wants to go. In the past few years, we've been at the berry farm early in the morning and have spent about six hours picking. By the time we have finished, we have filled about thirty three-quart containers and are exhausted. I have called Betty a "berry pickin' machine." I'm not sure which of us loves it more, but she insists I take most of the berries, keeping only a few of the three-quart containers for her. This year I took a plastic chair with me, and only ten containers, which we did not even fill. Even with breaks, an hour left me shaky and exhausted. Since the berries are mostly for personal use, I didn't need nearly as many as I used to—only enough for a few pies, and some jam and jelly. At this point, my life is on hold. I bide my time, counting down until I have my surgery. But, while I'm waiting, I try to find ways to feel as though there is some point to my life. I think about obituaries I've read in the paper, where some sixty-five-year-old woman has died after fighting a courageous ten-year battle with cancer. Could I really live like this for ten years? I just can't imagine it. I always said you can get used to anything if you have to live with it long enough. Maybe not.

Chapter Five

The Surgery

I actually have had very little experience with surgery. In 1975, I had a broken ankle that required a pin, which was then removed six months later. The orthopedist believed I would have less chance of having arthritis issues as I aged if the pin were removed. Whatever the reason, that ankle has given me no problems related to that fracture. In 1986, after eighteen and a half hours of labor, I had a C-section to deliver my second son, who weighed in at eleven pounds and six ounces. In 2008, I had arthroscopic surgery on my right knee. This was the extent of my surgical history. But I wasn't worried. I had complete confidence in my doctor. He had also enlisted the skills of Dr. Zureikat, a liver surgeon, to perform the surgery on my liver. Since this was not my doctor's area of expertise, he felt the chance of getting all the cancer was best if he had a specialist do the liver resection. He said that if someone in his family needed liver surgery, this was who he would want to do it. This further bolstered my confidence, both in my doctor and in the overall outcome of my surgery. He had thought of everything.

For the week prior to my surgery, I did a daily imagery process in which I envisioned my surgery. In this vision, my body readily gave up whatever the doctor needed to take. I had some ambivalence about giving up my sigmoid colon, which would result in my needing a colostomy. Dr. Sukumvanich told me he wouldn't know for sure if this would be necessary until he got in there. Although I felt it was most likely that it would be necessary, I hung onto the hope that, somehow, I could get through this with my sewage pipes still intact.

When I expressed how strongly I didn't want to have to go this route, he said, "I'm sure your husband would rather have you with a colostomy than not have you at all. It's not that bad." I couldn't look at either the doctor or my husband after the doctor said this, because at the moment I was thinking, *I don't give a shit what my husband would rather. He isn't the one who will have to deal with it. It will be me.* It's always easy for someone who doesn't have to do a thing to talk about it being "not that bad." I didn't believe him. Of course, I really did care how my husband felt, but at that moment I was so overwhelmed that I couldn't focus on that. I was not entirely convinced that it *was* better to have a colostomy than to be dead. I think the doctor who came up with this idea must be really proud of himself. Because of him, many people have lived a lot longer. I wanted to beat him up.

But I knew this was irrational. Nora, the PA, told me that there were people who chose not to have it; that they would take their chances and hope they didn't die because they refused to have a colostomy. This seemed plain stupid to me, yet I could fully understand how they felt. Still, I guess I was not ready to take that chance, so I signed the paper that outlined what all the doctor planned to do, giving him permission to install the colostomy if he deemed it necessary. Now I was as ready as I would ever be.

I'M READY!

This was the moment I had lived for. My life had revolved around the hope that six months of chemotherapy had decreased the cancer enough that the doctor felt it was reasonable to do surgery. I had one more scan, to see what the pictures had to say. The scan showed favorable results. Since the first scan on February 22, 2010, each following scan had shown, for the most part, a decrease in the evidence of cancer. This last presurgery scan was done on August 9, 2010. The tumor on my left ovary had shrunk by about half, while the one on the right stayed about the same. The tumor on the left ovary was wrapped around my sigmoid colon. This explained the difficulty I was having with bowel movements and the difficulty the doctor had getting the scope around the bend when he did my colonoscopy. Thank heaven it was a normal colonoscopy! All the ascites (fluid) in my abdominal areas was gone, while there was still a small amount in my pelvic area. There was no longer any fluid in my left lung. The tumor in the right lobe of my liver had remained about the same, but the peritoneal implants along the surface of my liver had diminished. Although there had been a decrease in the nodularity of my omentum (a body part I never knew until this surgery that I had—it is the fatty apron that covers the entire abdominal area), the cancer still covered the entire area. There was a lesion on my spleen that had remained the same throughout this six-month time period. There was no indication that it was cancer.

I had another blood test, and it showed that my CA-125, which started at 15,780, was now 176. It was still a far cry from the normal range of below 35, but it was also a far cry from the starting point. The number was in my favor. My blood work had met the minimum required levels for red and white blood cell counts and platelet count. What all of this meant was that I was ready for surgery. I felt triumphant. I felt better than I had for a long, long time—not physically, but mentally and emotionally. I did it. I was ready. My surgery was scheduled for August 23, 2010. Let's get this party started!

As my surgery date fast approached, I began to think about what it would be like. I began to feel embarrassed about my old, overweight body. I wondered what the doctor would think when he saw all that fat around my middle; if it would be disgusting to him. I cried. Then, as a way to feel better, I told myself that this was his job and that if he was any kind of doctor, and person, he would only be focused on seeing my cancer and getting rid of it. I reminded myself that when I was doing therapy with drug and alcohol clients, I never cared how "out of shape" they were mentally or emotionally. In fact, the more mixed up they were, the more intensely I would feel about helping them get better. I liked this analogy, and I clung to it, hoping my doctor would think this way too.

I allowed myself to daydream, and for that last week, I was on a high. I even began to think about all the things I was going to do after I recovered from the surgery. I knew that there would be chemo afterward, but I planned to breeze through that and get back to my life. The yo-yo was at the top of the string. It was secure. I had forgotten about the fine print.

OPTIMAL RESULTS

As I sat in the waiting room, anxious for my turn to be called back to get ready for my surgery, I was surrounded by my family. With me were Bill, Marc and Pat, and Carrie and Nikki. Later Joan and Michele, two of my sisters, and my friends Elaine and Lynn joined the group. We were all in high spirits. I felt like a little kid getting ready for bed on Christmas Eve, filled with anticipation for the excitement of the next day. I knew that when I woke up the next day, my surgery would be over and I would be on the road to recovery. We talked and laughed, telling stories to entertain each other. Finally, my name was called and I was taken to the presurgery area. Within a short period of time, I was in a hospital gown, with IVs inserted and medication running through my veins. In my little cubicle, I was visited in turn by everyone who had come to cheer me on. I was also visited by numerous medical personnel, and I soon lost track of who was there for what. They continued to prep me, and before long, I was wheeled down the hallway to the operating room. My surgery began at 11:15 a.m.

On two occasions, Dr. Sukumvanich reported to my family on the progress of my surgery. Around 5:00 p.m., he went out to report that the surgery was finished. He gave the best possible report: every bit of cancer that could be seen was removed; there was no visible tumor left. I had a complete hysterectomy, including removal of both ovaries. My sigmoid colon and part of my rectum were removed, and I had a colostomy; he was happy to report that it was temporary. All of my omentum was removed. I had a liver resection, removing the tumor and the surface nodules. In addition, my gall bladder was removed and my diaphragm was scraped. He said there was a lot of cancer packed between my diaphragm and my liver, and in getting it out, he caused a small pneumothorax. The lesion on my spleen was determined to be noncancerous, so that was left intact. In addition, the doctor had installed an intraperitoneal port under my left breast. The plan was that I would receive chemotherapy through this port to destroy any microscopic cancer cells left after my surgery. It is always assumed that there are some. These were optimal results.

"Optimal results" is a medical designation meaning that there is no cancer left behind that is larger than one centimeter. In my case, there was no visible cancer of any size. Outside of the need for the colostomy, this was as close to perfect results as a cancer patient could get. I spent the night in the intensive care unit, which is standard procedure following this kind of surgery. I was connected to the usual pain medication pump. Every time I woke up, I pushed the button that dispensed the medication. First thing the next morning, I was gotten out of bed by the nurses, and by afternoon, I was on the regular cancer floor.

My recovery went well, and speedily. I had many visitors every day. My family made multiple visits, and the windowsill and the air conditioning /heating unit were covered with flowers. I received many cards, both electronically and via snail mail. One of the nurses joked with me: "So, who is taking the next shift?" At first I didn't get it, and then I realized she was referring to my visitors. Apparently she was amazed not only that I had almost constant visitors, but that they also seemed to come in groups. I felt very loved and supported.

Bill was there every day, sometimes more than once. He looked tired, but I was glad to have him there, and I was selfish; I didn't want him to leave. Even if we didn't talk, his presence was comforting. His concern was tireless, and I loved him for it. I hoped I wasn't taking him or his love for granted. I knew I was very *self*-centered these days. Still, I did think from time to time about how he must be feeling, about how this whole thing affected him. I tried to be sensitive to his needs and make sure that his entire life didn't revolve around me and my cancer. I was sure he was overloaded with responsibilities, but he never complained. Often, I wished he would; I thought it would be more real. Or maybe it would just make me feel better and was more like what I would do. I hoped he was aware of my gratitude for his caring, and of my love for him.

After the first day on a new pain medication, I began to notice little visual hallucinations. If I focused on one spot for more than a few seconds, it seemed to separate from its surroundings and move over to the side somewhere in a little triangle. So if I was looking at my sister while she was talking, her head broke off from her body and sat somewhere to the side. It was a very strange feeling, but I didn't tell anyone, hoping and assuming it would go away when I discontinued the medication. Thankfully, it did.

Dr. Sukumvanich came to see me a couple times, but he already told me before the surgery that he was going on vacation, for which he apologized. I assured him that as long as he did the surgery, I was confident that others could follow up on his work. Before he left for the last time, he said the words I longed to hear: I could begin to eat again. I was excited. Getting used to eating again was a slow process; I threw up the first time I had semisolid food. But, gradually, I was able to resume more normal eating habits.

Bright and early Sunday morning, the nurse came into my room. She was finishing her shift for the day. She told me a male nurse whose name I forget would be her replacement. Since I had begun eating in small amounts, I had begun to have some deposits in the bag that was now attached to my stomach, slightly below my waist, on the left side. I asked the nurse about it, and how to take care of it. I had a visit from the colostomy nurse earlier in the week, but I remembered little of what she said. I was still heavily drugged at that time. Although it isn't complicated, I could barely think about it, let alone tend to it myself. I had not allowed myself to think in detail about it all week. Being drugged helped.

I told the nurse that I would prefer my poop be taken care of by her.

I posed my request to her very tentatively. The idea of anybody doing it was uncomfortable to think about. "I mean, if it were you, how would you feel having a man clean your poop from a bag for the first time?"

She agreed to do it but didn't seem very excited about it. I had been outfitted with the one-piece variety of bag, which meant it had to be emptied and cleaned repeatedly. The system was to be changed about twice a week. Although the adhesive was made of some sort of natural pectin mixture, more frequent changing was not recommended, due to potential skin damage. The nurse worked the small amount of stool to the bottom of the bag and then squeezed it out into a pink plastic container. She showed me how to use a huge syringe to squirt water into the bag and let it drain. Then she reclosed the bottom of the bag using the resealable system. She left the room without saying anything more, and I didn't see her again. When she first came into the room, she came to perform some task, which I couldn't recall. Perhaps it was to draw some blood or to check my blood pressure. Once she completed the task of cleaning my poop bag, she didn't do anything else. I felt certain that it was an unpleasant task, and I felt a little guilty that I asked her to do it. It made me feel unclean, both literally and figuratively. Maybe this was how the lepers in the time of Christ felt—dirty and unworthy of the people who were not so afflicted. I was worried that every time I went out among the general population, I was going to feel like a leper. Perhaps I should plan to dress in sackcloth and ashes so they would be alerted to my condition.

A little bit later that morning, the team of doctors came to see me and asked if I wanted to go home. I said, "If it's okay with you, it's okay with me." This was my seventh day in the hospital, including the past Monday, the actual day of my surgery. That meant I had recovered from a major six-and-one-half-hour surgery in five days. I had been told that I could be in the hospital anywhere from five to twelve days. I felt good about this, and although I knew I still had a long way to go to regain my strength, I didn't care. I was on the right path. I could handle anything of a short-term duration that was ever decreasing. I probably also had the idea somewhere on the verge of my conscious awareness that at least in this, I could show the doctors what I could do when I put myself to the task. I was back in the driver's seat, or so I thought. I felt proud, and I guess we all know what follows that.

My friend Elaine arrived with someone who wanted to do some sort of cellular balancing procedure. I didn't really understand, but I agreed to it; what could it hurt? Surely it was better to have balanced cells than unbalanced cells. All I had to do was relax, which I did. I sensed this woman moving around my body and touching me at various points. Then I became aware of some sort of melodic sound, which I found out later was a tuning fork. It was rather sharp to my ears, and startled me, but I forced myself to stay in a relaxed state. When the woman was done, my friend Elaine told me I had done very well. I was glad to hear this, but I still didn't really understand. All I had done was relax. After this, Bill came back into the room. He asked what I wanted to do with all the flowers. Elaine and her friend suggested I could donate them to the other patients.

"No!" I exclaimed immediately. "I want to take them all home with me." Somehow, they had helped me get through the week, and I wanted to keep them all with me as long as I could. I felt a little selfish, but at the moment, I didn't care. I was not quite ready for making charitable donations yet. I was still very *self*-centered and felt in need of charitable donations for myself. Bill said that was fine and began one of the many trips he had to make to load all the flowers into the car.

It took all morning for the medical staff to get everything ready for me to go home. From my experience, this is standard operating procedure. One of the doctors, or maybe a PA, came into the room to remove my drains. I had had two drains in my pelvic area since the surgery, and, fortunately, they were ready to be removed before I went home. The first one was removed in one long pull. I didn't know what to expect, so it wasn't too bad. The second one was not quite so easy. I knew what would happen this time, so I was a little tense. The doctor or PA began to pull on the tube. I let out an involuntary scream. She had to let go and grab it again, close to my body, and pull again the whole length of her arm. Finally it was out. That tube must have run back and forth a few times across my pelvis. I made a joke and told her that when I told this story, I would say the tube was six feet long. That's what it felt like when it was removed.

Gradually, things came together, and I put clothes on for the first time since Monday. I couldn't really bend over, so I needed some help. Bill helped me dress. I still felt pretty shaky with what seemed like a very small exertion, but I really didn't pay much attention to this. My happiness with my optimal results seemed to overcome all the pain and the ability to only make the smallest of movements at a very slow pace.

The drive home seemed to take forever, and I made involuntary sounds every time we went over a bump in the road. I spent most of the time on that trip thinking about how happy I was that my surgery went so well. It really seemed like I might get better. I daydreamed about what my life might be like in a few months. I had been assured by Chris, the oncology nurse, that I would have chemotherapy after my surgery. I didn't care; I just wanted to get it done and out of the way. We arrived home in due time, and Bill helped me get into the house and into bed. He left immediately to go to the pharmacy to get my prescriptions. I would have to give myself injections for ten days to be sure I didn't get any blood clots.

Later that afternoon, my sister Joan and her daughter Cassie came up to check on me, to be sure I'd settled in at home. They brought homemade soup. My friend Lynn stopped to be sure I was okay and also brought me food. I slept off and on the rest of the day and was up bright and early the next morning when the visiting nurses came for the first time. They checked me over and determined that all was well. All my incisions looked good, and my colostomy was working just fine. I spent more time in bed than not over the next few days, but gradually I increased my time up and around. Every day I felt a little bit better.

I was upset when I got on the scale and found that I had gained twenty-five pounds. This was after eating virtually nothing for a week and losing several body parts. I knew, though, that it was the fluid that I was retaining from being in bed all week. Over the next two weeks, I lost those twenty-five pounds, along with another eight pounds. I bottomed out at 182 pounds. That made me feel better.

On Thursday, I went to my doctor's office, and had my sixty-eight or so staples removed. Steri-Strips were placed over the incision, and I left them on until they fell off on their own. This took a week or so. The incision healed with no problem. I noticed, however, that I was hunched over when I walked and that I had a hard time straightening up. I asked if I could go to physical therapy, and I was given a script. I was anxious to get started, because I felt that the incision from my surgery was pulling my body into a curve, and it needed to be stretched in the opposite direction. I felt certain that this would improve once I got some good PT under my belt.

SETTLIN' IN

Within the next four weeks, my body healed, and I continued to regain my strength. I was right about the physical therapy; it helped tremendously. The girls were all wonderful, and Shelly, the physical therapist I always had, was so good at what she did. She actually listened to what I had to say, as though it was important for her to know my perspective before she began to treat me. What a novel approach! After a few weeks, I could see myself straightening up, and I felt stronger.

I thought to myself that I was on the verge of feeling like a normal person again. I had gone out shopping a few times by myself, and each time, I seemed to have a little more stamina. After about a half hour, I began to feel weak and needed to sit down. I felt frustrated by this, but as long as I continued to see and feel incremental improvements, I was happy.

It took some time for my digestive system to begin working again, but gradually I began to eat more normally. I learned to change my appliance, and with the help of the visiting nurse, I began to experiment with different items they make to accommodate the "imperfect" colostomy. I'm sure the imperfections in mine were due to the imperfections of my overweight, middle-aged body.

Exactly four weeks and two days after my surgery, I had an appointment with Dr. Sukumvanich. He told me that I had done really well with the surgery and that everything looked good. He said they "burned, scraped, and cut" until there was no cancer to be seen anywhere, but that they always assumed there were still microscopic cancer cells left behind. For this reason, chemotherapy always followed surgery. I felt very positive and was more than ready to move into this next (and, yes, I was thinking, last) leg of my treatment. My CA-125 was 182.

Dr. Sukumvanich began to talk about what chemotherapy options he saw, reviewing four possibilities. He carefully explained that since I didn't fit any of the studies, it was hard to say which one would be best. From my own research, and what he was saying, I concluded that the reason I didn't fit the studies was because there are actually very few studies done on stage IV ovarian cancer patients. Most of the studies focus on the three earlier stages.

But he decided that chemo via the intraperitoneal port would be the best route. I would have one treatment every four weeks, for six months. "In studies (which you don't really fit)," he said, "patients who used this form of chemotherapy after surgery lived an extra seven months before their cancer came back."

Suddenly, time seemed to stop. "Extra seven months" rang in my ears. The room got smaller, the air got a little closer, and it started to get warm. Out of the corner of my eye, I peeked in the direction where Bill was sitting. The yo-yo, which had been flying high, suddenly plummeted. I hung there, immediately jerked to a stop. "An extra seven months." Ah, yes, the fine print. It all started to come back to me. For that brief period of time, I seemed to have forgotten that I had cancer. I was acting like I was healing from something like an appendectomy. Nope! This was cancer—the land of the living dead.

The intensity of the feelings of deflation was overwhelming. I felt as if I was moving in slow motion. I tried to focus on what the doctor was saying. He was talking about the possible side effects of this particular chemotherapy. I could always read that later. It didn't really matter; I would do the chemo regardless of the side effects. Besides, the nurse would go over that with me, and I would have to sign a paper agreeing to the treatment. I'm sure he asked me if I had any questions, and I probably shook my head no. At this point, my husband piped in.

"When can she have the colostomy reversed?"

"Well, she has to be cancer-free for one to two years before we would reverse it. Generally, if the cancer is going to come back, it usually comes back within two years. If we reverse it and the cancer comes back, then she'll just have problems, and there is no point in doing that."

I shook my head and mumbled my understanding and agreement with such a reasonable plan. This just added to the deflation I was already experiencing. I think I really knew from the beginning that although it was technically reversible, it was extremely unlikely that a reversal would ever happen. Still, it was another blow to the world of dreams I had built. The hope of a normal life returning faded a little bit more.

The doctor left the room, and I got dressed. We went to Chris's office, where she handed me a paper with the information about the new chemo, including side effects. She reviewed the protocol, and I signed the paper. As my husband and I left the office, I walked out with little awareness of what was happening around me. I didn't really want to talk yet, so it was a long ride home, and a quiet one.

Denial is an amazing thing. As the days go by, I find myself ever so slowly sneaking back into the land of dreams, where all the clouds have silver linings. Once again I make myself believe that I will still get better. That seven months only applies to *most* people; okay, almost everyone. I could still be an exception. I am unable to stop myself from thinking that I am still going to have a real life somehow, someday.

Chapter Six

THE COLOSTOMY

I feel a need to issue a warning at the start of this chapter. If you are offended by or bothered by talk about poop, perhaps you should skip this chapter. My goal is not to offend, but to leave this information out would be to present an incomplete picture of my life with cancer.

At the first talk of a possible colostomy, I just closed my eyes, and everything in me sunk to the floor. The doctor explained to me what it was, but I already knew. I just wouldn't allow myself to picture this on my body.

In the end, as I think we all do when faced with something we would like to avoid at all costs, I knew there was no sense in avoiding it. Whether I accepted it or not, if it had to happen, happen it would. So as I did with everything else, I began my research. I found a wonderful website with photographs that gave a pictorial progression of the procedure itself. When I got to the end, although I was by myself, I exclaimed out loud, "Oh my God. It looks like the tip of a penis sticking out of her stomach!" I could not get this image out of my mind. I sent it to various friends, who thought this was funny. It was, but not really—not for me.

Still, after reading this article, and seeing an actual stoma, as the protuberance is called, I stopped crying every time I thought about it. I told this to my friend Betty, and she declared, "Knowledge is power." Yes! That was exactly how it was. The more I knew, the better I felt, even if it was bad news. Maybe it gave me a feeling of control, even if I really had no control, a sense of power where there was none. I had at least a vague notion of what exactly would be done to create this stoma. I talked about it with all the people I knew, telling them I would never leave my house again after this was done. Gradually, this segued into "I won't leave the house until I am sure of how to take care of it and I can feel confident that it won't leak everywhere when I go out."

I pictured myself wearing maternity tops for the rest of my life, to cover up what I decided to call "the beast." I couldn't imagine how I could wear normal clothing without the whole world knowing that I was not like them once again because I sported my beast on my stomach instead of at the bottom of my back, neatly tucked in that crease at the very top of the legs that we call "the crack." Chris, the oncology nurse, assured me that no, I would not have to wear maternity tops, but I didn't really believe her.

As I expressed all my fears to her, Chris said something like, "Well, can I tell you that yes, people do have occasions when they have leakages? And they do have embarrassing moments when they are out, but as you learn to take care of it better, these things will be less likely to happen." Somehow I felt better having my fears confirmed. After all, what is the likelihood that my transition from sitting on the pot to poop like everyone else to disposing of my waste in a bag hooked to the side of my stomach would go off without a hitch? At least she was being realistic.

In my first week dealing with the visiting nurses, Renetta, the wound-care specialist, was a godsend. I loved her down-to-earth manner. She wasn't crude, yet she "told it like it was." I complained that when I went to the doctor, they could see my poop through the clear plastic bag used to catch it as it made its way from the beast. "Nobody else has to display their waste like that, for the entire world to see ... or whoever happens to be in the doctor's office at examination time." "We have a solution for that," said Renetta. "You can get the opaque bags." Before she left, she ordered me a box of these new bags, and I felt better. Not only that, but I also got the small ones. Although the instructions said that you should not let the bag get more than two-thirds full before disposing of it, I never planned on letting mine get to that point. And so I learned all about the fine points of taking care of a colostomy. Renetta was there to show me all of it. Dr. Sukumvanich was wrong, though. It is that bad.

Better Than Being Dead

After a short time, I realized how convenient the system God set us up with is, and I developed a standard response to those who ventured to inquire about how I was doing with my colostomy.

"There is a reason God put our assholes in a place where we didn't have to have a bird's-eye view of everything that comes out of them," I would say. This always produced at least a good chuckle, if not an outright hearty laugh. I thought it was funny too, but I had a much deeper appreciation of the meaning.

I had gotten starter kits from three different companies, and with each one, there was an accompanying video that explained how to use each of their products. They also came with booklets that were meant to be inspiring. They recounted tales of people who, after having a colostomy, went on to live their lives accomplishing wonderful, amazing feats. There were people with a colostomy who climbed Mt. Everest. There were women with a colostomy who had babies. There were many people who became avid spokesmen or spokeswomen, extoling the virtues of having a colostomy.

Myself, I didn't want to do anything spectacular. I just wanted to get from one day to the next without having to worry about having poop leaking onto my stomach and, therefore, my clothing. I just wanted to get through the morning without having to experience things like projectile poop liberally spraying all over the sink, the counter, the front of the cabinets, and the floor, including my little bathroom rugs. This could happen without a moment's notice and in the ten seconds when I moved from the toilet to the counter to get a new bag from the cabinet under the sink.

As time passed, I became intimately acquainted with all the products, especially those made to accommodate difficult stomas. There are powders, pastes, sticks of putty, putty in the shape of a washer (the kind you use with a nut and bolt), wipes with alcohol, wipes with sticking power, drops to absorb odor, and different-sized bags. There are even decorated bags, meant to be sexy, made to be worn when you want to be intimate. There are "caps," with just the tiniest amount of space, for things like swimming or intimacy. Of course, here you have to have good timing, or be just plain lucky, and hope that you don't end up with more stool than there is room for in the bag or cap.

One of the biggest differences between the traditional method of disposing of solid bodily waste and the beast method is control. In the traditional method, you have control. As a child you learned that you could "hold it" or "release it." You learned that you were to hold it until you were in a place that was appropriate for releasing it. Those good old sphincter muscles were a thing of wonder, and through various methods of potty training, you became expert in the use of those muscles. I had come to learn a lot more than I ever cared to know about my digestive processes. Knowledge *is* power. Betty was right.

Unfortunately, the stoma has no nerve endings. I had no control over what came out when. Indeed, quite often I was completely unaware that anything was even happening. One time, I had just cleaned up and was walking from my bathroom to my bedroom to get a pair of underwear. As I reached into the drawer, I pulled out a pair of underwear and was surprised to find that it had poop on it. As I was standing there, trying to process this strange event, I realized that I had forgotten to put a new bag on. So I had left a trail behind me that I had stepped in, and I had deposited a small amount right into my underwear drawer. The amazing thing was that I was completely unaware of what was happening. In spite of how upset I was about all this, I had to marvel that I hadn't felt a thing.

At times, it was only the pressure against the bag that alerted me. I constantly checked it. I thought I'd gotten pretty good at it. Just a slight brush of the hand against the bag under my jeans, and I had all the information I needed. It didn't even disrupt my conversations. Of course, that was after a lot of practice. Begrudgingly, I acknowledged that having a colostomy was better than being dead—by a hair.

Slight Imperfections

The incision from my surgery has healed well, although the scar is wider in some places than others. It goes from the bottom of my breast bone to right above where my pubic bone starts, covering a length of seventeen inches. The otherwise straight line swerves to the right around my belly button; I imagine this is because it is less complicated to put back together. But where it swerves to the right, it pulls my skin from the left half of my abdomen, and this makes what we have come to call a slash through the middle of my colostomy site. The slash dips in like a tiny, dried-up streambed. The result of this was that when I applied the wafer portion of my appliance, the part that sticks to my abdomen, I didn't get a good seal. In addition, I sported an "inny," not an "outy"; that is, my stoma was concave, not convex. The stool would mostly just lie right there at the opening. What this did, then, was eat away at the seal, and gradually the stool lifted the seal and collected under the opening. As the stool collected, it didn't fall neatly into the bag. Yet, depending on things like pressure and amount, it could lift the entire wafer from my body. This was another reason I would either change or empty the bag after every deposit. But, mostly, I would just clean it from the opening. My husband said we should take out stock in Charmin. I used much more toilet paper than I had pre-surgery.

There was one drawer in our dresser that contained T-shirts belonging to my husband, but he also had T-shirts in another drawer in the closet. The dresser drawer was less than half full, and I hadn't seen him get anything out of it for a long time. I asked him if he'd be willing to move his T-shirts to his other drawer so I could use this drawer for my colostomy supplies. Of course, he obliged. At first, my supplies didn't come close to filling the drawer. But as time went on, not only did the drawer become full, but I also had to stash extra boxes underneath the dresser. With each new box of bags, I also received several blue plastic bags for disposal of the used colostomy bags. I have always been a strong believer in recycling, trying to keep my personal additions to the landfills to a bare minimum. There were not enough blue bags for individual usage, so I reopened the blue bag to add more used colostomy bags. I generally went through about two per week. When you become as up close and personal with your own poop as I have, reopening the blue bags was nothing. I thought about the landfills and felt good that I was doing what I could to not add unnecessarily to their bulk. I always said it's the little things in life that really make a difference.

Once, when my sister Therese was visiting, she was unlucky enough to be here when I was on a rant about my colostomy. I dragged her back to my bedroom and went through the entire drawer with her, explaining the use for each product. "And, in the end," I said, also coming to the end of my rant, "None of this stuff makes a fucking bit of difference. I *still* have the problem with leakage." She had been quiet, just looking at me, and watching my demonstration with ever-widening eyes. I wondered what was going through her mind. I apologized to her for having to be subjected to my temper tantrum. She told me it was okay, and it sounded like she really meant it. We went back out to the kitchen and continued what we were doing, as though that little visit to the colostomy store never happened.

When I first found out I had cancer, I asked Nikki, my daughter-in-law, to do some clothes shopping for me. I knew things were bad when I didn't even have the energy to shop! I needed some clothes that were flexible around the middle. With the ascites, I constantly felt bloated, and after eating even small meals, I felt full very quickly. Nikki came through like a pro and padded my wardrobe with knit clothing. At home, I would rarely be seen in anything other than sweats of some variety.

After my surgery, to accommodate the colostomy and its necessary equipment, I continued to be more comfortable in the same type of clothes. Once I started the heat-seeking chemo treatment, keeping my clothing loose became even more important. Quickly, I discovered that getting hot and sweaty around the waistline was not a good thing. The part of my incision that segued around my belly button would quickly become irritated, and I had almost constant sores there. Something like a paper cut, it would take weeks to heal. On one occasion, when there was a lot of irritation under the wafer part of my appliance, I called Chris and whined to her about all this irritation. "Am I going to spend the rest of my life sitting in a chair, wiping poop from my belly?" It was one of those occasions where the poop had leaked under the wafer, and by the time I was able to change it, the skin was an angry, flaming, diaper-rash red. I also had a sore at my navel. Chris scheduled me to see the colostomy nurse the following Wednesday, when I came for my appointment.

From Friday until I saw her that following Wednesday, things healed considerably. I'll never forget the look on her face when she removed the wafer from my stomach (which, of course, had just been put on a couple hours earlier, so it looked great, just like new underwear). She looked at it, hesitated, and said, "Oh." The unspoken words were "What? I don't get it. You're making a big deal out of this?"

"Well, it's a lot better now than it was when this all started last week." I felt a need to help her see how bad it had been. Perhaps relative to some of the things she was used to seeing, it was nothing. But for me, it was bad, and it was a constant source of pain and discomfort. There I was, splayed out on the exam table, with four medical people squeezed into the small room. The beast was exposed for the entire world to see—or at least those four people. It might as well have been the whole world. I explained about the sore around my navel.

"Yes, I see that. It looks like a paper cut." She went on to explain that there was a fabric she had that I could use to absorb the moisture and keep the sores from developing. She didn't have time to go and get it, so the medical assistant was sent on this errand.

When she returned, she had a large piece of fabric that looked something like Under Armour, measuring about a half a square yard. The fabric was meant to be installed in the folds of the skin to absorb sweat. What this meant was that if you had a fat belly, as I did, you were to fold this fabric in half and put it between the folds of fat, making sure that the end was exposed so that the moisture could be dissipated there. As I lay on the table, all three of them worked over my fat belly, tucking the fabric. I believe this was one of the most humiliating experiences of my life—just another consequence of overindulgence all those years. At the same time, as they worked on me, I think they were all oblivious to what I was experiencing. I say this as a compliment to them; they didn't seem to care at all about my fat. I was just another body that needed some help. This is the way it should be for people who do this kind of work. Otherwise, how would they bear it?

"Do I have to wear this to bed? I don't generally wear underwear to bed." In fact, I *hated* to wear underwear to bed.

"Do you sweat when you sleep?" It was all a matter of being very practical. You wear it when you are likely to sweat. Inside, I was screaming. I had to draw the line somewhere, and the idea of wearing underwear to bed seemed to cross the line. I envisioned myself in a straitjacket, being carted off to the psych ward while I screamed over and over, "I *will not* wear underwear to bed!" Just one more little inconvenience cancer patients are subjected to. A tiny little nudge on the slope of the downward spiral. Silly, right?

As a result of all my experimentation to try to correct the imperfections in my stoma site, I concluded that there was nothing I could do about it. The best solution seemed to be what I was already doing: cleaning it as soon as there was a deposit. Occasionally I got an e-mail from one of the companies that made the products, recommending some new, innovative product, so I would call them, and they would send me a few free samples.

In the end, none of these efforts led to any improvement. I was not angry with anyone about this. I think my doctors did a wonderful job. The placement, I realized, was optimal. I could wear jeans that fit snugly, with tops that were tucked in, or short, and there was never a revealing bulge where the beast resided. I could see my friends occasionally glance in that area when we were out, just to check. Some of the more bold ones would even comment; they were amazed that they saw no tell-tale signs of my colostomy. The problem, I was sure, was with my overweight, flabby gut. There is only so much you can do to accommodate this. I can't put the responsibility for the consequences of years of overindulgence on anyone but myself. This was just one in a long list of consequences for having no self-control when it came to sweets and the convenience of fast food.

THE EVERYDAY JOYS OF LIVING WITH A COLOSTOMY

As time went on, I did begin to feel some sense of control over my colostomy and its processes. I made sure that after each new experience, I made accommodations in how I handled it, so that I could systematically eliminate that problem from occurring again. What I soon began to realize, though, was that there was no end to the new experiences. Just when I thought I'd seen it all, something else would come up.

To begin with, can you imagine something that sticks so well you can even shower without fear of it coming loose? For me, though, it was virtually impossible to take a shower with the bag on. I know that all the rules, books, and videos say you can shower. They even send you little tabs to stick over the small vent hole to keep water from getting inside the system. But this just didn't work for me. I found that if I got really sweaty, instead of coming loose, the wafer would adhere even more strongly to my stomach, making it virtually impossible to remove without taking skin along with it.

Since chemo is hard on skin cells, and some varieties have skin cell destruction as an even more severe side effect, it seemed to take forever for those little sores to heal. In addition, my platelets were tending to run on the low side, so any time I tore my skin open, the sores would bleed for fifteen to twenty minutes, at a very slow trickle. So I only showered on the days that I changed the wafer portion of my colostomy system—in other words, twice a week. Of course, I washed all the important body parts on a daily basis. Since I had little to no hair, clean hair wasn't something I had to worry about. While I knew I was clean, it bothered me that I didn't shower every day. Besides, I always thought of a good shower as one of the finer pleasures in life. Just another minor adjustment necessary for life with a cancer-related colostomy.

When I read the booklets or watched the instructional videos, I became offended at some of the examples that were used. As a simulation for poop, they used glass beads! That's a pretty close analogy; they both flow at about the same rate and leave the same trail behind them as they pass through! When they demonstrated cleaning the bottom of the reusable one-piece system, they gave a little swipe with a piece of toilet paper. In reality, I felt like I used a quarter of a roll of toilet paper to clean around my stoma, and even then, it wasn't really clean.

I don't know how other people felt who watched this DVD, but I would have appreciated a more realistic demonstration. Let's think about who would be watching these demonstrations. Hmmm. It would be people who have to deal with real shit! What would be so horrible about using the real thing to demonstrate how to deal with … the real thing? Instead, I got to watch a neat and tidy demonstration that used nothing messy and one or two sheets of toilet paper. In reality, no matter how much toilet paper I used, I was never quite clean. All this demonstration did was make me feel dirty.

The first time I had a scan after my surgery (about two months later), I had horrendous cramps. They came in huge waves, not unlike labor pains. Traditionally, when I had a scan and had to drink the solution for the contrast dye, it was like I had done a colon cleanse, and before I went home, I was all cleaned out. This time, however, I had no discharge, just the cramps. By the time I left, I was in pain. My sister Therese was giving me a ride home, and I asked her to stop at the CVS. Feeling desperate, I wanted to buy some gas pills that had previously been recommended by Chris when I was experiencing bad stomach pains. I would try anything at that point for some relief. As I was standing at the checkout counter, I had an intense warm feeling on the front of my body that seemed to radiate down my left leg. In a panic, I looked down, and could see a huge bulge at the site of the beast. Since I was running into the store for a quick purchase, I had left my purse, with all my supplies, in the car.

I checked to be sure there was a restroom in the store and then carefully walked out to the car. Without bending over, I grabbed my purse while I explained to my sister what was going on. Fortunately, I made it to the bathroom without an eruption, but I can honestly say there wasn't room for a teardrop by the time I was able to remove the bag. I didn't need the gas pills after that.

I learned after that to drink the formula from a cup, as opposed to using a straw. Straws are not recommended when you have a colostomy. It has to do with accumulation of gas. While I don't know that this was the culprit, I never experienced that intense pain again when having a scan. Things seemed to flow more naturally after that. On another occasion, while I was waiting for my turn to be scanned, I knew my bag was filling up, so I went to the restroom. It was in use, and continued to be in use for another fifteen to twenty minutes. I mentioned to one of the nurses that if I didn't get into the bathroom soon, there would be some cleanup needed. Finally, a tiny little old lady emerged, dressed in a lovely blue flowered hospital gown. She had a big smile on her face, and as she slowly emerged, I dashed in behind her. The floor and the toilet seat were wet with what I can only assume was her urine.

I was struck by the incongruence between the look on her face and the situation we were in. She looked like she had just left a party where she'd been having a heck of a good time. In reality, she had been peeing for the last fifteen to twenty minutes, and hadn't even gotten it in the toilet! What could she possibly have been doing in there all that time?

Now I not only had to worry about extricating my poop bag from my body without making a mess, but I also had to first deal with her pee! And the hits just kept on coming.

Since my bag was already bulging, I tried to work quickly. Ignoring the urine, and leaning over the toilet, I detached my bag. Since it was overfull, some of it spilled on the toilet seat, and splattered on the floor. Unfortunately, before I could even think about putting another bag on, there was more stool spraying everywhere. As if that wasn't bad enough, the wafer was over half detached from my body. The pressure had pushed the stool under the wafer, so I needed to change the entire system. But at the rate that the stool was coming out, I didn't have time to change anything. I quickly put on another bag, hoping that things would slow down enough to get them under control.

To my advantage, there was a little bench in this oversized bathroom. I sat down for a minute and just cried. I had poop on my pants, not to mention that which had sprayed around the room in various spots. At this point, someone knocked on the door.

"Jamie, are you okay?"

"No," I said. "I'm not okay, and I'm going to be in here for a while. When I'm done, someone is going to need to clean this bathroom."

She left, and I got up. As best as I could manage, I began cleaning using the bulk of the paper towels that were in the dispenser. Somehow, I just couldn't leave that bathroom looking like it did. Then I set about the task of changing my colostomy system. Since things had slowed down somewhat, I worked quickly and was able to get the new wafer attached, with a new bag. I cleaned my pants the best I could. When I came out, I told the nurse that I had cleaned the bathroom the best I could, but that it needed serious attention. After about fifteen minutes, having seen nobody with a mop and bucket, I went back to the nurse. I told her in more detail about what had happened and let her know that I didn't think anyone should use the bathroom until it was cleaned.

"Oh," she said then. "Okay. I'll get someone out here." She went and put a sign on the door that stated it was temporarily out of service.

As I was being prepped for my scan, the attendant came to inject the dye. She asked if I had more bags, because she could see that mine was filling up pretty fast. It's always nice to know that someone can see you pooping.

"Yes," I answered. "I have lots of bags."

After that, I ordered a box of large bags, hoping to prevent a recurrence of this whole scene the next time I had a scan. Since I usually had to stop on my way home to use a public restroom, I was glad to have the larger bags. This gave me more security, since the distance from one public restroom to another varied so much.

When I have experiences like these (and believe me, there are many of them), I think about all the people who have said things to me like "Oh, lots of people have colostomies, and they do just fine," I want to smack them. I'd like them to go through one day of it and then see what they have to say. One of my good friends is a stickler for routines. Her house is so clean that you could pick the most remote corner in the most unused room, and it would still pass the white-glove test with flying colors. She even has pooping routines. She goes the same time every morning. Wow! That's pretty organized. Maybe there are lots of people like that. I'd really like to see them dealing with a colostomy. I feel 100 percent certain that they would not be inclined to leave poop in their bag until it had accumulated to the one-third full mark. They'd be in the bathroom as soon as there was any amount. After a day like I had with my scans, I think they might have to sign themselves in to the psych ward. I'd love to hear their feedback at that point. I bet they wouldn't be nearly so cavalier.

Once, driving home from Pittsburgh, I could feel the pressure against my jeans. I pulled off the highway to check things out. The bottom of the bag, as usual, was empty, but there was a large amount of stool right at the stoma that had worked its way under the wafer. I could feel it burning, but since I was on the highway, there was nothing that I could do but head for home, at perhaps a higher rate of speed. By the time I got home (another half hour) and cleaned everything, my stomach was red and raw, and it was burning painfully.

Diaper rash is not a fun thing to have, especially when you are fifty-eight years old. I couldn't stand the thought of sticking something onto that sore spot. So I left it bare, sitting in my chair with my stoma surrounded by toilet paper, and a washcloth handy just in case I needed to clean something quickly. I spent the next four days this way. Of course, at night, I had to put the appliance on, since there were generally deposits all night long. Fortunately, on this particular occasion during the day, things moved slowly, so I had no huge surprises. I had the brainstorm of using A&D ointment, since that was what I used on my kids when they were little and had diaper rash. This seemed to speed up the healing process, and any time I had a similar occurrence, out came the old A&D. It literally was the same old A&D—the remnants of the same tube I had used on my kids twenty-some years ago. It was the one and only tube I had ever needed. Thank goodness it was so old there was no expiration date on it! How odd that I was likely going to be finishing it off by using it on myself.

My sister Michele gave me rides home from chemo, and I enjoyed getting to know her in a new and different way. When I had a severe case of motor mouth once during chemo, I started on about my colostomy. Probably it was one of the times that I'd had an appointment before my chemo and there had been issues with my stoma. A new system was like clean underwear; I always made sure I had good ones on when I went to the doctor. I always got a shower and changed the entire system before my appointments. So when the doctor or the PA saw it, it always looked pretty good, because it was only a couple hours old by the time they saw it. I don't think they were able to grasp what I was dealing with, based on what they saw. So, after my sister arrived, I started complaining. This led to a product demonstration. I removed the travel pack of supplies from my purse, showing her each item and how it was used, and I then explained my difficulties. I could see the reality settling in by the expression on her face, and I can only imagine the prayers of gratitude she said afterward. Maybe that day when she got up, she hadn't had anything jumping out at her to be particularly grateful for. After spending a little time with me, I imagine she was grateful that she was able to sit on the pot and poop like most other people. As I have always said, it's the little things in life that really make a difference.

I could go on for pages and pages with more poop stories. Fortunately, I do have some friends who don't mind hearing these stories, and it does help to be able to tell people about them. It's always interesting to see the looks of amazement and shock on people's faces when they hear what I have gone through. Life with a colostomy is nothing remotely like life without one. Suffice it to say, if having cancer has resulted in the need for a colostomy, it is guaranteed to be high on the list of major adjustments necessary to live life with cancer.

I can honestly say that once I got through the initial adjustment, I have never cancelled any plans because of my colostomy. At the same time, I can honestly say that life as I knew it was over after this part of my surgery. I know that things can always be worse than they are. I did look at a website with photos of some colostomy problems. I can say that indeed, they looked much worse than mine. They had huge holes around their stomas and huge sores on their bodies. I worked hard to be sure mine never got that bad. I never wanted to find out what it would be like if it became worse. What I did have to deal with was plenty bad for me.

Chapter Seven

ON TO THE NEXT PHASE

After my meeting with Dr. Sukumvanich post-surgery, to discuss the next phase of my treatment, I had gotten a heavy dose of reality. As my friend Betty used to say, "The hard hammer of reality strikes again!" Indeed it had! But somehow I managed to quiet that "seven months before it comes back" phrase. I think after that, the yo-yo never seemed to quite make it all the way to the top of the string. Yet, I somehow managed to push the "fine print" back into some remote corner of my mind: a dusty place covered with cobwebs—a place I avoided.

The decision to use the IP port made sense. It was the latest rage in cancer treatments. It was used with a single drug, or drugs in various combinations. My doctor didn't go into the finer details of why he recommended the drug I would be receiving, but I wasn't concerned about that. I felt confident that he had made the best choice.

Once, Chris, the oncology nurse, had explained to me how these choices are made and how the protocols are developed. She told me there was a huge group of doctors and nurses who did nothing but pore through literature containing studies, experiments, and results of the use of various combinations of chemicals in chemotherapy treatment. They gathered together the pertinent information so that when someone (a doctor) needed treatment for a certain condition, that person would have at his or her fingertips all the necessary information. He or she could then make a decision about what was best for the patient.

Since I had done so well with the surgery, I was anxious to get my life back on track. Even after the doctor's comment about the extra seven months, I still envisioned some degree of return to my old life. I imagined myself gardening, enjoying the sun, perhaps doing a small amount of baking, and visiting some new national parks with Bill. We had talked about seeing them all together before we died. We still had so many to see. I was ready to roll.

I Can Do This, but Not Like That

When I arrived at the cancer center for my first treatment using the intraperitoneal port, my husband decided he would stay with me until my friend Elaine arrived. She would be with me for the duration and then take me home. This treatment was different from the treatment I had undergone for the first six months, before my surgery. Those were all given through an IV. The port, which had been put in place at the end of my surgery, was under my skin and below my right breast, and at the bottom of my ribs. There was a rubber pad through which the needle was inserted, which gave immediate access to the catheter. The catheter wound its way through my abdominal area. When the chemo was started, it would run through the catheter and then out the end, where it would flood my abdominal/pelvic area. This method of dispersal is thought to expose the cancer cells to ten to twenty times more medication than they would get through the traditional IV method. This sure seemed like a good way to knock out those cancer cells once and for all. In order for this method to work, it was necessary to lie in a bed at a forty-five-degree angle, and the process took up to seven hours.

The best description I can give for the side effect of this chemo was that it felt like someone had punched me in the stomach, full force and repeatedly, over the first week and a half. Anytime I ate, I had severe stomach cramps, usually followed by diarrhea. I made the executive decision to put myself on the BRAT diet: bananas, rice, applesauce, and toast. I remembered the pediatrician recommending this any time my sons were having difficulty keeping their food down or in. This helped some, but I still ate very little. Gradually the pain subsided. The turning point was the day my neighbor Icel brought me over a jar of homemade chicken noodle soup. I ate it all within a few hours. The next day, I called my husband, who was on his way home from work, and asked him to stop at KFC and get me a box of crispy chicken strips with potato wedges. When he walked in the door, I was in my chair with my plate and a bottle of honey mustard sauce. I said, "Just bring that right over here." I ate the entire meal within a half hour! I do believe I could have eaten a few more, but I refrained. I knew I was on the road to recovery when that meal did not lead to any pain.

The crispy chicken strips and potato wedges became my favorite meal, and I had it once, sometimes twice a day for weeks. When I told the physical therapist about it, she commented that I'd be better off with some grilled chicken. Of course, I knew that. But all I could say was, "It's the best I can do right now."

In my appointment after the first treatment through the intraperitoneal port, I met with Jackie and Chris. I told them about my experience with the sensation of being punched in the stomach over and over and not being able to eat. Two days later, I received a call from Chris. She recommended that I meet with the doctor and discuss switching to another chemo treatment. She felt that the side effects of this one were too extreme. I felt ambivalent about this but agreed to meet with Dr. Sukumvanich to discuss other options. The next day, when I returned home from an outing, I had a message from him, saying he had heard from Chris about the pain I had experienced and that he was sorry to hear this. He said we would discuss my treatment the next week.

I spent the next two days agonizing about this decision. I worried that if I quit this current treatment, it could mean that I might not be able to get rid of the rest of the cancer. What if I was "wimping out?" I had promised myself that I would be tough, that I would do whatever I had to do to recover, and what if that meant feeling like I was punched in the stomach for a week and a half, six times, through six months of treatment? I called Chris and told her that I had been thinking that maybe I should just stay the course. She told me it was up to me, but that she thought I at least owed it to myself to talk with Dr. Sukumvanich. I agreed.

It was a long week. As the days went by, I felt worse, emotionally. I began to feel my life was out of my control and that everything I had just gone through was pointless. Maybe I would never get better. Maybe I would be dead soon. Maybe I wasn't strong enough to get through this. Was there really any light at the end of the tunnel?

When the day of my appointment with the doctor finally arrived, I had organized my thoughts a little bit.

"At first, everything was geared toward getting through that first six months so I could have surgery. I did that and had the surgery. It went well, but just when I was starting to feel normal again, I started back on chemo. Then I ended up feeling punched in the stomach a hundred times in a row. It feels like a downward spiral, and every time I think I'm going to be getting better, something else happens, and I end up a little bit lower. Then I get used to that, and before I know it, I am once again on the downward spiral. Am I ever going to feel normal again? I just can't seem to do anything that normal people do." I was crying by this point.

"Yes!" he exclaimed. "You will!" He reached over and squeezed my arm. "You're going to go on vacation; you're going to do lots of things. You'll see," he said, with some emotion in his voice. He went on to talk about a different chemotherapy that he thought I should try.

This particular form of chemotherapy is a heat seeker. The cancer tumors are known to be hot, so this chemo works by seeking out hot spots in your body and destroying them. This is why you are advised to not create any heat/pressure spots on your body while undergoing this treatment. The chemo might mistake them for cancer, and try to destroy them too. As a result, I had to pay more attention to my day-to-day habits, and eliminate things like leaning on my elbows. Since the inside of your mouth is generally a warm area, drinking cool beverages and eating cool food is important. No more hot showers! No more shoes that rub your toes. Life became lukewarm, literally and figuratively. In addition, it carried the same common side effects as most chemos.

The biggest selling point for this chemo seemed to be that the side effects were less severe. Dr. Sukumvanich told me that the side effects were mild and that most women didn't even feel like they were getting treatment. I remember feeling very dubious about this statement. This sounded too good to be true. At this point, though, I was still worried that I was making a wrong decision. I told him of my fear that I should stick with the other and that I might be sorry in the end if I didn't. He assured me that there was no reason to think the other treatment was any better. So, heaving a big sigh, I agreed to switch.

At that time, it was also suggested that I have a PowerPort installed. This is a device that is placed under the skin and allows access to a vein so that there is not a need to use the veins on the arms and hands. By then my veins had been severely compromised. I had lumps in my veins at the sites where the needles were commonly inserted. Many places were unable to be used again. On one occasion, there were four attempts to find a usable vein before I could begin my chemo treatment. I decided to get the port. I was informed by Chris that there were people who had had these devices for over ten years.

"Oh, I don't want to keep mine that long!" I blurted out. I must have sounded so naive. Chris said nothing to this. Of course, the likelihood that I would be alive anywhere near ten years was very low. At the same time I had this PowerPort installed, I had the intraperitoneal port removed. It was December 4, 2010. I am glad I had it installed; it has saved my arm and hand veins. They have healed well; I have no more lumps in my veins, and after about six months, the bruising also disappeared.

It could take up to four months to determine if this new chemo was helping. My doctor recommended six cycles (months, in this case), and then he would evaluate how well it was working. The goal was to get my CA-125 below 35, preferably below 10. At that point, I would be put on a maintenance form of chemotherapy. This would be for at least twelve months, and if I were cancer-free at that time, I could take a break from chemotherapy. At the time of my first treatment with this new chemo, my CA-125 was at 66. I envisioned the proverbial light at the end of the tunnel. Maybe life by numbers wasn't so bad after all!

"We don't usually talk about these long-range plans." Dr. Sukumvanich, I believed, was giving me this information because he knew I wanted it. Perhaps I needed it, and I appreciated that he was willing to tell me all this. Even though at times, the information sent me plummeting far away from that thin thread of hope by which I hung, I had to have it. I needed the information. Knowledge was still power, even when it didn't make me feel better. Generally, any new information I got was quickly organized into the file cabinets in my brain. But, for some reason, information about my overall prognosis in fighting this cancer didn't seem to follow the normal pathways. Some of it was segued into a little pool off to the side. It was like the debris that collects in a creek. Perhaps a twig gets washed down and gets snagged on the top of a rock, the tip sticking up above the water. Then another leaf or two get stuck, and then another twig, and before you know it, there is a large diversion from the normal direction the water takes. Certain pieces of the information I was getting were dammed up, creating a small eddy, and God help me when it broke loose. I must have been exceptionally dense. I was slow to get the picture. Little pieces of debris that were stacked up, causing the eddy, were beginning to break free, but I worked hard to ignore that. Now, in the best-case scenario, it would be at least one and one-half years before I was done with chemotherapy—and that would only happen for a handful of lucky women. That was a long, long way off. Regardless, I still funneled those pieces off to the side and managed to see that pinpoint of light.

I was constantly being confronted with the issue of when my colostomy would be reversed. When I was asked by friends when I might be able to get it reversed, I told them it would likely never happen. Some of them had assumed it had already been done.

"Oh, I thought it was temporary," they would say.

"Well," I would explain, "it is, but I have to be cancer-free for one to two years, and the chances I'll be alive, let alone cancer-free, by then are slim to none. So I've just accepted that I'll have it forever."

When I was asked by the medical aide who took my vitals about getting my colostomy reversed, I gave this same explanation. "That's a very negative attitude," she replied.

"I think it's a very realistic attitude," I countered.

"You sound kind of depressed," she answered. "Are you taking any medication for that?"

"No," I said, "and I'm not interested in taking any, thank you."

Here we were again; my realism was being interpreted as depression.

I decided that I would get this clarified once and for all. The next time I had an appointment with the doctor, I posed the question.

"You told me I had to be cancer-free for one to two years before I could have the colostomy reversed. Is it one, or is it two?"

"Well," he answered, "two. But that's not carved in granite; it's just my personal preference." He explained again his reasoning.

"So have we started counting yet?" This really was the $64,000 question, in my opinion.

"No."

"So when do we start counting?"

"When you start the maintenance chemo." That was so far away that it wasn't even worth thinking about.

I rest my case.

Settlin' In Once More

I thought of my inability to deal with the side effects of the chemo through the IP port as a personal failure. When this whole thing started, I had made a vow to myself that I would be as tough as I needed to be. I didn't care how rigorous the treatment was; I would get through it. I would make sure I had done everything in my power to stay alive. When I agreed to change to a different chemo treatment, it was a mental defeat. I tried not to let it affect me, but I know it did. I guess I will never know if it could have been a determining factor in the outcome of my struggle with cancer. In a situation where I felt powerless, it was like I had given up a tiny opportunity to have some power over what was happening.

After the decision to abandon that treatment, things seemed to slow down. It was gradually beginning to sink in that I would never be going back to any old life. This was my life now, and it seemed likely that it would not really get much better. Still, it was more of a nagging thought that only surfaced here and there. I wanted/needed to believe that I was going to get better. I could not accept the idea that the things I enjoyed in life were nothing more than a distant memory. It seemed that I had been relegated to spend the better part of my life sitting in a chair, watching TV or movies, doing crossword puzzles or word searches, or reading books. There had to be more than this.

Starting in November 2011, I gradually got used to the new chemo.

I did everything that was recommended to deal with the potential side effects, and as usual, I had most of them. I guess I was not in that group Dr. Sukumvanich had talked about that didn't even know they were on chemotherapy. I knew I was getting chemo treatments. Living a lukewarm life, in more ways than one, while not energizing, wasn't nearly as difficult as my first six months. Yes, I was slowly losing my hair, but I had been there before. While it did nothing for my self-image, it had no physical impact. Yes, I was eating the menu of an eighty-year-old woman, keeping my foods bland and lukewarm, but this could not be considered earthshattering. Those piping-hot showers I'd always enjoyed had become a distant memory. Yes, my skin was dry, my sinuses were in a constant state of irritation, and my nose would bleed from the sores within. When I awoke, if I was lying on my side, my ears would be stuck shut. After I lifted my head from the pillow, I could feel them slowly become unstuck.

I was very careful about where I sat and what kind of shoes I wore, as well as not leaning on my elbows and not letting myself get too hot. I was glad I had started this particular chemo during the cold weather months. I was fortunate to never have developed hand or foot sores, but the tips of my fingers had a constant burning sensation. The nails on my toes turned brown, and they became thick and flaky. The skin around them was red, extremely dry, and the outside edges of my little toes were very sore. As soon as the weather got a little bit warm, I tried to wear sandals that didn't actually touch my little toes. Dr. Sukumvanich suggested I get a couple pairs of Birkenstocks. "A lot of my patients really recommend them. They're a little expensive, but they are worth it. Don't wear shoes that go in between your toes." That wiped out about two-thirds of my sandals, including almost all of the ones that didn't touch my little toes. So I added two pair of Birkenstocks to my shoe collection.

I, as usual, experienced body aches and joint pain. My theory was that the side effects each person experienced were related to problematic body areas. I had rarely had any stomach problems, so I thought this explained why I never had nausea as a side effect. However, I'd had joint pains for years, so I thought it was no surprise that the side effect of joint pain was an issue for me. All my usual areas of joint pain seemed to be much worse.

After my second post-surgery scan in February 2011, there was still no sign of cancer. I became obsessed with my CA-125, which was then at 42. Jackie was quick to point out that they didn't just go by the number; they strongly took symptoms into account. I had so many symptoms; how could I tell which came from the chemo and which might be from cancer? I became angry with the number—very rational! The month before, it was 36, and I was told that was considered "as good as" 35. Apparently not, because I still had not been declared cancer-free.

The magic number of 35 lay just out of my reach. And so I settled into living on the edge—the edge of normal. It was not a matter of choosing a life; it was a matter of getting used to things being a certain way. During this time, more than any other, I began to grasp the notion that this was my life, this was life with cancer. That little clog in the stream was gradually eroding, leaf by leaf, twig by twig.

Somewhere in March 2011, after my fourth cycle, I had an appointment with the doctor.

"Well, your number isn't coming down as fast as we had hoped." I mentioned that I had read that it took four treatments before it really started to work.

"That's true," he said, agreeably. "That's true."

I felt a little better. After all, maybe my normal CA-125 before I had cancer was 34, or at the high end. In that case, my 42 could be thought of as a single digit. Maybe now that I had the four cycles under my belt, the number would start to come down. Apparently that wasn't the way the doctor was looking at it. While I knew it was not a good sign that my number hadn't dropped to the desired level, I was always looking for alternative explanations as to why. Of course, I was sure he had seen cancer take this kind of path in one variation or another many times. Once again, I was happy that he gave me the unpadded version of how I was doing. I didn't want to be given false hope. I wanted to know exactly where I stood. The fact that I could count on him to tell me that was reassuring.

Life by Numbers

Math was never my strong suit. In high school, it was usually the end of the semester by the time I caught on to things like geometry, algebra, and trigonometry. I never dared to think I could tackle calculus. Yet now my life revolved around numbers. Sometimes these numbers were as hard to understand as the ones I'd had to tackle in high school. Floating around in my head at any given moment were numbers reflective of frequency of treatment, time between treatments, values of all aspects of my blood measuring white and red blood cell counts, and the values of various other bodily functions.

Adjusting to having chemo treatments once a month was harder than I thought it would be. In fact, I hadn't really given it any thought until it actually happened. In those first six months, going to Magee three weeks out of every four was pretty intense. Yet I wanted that. It made me feel I was working really hard to get rid of my cancer. I still didn't feel good enough to go back to my old life; I was still trying to get better. With only one treatment per month, I felt like I was being lazy, somehow not working hard enough. As I write these words, I am struck by their irrationality, yet there it is.

When I did therapy during those twenty years at ARC Manor, I was the queen of rational thinking. I loved the concepts put forth by Albert Ellis regarding his rational emotive therapy. It just made so much sense to me. Once the irrational ideas were identified, it was simply a matter of systematically replacing them with more rational thoughts.

Not so simple. Here I was, desperately looking for and hanging on to the thinnest of threads that left me with some feeling of hope. I didn't care if the thread was anchored in irrationality. As time slowly ticked away, I felt my life force ebbing right along with it.

Once a cycle I would have my CA-125 checked, and the length of a cycle depended on what type of chemotherapy I was receiving. Generally in my treatment, a cycle was three or four weeks. The CA-125 was generally checked toward the end of the cycle, thus giving information about the impact of each cycle on the cancer growth. Through my own research and through constant reminders and explanations from the oncology team, I knew that the CA-125 was not an exact science, since many other things besides cancer could cause it to change. Still, it gave a general idea.

Certainly this was the most significant number in my life. I lived for the moments when I would hear what my new number was. I couldn't wait to find out. I tried to tell myself that it didn't matter, but I was unable to stop myself from dwelling on the value. I felt sorry for

Chris, and then Melissa. They always had to take my calls and give me the latest number, good or bad. When it went up from that low of 36 to something in the 40s, they assured me that they considered this the same number. I didn't believe them.

From the blood work done before each chemo treatment, the medical staff could be sure that I was still stable enough to have the next treatment. Since a low white blood cell count was a common problem with most chemotherapy regimens, this was always checked. A low white blood cell count (WBC) was a medical reason to cancel the chemo until the number rose to the acceptable level. To be sure the WBC count didn't get too low, I received injections of a drug that is used to boost WBC production. There were two potencies. For the stronger version, there had to be fifteen days between chemo treatments, and the less potent variety was used if there was less than fifteen days. Only one shot of the stronger version was needed, while I got two to five shots (per day) of the less potent of the two. Neither one could be given until at least twenty-four hours after a chemo treatment. I learned to give myself the less strong potent shots, which saved me anywhere from two to five two-hour trips to get the shots at the cancer center. When I had to get the stronger shots, I only got one per cycle, and that had to be done at the cancer center. This was due to the high price of these shots, somewhere around $11,000 per shot. On my insurance EOB, it was listed as $9494.50.

Other numbers of significance were the red blood cell (RBC) count, and platelet count. They could be lower than normal, but not too low. For example, a normal platelet count was somewhere between 150,000 and 370,000. As long as it didn't go below 100,000 I could still have a chemo treatment. I haven't had a normal RBC count for a long time, but it was only low enough that I needed a transfusion one time.

Then there were the liver enzymes, which were checked once a cycle. One in particular, the alkaline phosphatase, hadn't been normal since before I found out I had cancer. Apparently my PCP hadn't thought the elevation in this number was anything to worry about, because he had done nothing in response to my high value. A normal value is between 50 and 136. Since November 2011, mine has been between 155 and 306. Once again, it is a number that can be impacted by a variety of things, and certainly cancer is one of them.

These numbers floating around in my head were a huge focal point in my life. I became much more educated about the significance of the values than I ever cared to be. But they were the determining factors in my treatment, and so I watched them. With chemo treatments only once every four weeks, I began to feel like I was doing next to nothing to fight my cancer. All that time in between treatments left me in a sort of time warp. My life seemed to be moving in slow motion again and going nowhere fast. The idea that I might ever get better became more difficult to hang on to. If you have a broken bone, you start physical therapy fairly quickly, and this gives you the feeling that you are moving forward. If you have surgery to remove a body part that doesn't work right anymore, you gradually regain your strength and get back into the swing of things. Neither of these ideas seemed to apply to my situation.

I tried to give myself artificial incentives. Especially after my surgery, I had frequent and intense hot flashes. I always had a sweater on hand that could be removed and put back on with little effort. I had an old blue sweater that I loved—a Liz Claiborne sweater that had hung in my closet for about fifteen years. It was made of a sweatshirt-like cotton fabric, but it buttoned down the front. It was one of those things you become attached to and can't bear to part with even long after it has turned to rags; I think everyone has one. I stitched it up here and there, just to make it easier to get on and off. I decided that once my CA-125 got below 35, I would have a little ceremony and burn it in our outside fire pit. For some reason I had set May as my target month. May came and went, and my number, still uncooperative, remained in the unacceptable range. The old blue sweater still hangs in my front closet, but I don't wear it anymore.

As my CA-125 continued to waver, so did I. Every time my number went up, I went down. I was so close, yet so far away. I would turn myself inward, trying to see the cancer. It was hard to know where it might be. In the first six months, from the scans, I knew where it was. When I did my healing imagery, I knew where to focus, where to look, where to shine the sun. Now I had no idea where it was. If I couldn't picture it, I couldn't chase it away. It was like a little kid, playing hide-and-seek with me, and no matter how hard I looked, I couldn't seem to pin it down. It doesn't seem like this should have mattered, but it did. Life by numbers was exhausting.

Dr. Sukumvanich told me more than once that this was considered good control of a bad disease. Maybe by the tenth time he uttered these words, I began to hear him. It must have been very frustrating for him to see me doing so well after starting out so near death. There I was, though, acting like I was still waiting to get better. I wonder if all his patients were so dense, or if I was a new experience. I tried to explain to him my notion of the downward spiral, but he had a contrary perception of me as someone with a very bad disease that he had been able to stabilize.

The holidays came and went, the cold months gave way to another spring, and spring became summer. Through all these months, I moved along, still waiting for something big to happen. As time crawled along, any hope I was hanging onto slowly faded. The yo-yo was still, and I was dangling at the bottom of the string. Dare I think I would stay here? Was this it, then? Had I fought the good fight, and won? Had I fought the good fight, and lost? Perhaps it was all a matter of perspective. Would I continue this chemo for the rest of my life? How long might that be? Should I settle in? Should I think like the doctor … that I had good control of a very bad disease? Could I live like this, indefinitely? Did I really have a choice? Lots of questions, all without any real answers.

Chapter Eight

————

THE CRISIS

In June 2011, my CA-125 jumped up to 100. When I heard this at my appointment, I could feel myself slump, both in body and spirit. I tried to control myself; they already had seen me a basket case enough times. After being in double digits for the previous nine months, I couldn't believe I was again in triple digits. The June 20 scan revealed no evidence of metastatic or recurrent disease. In addition, because of a severe headache I'd had that had caused me to throw up several times and had left me feeling nauseated for several days, Chris had scheduled me to have a head scan. This had also been negative. The CA-125 of 100 was the biggest sign of cancer I had received since my surgery.

"I don't understand ... I just had a scan, which showed no signs of cancer."

"Well, that's only one of the things we use to evaluate how you're doing. We also use the CA-125 and your own report of how you feel."

Of course, I knew that. I had been told this many times. Somehow, though, when the time comes to get this kind of news, it doesn't make sense. There was no change in how I felt, and the scan was good, yet the number had climbed. How do you process something like that? All along, though I knew I was living on the edge, living a very limited version of life, at least I was alive. Although I constantly lamented that I was unable to do much at all, at least physically, I knew I wanted to be alive. It wasn't much, but it was a life. I would find a way to make it meaningful. Yet here, in the course of a few minutes, somehow that tenuous grasp I had on life had been snatched away from me. I teetered on the edge. How could fifty points make that much difference?

"This is not the big kahuna," I heard Chris say, her voice breaking through the haze. She was trying to tell me that death was not right around the corner, not this time.

"Let's get Dr. Sukumvanich in here and see what he wants to do." This time it was Jackie. Yes, that was a good idea. He would know what to do. He would fix this. He knew how to deal with situations like this.

While I was waiting for the doctor, I began contemplating what was happening within my body. The feelings of betrayal surfaced again; my body was once more letting me down. I thought I had straightened it out; I thought we were on the same page, working toward a common goal. Even though my number had never arrived at the desired level, I still imagined that I was routing out those last few cancer cells, doing the final cleansing. Apparently not. At some point, when I wasn't watching, they had sneaked in and begun to take hold once more. Maybe I had let my guard down; maybe I hadn't been careful enough. I must have done something wrong. How else could the cancer have started to grow again? I must not have been careful enough.

Jackie and the doctor came in together. When he saw how distressed I was, he assured me that he hadn't given up on me, and he recommended that I switch to a different chemo.

"I thought that was considered a maintenance drug," I said, remembering when he told me I would be receiving this particular chemo when I was cancer-free, as a maintenance drug.

"Well," he answered, "that doesn't mean that it isn't still working on cancer cells."

Of course, I would do it, but that little detail hadn't escaped me. Here I was, once more moving on the downward spiral. I felt off balance already.

Somehow, this seemed like it didn't really pack much of a punch. I needed a real killer in there. Those cancer cells were on the move once again, and I needed more than a maintenance drug to make sure they didn't take hold. Yet I knew the doctor was the expert. He had seen the cancer cells take this kind of path before. He knew the best course of treatment. I trusted him. He had never given me a reason not to trust him. I knew cancer still had a lot of unknowns, and in spite of all the tremendous knowledge of modern medical science, sometimes there were no clear-cut answers.

I remember when Marc, my oldest son, realized that people die. He was about seven years old. It was Christmastime, and we were talking about Jesus. I explained that Christmas was a celebration of Jesus's birthday. Marc was always a thinker, and I could almost see his brain clicking along, putting new information in the cataloging room so that it could be filed in the appropriate place. As we talked, he quizzed me so that he could be sure he had enough information to make sense of what I was saying.

"How old is he?" He needed to be able to see this Jesus person, probably imagining him to be about the same age as he was, excited at the prospect of a birthday party where he'd be getting lots of neat toys.

"Oh, he's not still alive. He lived a long time ago." Still with no clue where this was all going, I began painting a brief picture of Jesus: you know, the stereotypic one we all have—the thumbnail sketch of his life, as if it were obvious and there was nothing shocking about it. I mean, it would make perfect sense to a seven-year-old boy that the entire world would go crazy every year celebrating the birthday of a dead man, right? Over and over, year after year?

"What do you mean?" he asked, clearly confused.

And, so, I explained the whole BC/AD thing, with Jesus's life being the dividing point. I talked about what people believe about Jesus that leads them to celebrate his "birthday" year after year.

"You mean people die?" He had the most betrayed look on his

face, as if someone had destroyed his faith in humanity. I was horrified to think that my innocent conversation about Jesus's birthday could have done this to him. What was I thinking? Apparently, not much of anything. I did my best to salvage the moment and make something positive come out of it.

"Well," I started tentatively, "most people live a really long life. Their bodies just plain wear out. Like an old, old car. Like Grandma Bentley, and Grandma and Grandpa Schneider. They're old and still haven't worn out. They'll be around for a while. So you don't have to think about it now. When you get sick, or break something on your body, the doctors can almost always fix it for you. It is only if you get a really bad sickness, or if your body gets broken very badly, or something really big on your body gets broken, that it can't be fixed, and then you die. But that doesn't happen very often." I went through lots of examples of things like broken arms and legs, flu, and chicken pox—all things that could be fixed by those amazing doctors. By the time we were done, he seemed more relaxed. And I could see his mind filing things away again.

Although the final hand had yet to be played, it didn't look good, and with this new jump in my number, things looked a little worse. Generally a person who was very cool in a crisis, I was falling apart now that I was the center of it. I was one of those people with a really bad disease—one that doctors often could not fix.

"I haven't given up on you. There are still lots of things we can try." Dr. Sukumvanich looked a little confused. Apparently it was way too early in this process to be getting this upset. Ever the voice of reason, what he said calmed me—slightly. He went on to tell me that this new drug I would be taking had very few side effects. The three big ones, which were uncommon, were headaches, high blood pressure, and perforated bowel. If the latter happened, it would be an emergency, and I would need surgery right away. But that was in the "rare" side effect category, occurring less than 1 percent of the time.

I quickly dismissed those three bad side effects from my mind. I started to think, and that helped me calm down too. When I had seen him for the first time after my surgery, and he had explained the four options he considered viable for my continued treatment, this had been one of them. I remembered thinking I liked the way it worked. What it did was destroy the blood vessels in the tumors, thereby cutting off their lifeline. I liked the logic of it. So maybe this was a good thing in the end.

AT LAST

I met with Chris once again, to review the information and sign the paper consenting to the treatment. She reiterated the three big side effects. The other side effects were those common to most chemotherapies and known to occur more than 30 percent of the time. They included generalized weakness, body pain, abdominal pain, nausea and vomiting, poor appetite, constipation, upper respiratory infection, low white blood cell count, proteinuria (a kidney problem), nosebleeds, diarrhea, hair loss, and mouth sores. At this point, I only half listened to the side effects. I had pretty consistent side effects from one chemo to another, so I assumed this one would be more of the same. I was most concerned about the high blood pressure, since I already had that. I had been taking medication for it since about 2000. It was under good control, but that being listed as a side effect didn't seem to bode well. I tried not to think about it.

Like the other chemo treatments I had received, this one was given through an IV. I would receive it once every three weeks. After my first treatment, my CA-125 had come down from 100 to 50. This was very exciting! I had my appointment that week with Jackie, but at the end Dr. Sukumvanich peeked his head in the door, and said that was very good. "This is going to work." He clearly was very encouraged by my response to this new chemo. I could hear the excitement in his voice. It seemed we had finally found the one that was going to do the trick.

By the second cycle, however, my blood pressure was on the rise. I was to work with my primary care doctor on this, so I immediately scheduled an appointment to see her. She increased my medication. With each successive treatment, though, my blood pressure continued to rise. As it went up, my CA-125 came down. By September 12, I was at the magic number—35! Unfortunately, my blood pressure was continuing to rise. My PC had already made several adjustments to my medication, but they didn't last. In addition to this side effect, I had severe body pain. Dr. Sukumvanich didn't feel it was from the chemo, but I did. He explained that as people get older, things tend to get worse, and it is easy to blame it on the chemo when it could be due to aging. The information from the company that made this drug did mention body pain as a side effect, but Dr. Sukumvanich felt that sometimes what was listed as a side effect was questionable. I was used to body pain with all the arthritis I had, but this was so much more intense than anything I had experienced; I knew it was more than just getting old.

There was not a spot on my body that didn't hurt. Getting up and down required real effort; walking was painful. My right foot burned and burned. I could have sworn I broke something in it. I even went to a foot doctor. She was wonderful. It was her practice, and she did everything herself; she answered the phone, did the scheduling herself, and ordered tests herself. This resulted in some interruptions during the appointment, but she took her time, explained everything thoroughly, and made me feel like she really cared about my pain. She ordered an MRI, which showed arthritis as the culprit. I was fitted for orthotics, which helped me tremendously. I also had physical therapy, which didn't really help. In the end, I think it was arthritis severely aggravated by the chemotherapy.

My hands and fingers burned with arthritis pain, and my arms and shoulders were painful with the smallest movements. My neck had very little range of motion. I think my face hurt the worst. I had an almost constant sinus pressure headache. Mary, my tai chi instructor, stopped at my house several times to do massage and Reiki. This helped tremendously. She showed Bill how to massage my face and neck. He would do this several times a week. I limped and moaned my way from one position to another, crying about the idea that the thing that actually might cure me was at the same time making me hurt so badly. What a paradox this treatment was!

Bill and I had planned a vacation—something we both sorely needed. We were going to one of our favorite national parks, Smoky Mountain National Park. This was our fourth visit, and our first in the fall. We had many favorite spots, including some of the park hikes as well as restaurants in downtown Gatlinburg. Our typical pattern was to get up at a leisurely pace, pack a good lunch, complete with energy boosters (snacks), and head out for a day-long hike. Bill would always peruse the book we had purchased on our first trip and find a suitable hike that worked for the entire family. This meant it couldn't be too hard, or if it was hard, it couldn't be too long. He was expert at accommodating all the different levels of physical fitness within the family unit. He managed to incorporate nothing too strenuous for Mum (me), and several points of interest for the boys. Waterfalls were always considered a good selling point.

We had done everything from camping in a tent to renting cabins and condos. In our younger years, we loved the camping lifestyle. The rustic accommodations were all we needed. Cooking dinner over the campfire was an adventure, and we enjoyed coming up with inventive meals that were mostly simple, but occasionally elaborate and expensive. We always left room in our schedule for a couple nights in town, where we would wander the streets like typical tourists, buying cheap trinkets or T-shirts to commemorate our trip. All in all, it was a wonderful, rejuvenating time. We loved the physical challenge of the hikes, followed by a relaxing evening around a good meal, be it homemade on the campfire, or at one of the restaurants in Gatlinburg. The bonus was that all this took place surrounded by Mother Nature.

As we drove south, heading first for Nashville, to visit my nephew Alan and his family, who had moved there a few months before, my mind drifted through these little pockets of warm memories. When I thought about how this trip would be different, it was hard to stop myself from crying. I wanted things to be good, for Bill. I wanted this to be a real vacation, not a trip on which Bill had to spend all his time taking care of his sick wife and would be unable to enjoy himself. The trip was his idea, and I knew that, ironically, he was thinking the same thing about me. He wanted this to be an opportunity for me to relax in a place he knew I had always enjoyed and loved. I knew it wouldn't be anything remotely like our past trips, but I was determined to make it as good as I possibly could. I forced myself to focus on the pleasant things.

We had always talked about visiting Nashville, the home of country music. We had both come to enjoy the sound of country, more so as we got older, and we each had our favorite singers. When we had received a card in the mail with the new address of the "Nashville Bentleys," we were excited at the opportunity to visit them, as well as to get a little taste of Nashville. We spent two days there with them and enjoyed the visit tremendously. Alan and his wife, Melanie, and their kids, Evan and Erin, made us feel right at home.

We were lucky enough to be there for the outside, downtown kickoff of the World of Bluegrass week, a free, informal affair that preceded Del McCoury and Friends being inducted into the International Bluegrass Hall of Fame. We watched the performances for about one and one-half hours and then left. It was more than enough time for me to be standing, and then sitting sideways on the cement wall in a little outside park across the street. After hearing Vince Gill sing, we made that the high point of the concert and headed into town for lunch. Later that night, we came back to town and perused several of the bars, listening to the hometown performers. It was a fun time. I took more pain pills than usual to help me feel comfortable enough to last through the evening. I went so far as to order a beer in two different places. I sipped at it slowly, and by the time we left each place, I had cleared the long necks of the bottles. I didn't really enjoy the taste of beer anymore, but it made me feel more like we were a normal couple, having a normal evening in downtown Nashville. Bill was more concerned about wasting all that beer, so he finished my second one.

From there, we rented a cabin in the mountains outside of Gatlinburg. Patrick, our younger son, and his dog, Dexter, were the only ones who were able to get away to join us for a few days. While not completely isolated, the cabin was nestled in the trees, surrounded by silence. The leaves hadn't started to change yet, but there was a quietude that was peaceful—just what the doctor ordered. While I didn't feel well, I enjoyed being there. We took some short hikes; I was unable to do more than that. I had my trusty hiking stick. Bill had bought it for me at the Annual Fort Armstrong Folk Festival held each August along the river in Kittanning. I had taken it when we went to Yellowstone, and it was a tremendous help on our hikes there.

Bill and Patrick went for a longer hike to the Chimney Tops. This was a family favorite. Our first trip to the Smokies was in 1982, when I was three months pregnant with Marc. Bill and I had hiked to the Chimney Tops. It was a long uphill hike that ended on the exposed rocks for which the mountain had received its name. The 365-degree vista provided a breathtaking view. It was truly a wonder of nature. I was much braver then. We all went together when Marc was about seven and Patrick three. The next trip, I only went about halfway and then went back down and waited at the creek for the "boys" to return. This time, Bill and Patrick went together, but Bill admitted it was a little rough on him. Patrick, of course, had no trouble with either the climb or the exposed rock. I spent the morning relaxing at the cabin. It was hard to believe that there had been almost thirty years between the first visit and this one. Certainly the Schneiders had gone through changes, but it was nice to know the park had remained virtually the same.

As soon as my blood pressure had started to go up, I had purchased a BP cuff so that I could monitor it on a daily basis. I had been doing this at home for a few weeks, and I took the BP cuff along on our vacation. My blood pressure had continued to stay in a high range, running around 180/90. My last chemo treatment before we left for Tennessee was on September 14, and I would have my next one on October 5, the day after we returned home—as long as my BP was below 150/100.

The last time I had seen my PCP, she had started me on a new blood pressure medication, which she called "the big gun." She explained that the dosage could easily be changed. As I sat in the cabin in the Smoky Mountains, I became more anxious about whether or not I needed to add pills. I decided that I would call and report my BP after we got on the road to head home. She had told me that if my BP stayed at a range of 180/100 for two days, I should call the office. I seemed to be fast approaching that range. I knew that anxiety didn't help keep my blood pressure down, so I tried to calm myself. I listened to my relaxation CD on my iPod. I was generally able to tell when my anxiety was heightened, and I believed that, at the time, it had little to do with the range of my BP.

We got an early start home, and I called my PCP's office as planned. I was told to take one more of the new pills, and at the same time, I was told that I was being referred to a heart doctor but that I could still call my PCP until I had my first appointment with the new doctor. I was unable to have my chemo treatment that Wednesday as scheduled, since my blood pressure was above the acceptable limit. The following Saturday, Bill and I went to Pittsburgh and had dinner at the Cheesecake Factory. Armed with enough leftovers to feed myself for at least three days, we returned home that evening and made an early night of it.

It All Comes to a Head

When I awoke Sunday morning, I had such intense head pain that I could barely stand to get up out of bed. I came out to the kitchen to take my blood pressure and got a reading of 205/105. It only took one suggestion from Bill, and I was on the phone calling my PCP's office. The doctor on call instructed me to go to the local emergency room. Each movement sent sharp, heavy pain through my head. The light was blinding, so I put on my prescription sunglasses and didn't remove them for three days. Upon admission to the ER, I was given a shot for the head pain. It had no impact. I was given a head scan, which showed nothing. I was given nothing for my blood pressure, which at that point was 218/113. In addition, my heart rate was running low. When the doctor felt I should be admitted, we called Magee to see if I should go there, and I was taken by ambulance to their emergency room.

Within twenty minutes I was put into the intensive care unit, where I remained for two and a half days. I was unable to lift my head without getting severe nausea and at times also throwing up. Those two and a half days were a blur to me; I drifted in and out of a drug-induced sleep, moving as little as possible. I know I was visited by different doctors; neurologists, heart doctors, and Dr. Sukumvanich. I had an MRI, MRA, and MRV of my head all at the same time. In addition, I had a heart scan. All of these tests came back normal. The diagnosis of hypertensive crisis was linked to my chemo treatments. As a result, I had to discontinue the treatment I had been on. It went on my "do not use" list. The chemotherapy that had finally lowered my CA-125 to the acceptable level would be used no more.

I was devastated by this turn of events. But, at the moment, I had to focus on getting my blood pressure back under control.

Aside from the scans, with frequent monitoring of my blood pressure, I was given medications to keep my readings at an acceptable level. Since I was unable to void in a bedpan, and since being in an upright position produced such severe head pain, a catheter was inserted the evening of the day of my admission. Since I wasn't eating at that time, I didn't have to worry about my colostomy appliance. In fact, I had forgotten all about it.

I was admitted on a Sunday afternoon. In the wee hours of Tuesday morning, the nurse on duty came into my room and told me that if I wanted her to, she would be more than happy to bathe me. I said thanks, but no thanks. The idea of someone washing me was more than I wanted to imagine. It was something old people had to have done. As I drifted in and out of sleep, I became aware of an odor. It seemed to come and go as I moved. Suddenly, it dawned on me that I hadn't looked at the beast since I had been admitted to the hospital. I peeled back the covers, and there it was, about half attached to my body. The other half had lifted, with stool pressing out around the edges. That was the source of the odor and, I'm sure, the thing that prompted the nurse to make her generous offer. I lay there for several minutes, considering my options. I had so many wires hooked up to me, a catheter in place, an IV running; I knew there was no way I could wash myself. So I swallowed my pride, and pushed the nurse button.

She cheerfully answered the call button, and was in the room in less than five minutes, armed with all the necessary supplies.

"I went to one of the nurse's lockers to get some nice-smelling soap for you. I don't like the stuff they give us for patients." She was really serious about this. "I love to give the patients baths."

I was thinking that there must be something a little odd about her. Who could like such a chore?

But as she began to bathe me, I began to relax. I could feel my embarrassment fading, and I let her do her thing. She did one side of my body at a time. When she got to the half with my colostomy, I explained that I needed to change the whole thing and apologized for the odor. She just ignored that and asked how she could help. My husband had brought me supplies, so she brought my bag to me, and the necessary cleaning supplies, and stood back while I took care of the beast.

Then, without my having to leave the bed, she changed the sheets and brought me a new robe. I felt like a whole different person and couldn't think of a way to thank her. When I had gotten my supplies from my bag, I noticed that my husband had brought me a new bottle of shower gel, one with a nice, fresh scent, something like pear and eucalyptus. I asked the nurse if she could accept it as a donation— something she could use on other patients. She was thrilled and readily accepted it. It didn't begin to repay her, but it was all I had at the moment.

Things looked up from that point. It was a wonderful way to start the day. I even took off my sunglasses. In the late morning, I had a visit from the doctor who had been in charge when I was admitted to the emergency room.

"Well, it's nice to see your eyes," she said. "You must be feeling better."

"Yes, I am beginning to feel better, thank you."

"You had us pretty worried when you first got here."

My husband was visiting at that time, and he mentioned some things to her about the care I had received at the other hospital ER, and the fact that I had not received any treatment for my blood pressure. When we had arrived here, within twenty minutes, they thought my condition was bad enough to put me into the ICU.

"That is being investigated," she said. "It's not the first time we've had trouble with that place." She then turned to me. "How would you like to move to a regular floor?"

"I would *love* to!"

My catheter was removed, and I had the opportunity to use the hidden pull-out toilet stashed under a metal cabinet in my ICU room. Who knew they had such things? By the middle of the afternoon, I was settled into my new room on the cancer floor. The first thing I did was sneak into the bathroom to wash the body parts that had only gotten a cursory swish that morning. I'm sure it was done that way for my comfort, rather than an oversight by my thoughtful nurse. When I came out of the bathroom, my new nurse was just coming in the door.

"Oh, you're already up!" There was a tone in her voice that left me feeling like I had done something wrong.

"Was I not supposed to do that?" Maybe I didn't know all the rules.

"Well, no, it's okay." she said, sounding a little like I *had* broken a rule. "I haven't seen you yet."

Ah. That was the unspoken rule I didn't know about. She wanted to check me in, or check me out, before I started going off on my own.

"Well, I had to pee pretty badly." I was trying to salvage the situation and keep from getting off on the wrong foot with this woman who was in charge for the time being.

"Oh, that's okay." Now that she was back in charge, things would be fine.

"I'm supposed to get some medications at three p.m." Oops! There

I was again, stepping on her feet. Since it was already 3:15, I was just trying to help her out.

"Okay. I just need to get a few things done first." It was after 5:00 p.m. before she came back around with my 3:00 p.m. medications.

I was so happy to be out of the intensive care unit that I didn't really care about anything else. I was also allowed to start eating real food that day. Although I couldn't eat much yet, just the idea was exciting. I felt as though I were back in charge of myself and my life, at least in some little ways. Tuesday is the first day I remember clearly. My sister Joan dropped by to visit that evening. We chatted about nothing and everything. As our visit drew to a close, I noticed that my face felt hot and that my heart seemed to be racing. After she left, I went to the bathroom, and when I looked in the mirror, I realized that my face was beet red. After a quick examination, I noticed that my arms were the same way; a sort of rash covered them, and it began to itch. I was beginning to get the head pain back as well. When I got back in bed, I rang the call button and asked if someone could come and check my blood pressure. It was running high, so I was given more medication, which I was still receiving through the IV. I reported to the nurse that I felt a rapid heart rate and a sensation of buzzing, and that my head was hurting again. She told me she would get the resident on call.

The resident was a large young woman with a thick build who looked to be in her twenties. She seemed to be very conscientious. She asked me some questions and then asked if I was taking any medication for anxiety. I told her no and said that I didn't want anything like that. She assured me that if I didn't want it, I didn't have to take it. I was receiving pain medication. I tried to lie still and relax myself to sleep. By morning, I felt better. Still, I wondered what had caused the symptoms of the night before. I was not convinced that it was anxiety.

Wednesday went by without any problem, and the head pain from the night before dissipated through the day. I took my time exploring the menu, and ordered a wonderful grilled vegetable pita bread lunch. There is nothing like a little deprivation to make you appreciate food. While my blood pressure was coming down, it wasn't staying at an acceptable level long enough for me to go home. I began to feel perky. Without any conscious awareness, I was once again in danger of feeling hopeful. Here I was, in the middle, or maybe on the downside, of a serious medical crisis. I had come through it without having a stroke and without any damage to my heart. Yet, in the process, I had lost the one thing that had finally given me a real reason for hope; I could no longer do the chemo treatment that had finally brought me to that magical number—a CA-125 of 35. Just when I was about to ride back to the top of the yo-yo, I had been jerked to a stop. Whoa, Nelly! Where do you think you're going?

DEFCON 1 HEADACHES

On Thursday evening, my sister Joan once again came to visit after work. For whatever reason, we got on a roll talking about people we disliked and different situations we had been in with them. This was hilarious and entertaining in a way that was a wonderful release of tension. As the evening wore on, I once again noticed that I could feel a tremendous amount of heat emanating from my face. I looked at my arms, and they were red, hot, covered in a rash, and itchy. A quick look in the mirror confirmed that my face was in the same condition. I felt buzzy, with the same rapid heart rate. Joan decided to take her leave.

Within a short time, I became very stressed about my symptoms and once again used the call button to get someone to check my blood pressure. It was elevated, but I was more concerned with the feeling that my heart was about to beat out of my chest. An EKG was ordered, which came back normal. I was on the verge of panic and had to get up every few minutes to pee. Finally, the same resident on call was summoned to check on me. We had a similar conversation to the one we had had on Tuesday, revisiting the whole issue of anxiety attacks.

"But I was very relaxed, really enjoying myself, having a great visit with my sister."

"I know you said you didn't want to take anything for anxiety." Once again, the resident explained to me that anxiety attacks don't necessarily come when you are anxious in real time.

"That's right; I don't. But I also don't want to be stupid about it either." Although I still doubted that anxiety accounted for my symptoms, at this point, I had to at least consider the possibility. There didn't seem to be any other explanation. The idea that I was losing control in this manner was more upsetting to me than I could accept. At the moment, though, the resident told me she would consult with the doctor about my situation.

The doctor came into my room clearly interested in getting in and out as fast as possible. He got right down to business. I was getting back into bed after another trip to the bathroom.

"She's all right." He turned to the resident as he was speaking. "People who are dying of a heart attack don't get up and go to the bathroom."

"Well," I replied in the same vein, "If you think you're gonna die, you don't want someone to find you in a pool of pee."

I could see that he was stifling a chuckle. "Okay. Tell me what's going on." As I started to go into the details, beginning with my visit with my sister, he interrupted me. Clearly, he didn't want *that* much information. In the end, he turned to the resident and said to her, "Her blood pressure *is* elevated." He directed her on what medication to give me, and when to recheck it, and then he left the room.

By this point, the head pain had returned and was at an all-time high point. The resident stayed with me for a few minutes. I thanked her for her time and her concern. As I looked at her closely for the first time, I could see that she appeared exhausted, both physically and emotionally. Slowly, it filtered into my conscious awareness that while I was in the middle of my own crisis, there had likely been one of much greater proportions going on somewhere down the hall. I told her that she looked bone weary and that I was sorry to have added to her load. She assured me, in proper fashion, that it was okay; it was what she was there for. She seemed a little upset that she hadn't looked professional when she entered my room and that her feelings had shown through. She told me that I was the brave one, dealing with cancer as I was. We had a moment or two of silence, where I believe we courted some mutual admiration.

After she left, I lay in my hospital bed, trying to arrange all the wires so that they weren't pulling and so I could get as comfortable as possible. I moved very cautiously, as my head was sensitive to the slightest change in position. It seemed to be on fire, as if someone had somehow attached thousands of tiny electrodes to it and the smallest movement would set them off, causing them to twitch and pulse with energy so that I thought my head might burst at any moment. I tried not to move. I had already been given pain medication, which seemed to have no impact.

After what seemed like forever, with no change, I began to think about what I could do. I had to find some way to get some relief from this pain. I pushed the call button once more, and asked if my husband would be allowed to stay the night with me. "Sure!" was the answer. It was 11:15 p.m. I hated to call him at that hour, but it was the only solution I could think of.

"Bill, would you be willing to come down and spend the night here? I'm okay, but my head hurts so bad I just don't know what to do."

"I'll get ready and be right there." There was no discussion needed. I tried not to think about how tired he must be, or how tired he was going to be in the morning, when he would have to go to work. All I knew was that I needed him there with me.

Bill arrived sometime between 12:30 a.m. and 1:00 a.m. I told him that I would explain later what had happened; I couldn't talk at the moment. He said he didn't need to know; he would be there for me. I asked him to get my sunglasses and then asked him to massage the back of my neck and face like Mary had shown him to do. He asked if I thought a cold cloth would help. It did, and he kept rewetting it in cold water. There was so much heat emanating from my face that it didn't take long for the washcloth to become heated up. I listened to the relaxation imagery CD I had on my iPod. Gradually, I began to feel myself getting sleepy. With my head still pulsing and pounding with pain, I lay still, willing it to feel better.

In a short time, I woke up from my drug-induced sleep. I don't really remember falling asleep, but I must have, because I woke up. And it was there waiting for me, ready to once again wrap itself around me, enveloping my head in an explosive, pulsating capsule of never-ending pain. Even with the dark glasses on, my eyes burned and throbbed as though they had been too long in the searing heat of a mid-August sun at the beach. The vise around my skull tightened with the slightest movement, and the sharp pain in my neck was unforgiving. I gave a tearful little moan.

Bill was immediately awake and up at my side. He began once more to give me those little treatments, which all together produced a small amount of relief. I asked him to check the time, to see if I was able to have another dose of pain medication. "Soon," he said. "Another half hour." As we repeated this sequence off and on through the night, dark gradually gave way to light. The pain had dissipated to at least a manageable level, and I assured Bill that I was okay and that he could go to work. I stayed in bed, postponing breakfast, as I continued to drift in and out of sleep.

When she came in for the third time, Maria, the student nurse, asked if I was going to eat breakfast. She was a stickler for details, and we had talked the day before about the importance of eating well-balanced meals. She always noted what I ate and when I ate it. I assured her that I would, and I then explained why I was moving so slowly that morning. I gave her the details of my adventure from the night before. Immediately, she stopped what she was doing and began to shuffle through the papers in her folder.

"I think those are side effects of one of your medications," she commented as she continued to shuffle.

"What?" I asked, dumbfounded by her comment.

"Yes, I think those are side effects of one of your medications," she repeated. "We are supposed to have a working knowledge of all the medications our patients are taking, and I had to look some of yours up because I was unfamiliar with them."

"You're kidding!" I said, beginning to feel angry.

She continued looking through her papers for a few more seconds. "Yes, here it is." She had the information about one of the blood pressure meds I had been put on. She began to read from the paper:

"The severe allergic reactions include rash, itching, difficulty breathing, and tightness in the chest. Other serious side effects include feeling like you might pass out, shortness of breath, fast or pounding heartbeats, numbness or tingly feeling, chest pain or heavy feeling, headache, warmth, redness, urinating more than usual …" She went on, but all of those symptoms were mine. The paper recommended medical attention if those symptoms occurred.

So there I was, in a hospital, having a severe reaction to a medication, surrounded by medical people, not one of whom ever considered that I might be having a severe reaction to a medication! It was only the student nurse, who was so serious about her responsibility for knowing about the medications her patients were taking, who had been alert enough to identify the problem. Amazing! And I had been ready to give in to the idea that I was having an anxiety attack! Now I was angry.

As I write this, I am struck by the fact that I did nothing to follow up on any concerns I had about this medication. Did I ask to speak with the nurse or, better yet, the heart doctor who had prescribed this medication? No. I never said a word. That meant I would continue to receive this medication. What was I thinking? I guess I was being the patient. I was not thinking clearly; I was not in a position to take charge. While I generally was on the lookout for inconsistencies, lack of follow-up, or any other sign that someone was not following through with the established course of treatment, or that there was a problem with the established course of treatment, on this particular occasion I did none of these things. I moved on and ordered my breakfast. Then I rang the call button so I could take a shower.

Nails! or Comic Relief

Maria, the student nurse, answered my call. I was happy to see her. Here was a young woman who was going to do great things; she could be counted on to do her job. There were no shortcuts for her. I could tell by the way she did everything. She took the time she needed to do things right. Perhaps they all started out this way, dedicated to taking care of people, wanting to do their very best. Perhaps it was only after they spent time in the system—the one that made unreasonable demands on them, that required them to use equipment that didn't work half the time—that they began to take shortcuts and miss things that were important.

I had watched them, day after day, night after night. When they came around to give out medications, first they had to scan my hospital ID bracelet. This would enter my information into the computerized system, and then they would scan the medication. The two were forever linked together. I felt a bit like a product in a grocery store, but it was a good system—in theory, anyway. In my estimation, the scanners didn't work at least half the time. Sometimes it was simply a matter of replacing the batteries, but other times it seemed that no matter what they did, the nurses couldn't get the scanners to work. That had to be frustrating. If they couldn't even do a simple, basic task like giving out patient medication without high levels of frustration, what happened when they had to do something more complicated? No wonder they didn't have the energy to think outside the box and consider the possibility that a patient's symptoms were a reaction to a medication.

Of course, this was only what I saw. There is always more when you scratch below the surface, so I'm sure there were elements I wasn't even aware of that contributed to their difficulties. It is also possible that there were elements they were skipping that might have made their job easier. Systems are only as good as the people who work them, I have always said. Even so, systems can be so cumbersome as to become unwieldy. Anything involving a computer has that potential. That, of course, is the perspective of a computer illiterate.

I told Maria that I wanted to get a shower. I was never good at time management, always underestimating how long any given task would take to complete. I could remember when I started college in January, 1970, at the Kittanning branch of the Indiana University of Pennsylvania. As you can imagine, it was a tiny place. There were two girls' dorms, with one building for classes nestled in between. My biology teacher actually took roll call. When he called my name and I didn't answer, one of my friends said, "She's in the shower, she'll be right here." They enjoyed feeding me these tidbits later on. But they were right. It was not uncommon for me to get up at 8:50 a.m. for a 9:00 a.m. class and get there at 9:05 a.m., my hair still wet from my shower. Those were the days!

The process of getting a shower now was a bit more complicated. First Maria had to go out to the nurse's station to alert them that I was getting a shower, so they could turn off the monitors connected to all my wires. If they were busy, it might be some time before they were able to flip that little switch. Then she would come back to my room and remove all the wires, along with their accompanying sticky pads. Since I was using my PowerPort both for all my IV medications, as well as to have blood drawn for lab work, she had to tape a plastic cover over the needle inserted into the port. Once I got in the bathroom, I had to remove my colostomy appliance and clean that area.

After all that, I was ready to step into the shower. The first one I had after being in the hospital for four days was like heaven! I had asked for a shower chair, since I was still feeling rather weak. As I let the water run over my body, I gave myself up to the heat and the steam that it generated. I wanted to sit there all day. At least I wasn't still on the chemo that forced me to take lukewarm showers!

Once I stepped out of the shower, the first thing I did was reapply a new colostomy appliance. Experience had taught me that any lag time could produce disastrous consequences. The next step was the moisturizer. Shortly after I found out I had cancer, my sister-in-law Mary

Ann sent me *Anticancer: A New Way of Life*. This was a wonderful book, written by David Servan-Schreiber, MD, PhD. I found a tremendous amount of helpful information in this book, and it was the starting point of many healthful changes in my lifestyle. Before I was diagnosed with cancer, I had a rather lackadaisical attitude about a lot of things. While it's impossible to know how important each of these elements was, I decided there was no point in taking any chances.

One thing that the book mentioned as a possible contributor to cancer is body products containing estrogen or placental products, or parabens or phthalates. I started buying my bath and body products at The Body Shop, where products are made without phthalates. How important was this in the overall scheme of things? I decided it was worth a little more money to eliminate even the possibility of making it easier for cancer cells to grow. So, after showering with the pink grapefruit shower gel, I used the matching body butter to moisturize. I went through these body butters fairly quickly because the chemo dried out my skin so badly. I didn't even bother to think about how much money I was spending on these products, as compared to the odd brands I used to buy at a discount price at TJ Maxx or Marshalls.

When my actual shower, along with moisturizing and colostomy changes, was completed, I rang for the nurse once more so that she could reattach all the wires to my body. As I sat on the edge of my bed in a clean hospital gown, waiting for the nurse, I rested. Who knew that a shower could be so exhausting? All that relaxation I felt sitting in the shower had been replaced by sweat and shakiness. I stretched my hands out in front of me and was pleasantly surprised to see how long and lovely my nails looked. It had taken about one hour and forty-five minutes for me to complete my shower, and I wasn't quite done. As I admired my nails, I was struck by the humor of the moment and began to laugh, shaking the bed. Regardless of the time factor, and my state of exhaustion, it was all worth it. My nails were great! I couldn't remember a time when I had such nice-looking fingernails. When Maria finally arrived to hook me up, I explained why I was laughing. Strangely, she didn't seem to have the same appreciation for my nails as I did. I guess you had to be there. After the night I had been through, and the two-hour shower, it was the comic relief I needed to put it all behind me.

Chapter Nine

—·—

STARTING OVER—AGAIN

I managed to get through Friday without any problems. Throughout the day, my head pain gradually faded, and I woke up Saturday morning feeling good. I was unaware of the side effects of that blood pressure medication, and Maria had only mentioned the ones that were related to my symptoms from Tuesday and Thursday evening. She hadn't arrived on the scene until Wednesday, and she left at the end of her Friday afternoon shift. I had a meaningful conversation with her, letting her know how impressed I was with the high standards she held herself to. I told her that if she stayed that course, she could only have a brilliant career ahead. I stressed the idea that she should never let being busy stop her from doing everything she needed to do. She seemed embarrassed at the compliments, which, in my opinion, only served to make her an even more valuable asset to the nursing community.

Saturday morning, I was told I could go home. The doctor from the heart clinic expressed that I seemed to be an intelligent person, and he felt confident that I could handle the rigorous schedule of meds I would need to follow upon returning home. While I appreciated the compliment, I wasn't exactly sure what I had done to engender it. He went on to review with me how I should take the pills, some of them depending on my blood pressure reading at the time I was due to take them.

I also had a visit that morning from Dr. Sukumvanich. He was happy to hear I was going home. I asked him about my chemotherapy treatment and if he had an idea of what new chemo he might try. Also, I asked what we were going to do about my platelets. They were continuing to run low—below 100,000, which is the level needed for chemo.

"Well, I'm going to have to do some thinking about that and see what magic I can pull out of my hat." He seemed stressed, and I had the impression that it would indeed have to be magic. This little bit of tenuous reality barely filtered through my positive frame of mind, regardless of the source.

The side effect of the new blood pressure medication that I wasn't aware of, but am now pretty sure was playing out, was "mental or mood changes." It is possible that my euphoria was self-induced, but I believe it was at least contributed to by the drug. I was feeling just a little bit too good. While Bill and I waited for everything to come together for my discharge, I suggested we take a walk down the hall. I felt like I had so much energy that I needed to do something physical. Besides, the day before, when I took the same walk, I had enjoyed the view out the windows that lined the hallway. The street I looked out upon was lined with small trees, each wearing a brilliant yellow for its autumn dress. It was quite lovely, and I imagined I wasn't the only traveler to be cheered by the beautiful fall foliage. With the sun shining brightly and the gentlest of breezes, the leaves shimmered, and I imagined them tinkling like gold coins.

As we headed down the hall, I was disappointed to see that apparently, since my last walk, there had been more than a gentle breeze blowing. Most of the leaves were gone; there were just enough left to show what had been a glorious fall scene. But, at the moment, Bill was more attentive to the scene playing out inside. He looked at me in amazement, saying "Slow down!" He could barely keep up with me; my pace was accelerated in comparison to before my hospital admission. Still slow by Bill's standards, it was much closer to normal. It had been quite a while since I had been able to move that fast, and with such a small amount of pain. Yes, I did it again; I began to feel hopeful. I seemed to have no control over this. It was always too late by the time I realized I had done it. Perhaps this time I had a little help from the medication. We came back to the room, and within a few minutes, the nurse was there to review my discharge instructions.

With all my energy, my request to walk out on my own was honored—no wheelchair ride for me! I did, however, agree to sit on the bench in front of the hospital while Bill went to get the car. As I waited, I opened the envelope to look at my discharge paperwork. As I began to read, I was confused at the information at the top of the first page. The diagnosis was completely unfamiliar, and it took me a few glances to notice that it didn't have my name on it. Hmm!

Making the trip back to the second floor tapped a little more deeply into my energy reserves. When I approached the desk, the person behind it smiled pleasantly up at me and asked what I needed, recognizing me immediately. I explained that I had received the wrong discharge paperwork, and I showed her the name at the top of my packet of papers.

She had a look of nervous surprise on her face. The nurse came over and asked what was going on. As I explained it to her, she smiled and said, "No problem, we'll take care of that." With that comment, she took the papers from my hand, put them through the shredder, and proceeded to get me my discharge papers. They got me the correct packet, and I was on my way.

I knew there were protocols that needed to be followed any time there was a confidentiality violation. Of course, I have no idea what they did after I left, but my impression was that they would pretend the incident never happened. I'm sure that would be much easier. I have absolutely no recollection of the lady's name, and if I did, there would be no reason for me to ever talk about it. Still, it was a confidentiality violation. I only hope they took the time to figure out how it happened and put some steps into place to be sure it didn't happen again.

When I worked at ARC Manor, this would have been a relatively serious error, with relatively serious consequences. With all the hype today about confidentiality, an error like this should not be brushed off lightly. Some of the procedures we have to endure in the name of confidentiality are quite annoying, yet here was a blatant violation, and it appeared it would be swept under the rug. So much for all the new HIPAA laws.

I have recounted several errors made by various hospital personnel while I had my six-day stay there. This is not to assign fault or to be picky. It is to say something like "Everyone makes mistakes." In my case, none of these errors turned out to be serious or life threatening, but they had the potential for that kind of consequence. What this means to me is that on any given day, even when people are doing their best, mistakes happen. They can be little or big, and the consequences can be minor or far reaching. You can never let your guard down. You must always pay attention. Life is in the details, and details can kill you if you don't pay attention to them.

We left the hospital and drove to the end of the street to have lunch at Panera. By then I was more than ready for lunch. I downed my lunch in record time. Bill was still looking at me in amazement. For the past few months, getting in and out of the car had been a painful process for me. I had to break it down into segments. When I got out, I had to stand still for a few seconds before taking any steps. Then, each subsequent movement had to be done slowly, and with deliberation, to minimize the pain. That day, I popped in and out like a normal person. I wasn't aware of this change until Bill pointed it out.

We stopped at Macy's on the way home. As we started out, I felt like I could shop all day. However, in spite of my high energy level, I began to feel shaky and tired within thirty minutes. We cut the trip short and headed for home.

Bill had prepared one of my favorite comfort foods: a stuffed chicken with mashed potatoes, gravy, and corn. He had it all ready to put in the oven when we got home. That evening, as I sat in my chair, relaxing, I enjoyed the smell of the chicken in the oven, letting it waft over me. When it was finally ready, Bill fixed my plate and brought it over. As usual, he had way too much food on it. I would eat as much as I could, and the rest could always be saved for tomorrow. I sat and took my time, relishing every bite.

Although I was excited to be home, I did have some concern about my blood pressure. My medication schedule for the high blood pressure was rather complex. Some of the doses were dependent on blood pressure readings, which were to be taken at scheduled times. The medication schedule seemed to cover multiple possibilities, and I hoped nothing would happen that fell outside these parameters. Within the next few weeks, I had what I considered to be two crises with my blood pressure. I had to call in the evening to get advice on what to do when I had elevated readings. Each time, I was directed on what to do, and I got through with minimal disruption to the treatment plan. In addition, on two occasions, I found an undissolved pill in my stool when cleaning the beast. Both happened to be the same type of pill that had caused the symptoms while I was still hospitalized. These pills were very distinctive, so there was no mistaking them.

Dr. Piccone instructed me to discontinue that pill, and I was instead prescribed one-half the dose. When I talked with Dr. Piccone about the side effects, she wanted me to see if I could tolerate them, saying they sometimes lessened with time. She thought this pill was important for me to take at this point in my treatment. The symptoms did decrease, but they never went away entirely.

On Monday, I was on the phone first thing in the morning, scheduling my follow-up appointments. There were three: one with the cardiologist, Dr. Piccone, at Magee Heart Center; one with my PCP, and one with Dr. Sukumvanich.

I saw Dr. Sukumvanich, accompanied by Nora, on Wednesday, October 19, the fifth day after my discharge from the hospital. Everyone seemed to be sharing my good mood. Everyone was glad I had come through my hypertensive crisis so well. I asked the doctor if he remembered me talking with him in a previous appointment about my severe body pain. He didn't seem to recall that.

"Well, I don't know why, but for some reason, I feel remarkably better. It has only been two weeks off the chemo, so it doesn't seem like that would make that much difference, but the fact is that I do feel a lot better."

"See, I told you that the women were saying this chemo was causing severe body pain!" Nora said to the doctor. She jumped right on that one!

Dr. Sukumvanich just shook his head. I wasn't sure what that meant, but clearly this was an unresolved issue. Obviously, there were differing perspectives on the side effects of this chemo. I didn't really care about that. I was just glad to be feeling that much better. And I was anxious to hear what the plan of attack was. I was ready to move on.

"I think we should try another chemo. I am concerned about the platelets, but we'll try it, and see how it goes."

"Okay." There was not much to discuss. I just wanted to get started.

I had my follow-up appointment with my PCP on Tuesday, October 25. When she walked into the exam room, her whole manner was different from the way it had been on previous visits. She appeared to be red in the face, and it got redder as the visit went on. Her comments were curt; she seemed clearly angry or upset about something. I began to ask her about some things I had discussed with my physical therapist, related to the possibility that I might have rheumatoid arthritis. At this, she flipped her hands in the air, shook her head, and spoke in a very loud voice. "You don't have rheumatoid arthritis. There's no way you are having an RA flare-up. The treatment for rheumatoid arthritis is chemotherapy, which you are on, so there is no way you could be having an RA flare-up."

"Oh," I said. "I didn't know that. So rheumatoid arthritis is treated with chemotherapy?" I was searching my mind for the commercials I had seen about new drugs used to treat RA. I couldn't recall ever hearing anything about chemotherapy. But maybe they just hadn't used that word.

"Yes, well, it's …" I can't really say what her reply was, but it seemed that she was being more specific in her answer. Maybe it was sort of like chemo, or some form of it—something like that. She clearly was not open to a discussion of the issue. I was surprised. I had only been seeing her for about one and one-half years. My son had recommended her, and I liked her from the beginning. She seemed very open, and like she was willing to explain things to her patients.

"Okay. So I guess we're not going to talk about this anymore, then. I guess we're done with that."

While I was speaking, she was vehemently nodding.

"Okay. Well, then, I was interested in the results of my blood work." At my last visit, when I was having the severe body pain, I asked if there were any vitamin or mineral deficiencies that could produce those symptoms. She said there were a few, and that they could check for them. I had never been told the results, though. That generally can be taken to mean there are no significant findings, but I didn't want to make any assumptions. While I was feeling much better, I still had a good deal of pain in my feet and my knee. I knew that my knee was not in good shape to start with, but I was looking for relief anywhere I could find it.

The doctor pulled out the paperwork with my lab results and firmly laid them on the table in front of me. She spoke with such vehemence that I was afraid to say anything. All the labs that checked the vitamin and mineral levels were within normal limits. That was all I was interested in, but she went over every single value, even those that were clearly being impacted by my chemotherapy treatments, such as white and red blood cells, and platelets. When she finished, she handed me not only my copy but also her own, as well as the discharge paperwork from the hospital that had been sent to her directly. I could feel my face burning; it was probably as red as hers was, but for different reasons. I was embarrassed for her but a little frightened for myself.

Cautiously, I said, "Well, the plan is that once my blood pressure is under control, I will be referred back to you. Is that okay?"

"Yes, that will be fine. Good luck." She turned and left the office. The appointment was clearly over. I got up and left the office, in a state of shock. I was astounded by what had just taken place. I was certain I had done something to upset her. As I drove home, I tried to understand what had happened. She was already upset—or whatever she was—when she came into the exam room. So whatever I did, I must have already done it before I got there. I couldn't think of what it was. I am not generally taken off guard by things like that; I normally know when I've crossed over a line, usually just by being a blundering idiot. I was totally perplexed by this situation. I wished that she could have just come out and told me what was bothering her. But, I guess that skill is not generally included in a doctor's repertoire.

My first reaction was that I never wanted to see her again. That would mean I would have to find a new PCP. I didn't like that idea; it seemed like a lot of work I really didn't have the energy for at that time in my life. Then I decided that when I needed to see her, I would schedule one more appointment and see if we could resolve what had happened that day. I wanted to give her the benefit of the doubt. If she tried to act like she didn't know what I was talking about, then I would have to find another PCP. If she were willing to explain herself,

I would be very interested in hearing what she had to say. If I had been out of line, I would accept that. I wanted to learn. I knew I wasn't always diplomatic about things; tact was not one of my strong points. Marc, my son, had once told me I was the bluntest person he knew. He didn't mean it as a compliment at the time. But I felt that the doctor's behavior was beyond unprofessional. I just hoped that I wouldn't need to see her for a long time.

I saw Dr. Piccone on October 26. I had kept a log of my blood pressure readings, thinking this was the best way for her to get a handle on what was happening. She seemed to appreciate this. She was pleased with the direction things were going in, and she told me I looked much better than I had when she last saw me in the hospital. She said my color was much better. We reviewed my medications, and she made some changes. The medication that caused the unwanted side effects was cut out completely, which didn't disappoint me at all! She adjusted some of the other medications and reviewed the instructions with me. She was very thorough and wanted to make things as easy as possible for me.

I was pleased to be taking less medication. I was also pleased that I had lucked into such a good doctor. She was pleasant, exuded a positive energy, and was easy to talk to. I could tell she was very busy, but she never let that show through in a rushed attitude. Although she was very late for my appointment, I didn't mind. I could hear her through the door, working with someone else, and her manner was one that stated very clearly, "I will take the time I need for each patient." What a pleasant change from the encounter I'd had the day before with my PC. And for my wait, I was given a certificate for free parking that day. What meant more than the free parking was the acknowledgment that they were late and that the lateness inconvenienced me. The parking certificate was a token of apology. This is not common practice, and it speaks to the little things that make one medical practice stand above the rest.

Eking, but with Less to Eke With

On October 27 I had my first and only treatment with this fourth different chemo regimen. Blood tests showed that my platelets had dropped yet again, and there was a rise in my creatinine level. These issues moved it immediately into the "do not use" category. I was beginning to get a clearer understanding of what is meant by "unable to tolerate side effects." This didn't just mean "she isn't tough enough to handle this"; it meant that medically, my body wouldn't stand up to the side effects. Here was one more thing over which I had no control. I felt myself slip down another notch on the spiral. There was nothing left of that euphoria I'd had when I left the hospital. I was back in the real world. The hard hammer of reality had struck again.

My next appointment with the oncologist was short and sweet. I was to move on to regimen number five, with one of the two chemos I had received in the first six months. This was a once-a-week treatment. He reiterated the concept that this was considered good control of a very bad disease. It would be a much lower dose than I had gotten in that first six months. Once again, he told me that the side effects were minimal and that some women didn't even feel as though they were on chemo.

"You say that every time. I don't believe you anymore," I said, half-jokingly.

The appointment ended with a hearty laugh from him. I was glad he had responded thusly to my attempt to inject some humor into an otherwise disheartening situation. My CA-125 was 50. I had enjoyed one brief, fleeting moment sitting at the magic number of 35, but I had never gotten below it. The possibility that I would ever be in single digits became more remote with each passing day. I was becoming increasingly aware that life as I knew it was over; that I would never be going back to my old life. I tried to subdue the panic I felt rising inside me.

It seemed strange to me, but I had less enthusiasm that year as the holiday season approached. Perhaps Christmas was more exciting during my first year of cancer because at the beginning of that year I was pretty sure I would not make it until Christmas. So when I got through that first six months of chemo, had a successful surgery, and made it to Christmas still with much hope that I was going to beat my disease, I had reason to be optimistic. But as December again approached, I knew I was settling into my new life. I couldn't even foresee that the yo-yo would ever make it to the top of the string again.

When you're little and you try to use a yo-yo for the first time, it's a slow process. As I recall it, there is a lot of jerking and a lot of bumpy rides, and just getting the yo-yo to travel the full length of the string is quite a task. Getting it to go down and then come all the way to the top and back down seems to take forever to master. Here I was, at the ripe old age of almost sixty, and I felt as though I was just learning to use a yo-yo. My life had become one unsuccessful, jerking ride, and it didn't appear that I was in for any smooth travels again.

Looking ahead, all I could see was one day after another of unfulfilled life, sitting around, waiting for something to happen, but with little hope that anything of value would come my way. Yet all I could do was plod along, dragging myself from one chemotherapy session to another. I settled into the cycle, and watched as my life ebbed away. My hair fell out, and once again, I donned the wig.

I did less shopping for gifts than I had the year before. I told Bill he was going to have to help me shop. In the past, because I loved to shop and Bill didn't, it hadn't been a problem for me to do all the Christmas shopping. Even with our newfound enjoyment of hitting the sales at Macy's, Christmas shopping was a whole different level. Thinking about what to buy other people required a different strategy than just shopping for ourselves and each other.

But Bill rose to the occasion. We set out on a Saturday morning, and within a half a day, we had most of the gifts bought. This was a record of some sort, for sure. Of course, I would still be stopping on my way home from my appointments to buy more little things for the kids, and for Bill. The kids helped out by sending me e-mails of things they had seen online. It was a banner year for mail-order gifts—or rather, online ordering. I couldn't go wrong. Point and click. They had already selected sizes and colors. Patrick e-mailed me Carrie's wish list. This Santa would fulfill all her wishes at Maurices.

I struggled through the holidays, trying to maintain a cheerful facade for the sake of my family. I wanted them to have a good holiday. If this was to be my last, I wanted them to have a pleasant memory of it. Since my birthday falls on the day before Christmas, we always have the same thing for dinner: ham, scalloped potatoes, and green beans. This is one of my favorite meals, and it just seemed to go with the holidays. I had taken to ordering my own birthday cake. My husband had tried for years to satisfy me by baking my cake himself or ordering fancy ice-cream cakes. To his dismay, what I enjoyed most was a bakery cake, decorated with thick, sugary buttercream icing. This was the opposite of what he liked, but I maintained that since it was my birthday, I should have the cake I wanted. I had little perception of taste at that point, but I ate the same meal, trying to enjoy it from memory, since in reality I got very little flavor when I ate it. Somehow, I still enjoyed the cake. At least the busyness of the holidays helped to fill in the emptiness. Not that I personally was busy; I am referring just to the spirit of the season. I tried to absorb this feeling to make my empty days seem more meaningful. I had finished up my second online writing class at the beginning of December, so I didn't even have that to make my time feel more valuable. I had told my husband that I wanted another online writing class as my big Christmas gift, but that wouldn't start until February—a long way off. At least I would have some semblance of purpose through the holidays; everyone knows that just getting through the holidays is a feat all by itself. Many complain about the busyness. I always loved it. Not being busy this time of year meant you had nobody to shop for, no decorating to do, no wonderful holiday cooking/baking to do, no parties to go to; it was just like any other time of the year. This would have been a sad life, indeed, in my book.

Although I had very little energy for these things this year, I did manage to make a couple different kinds of cookies. While Bill did the "heavy" decorating, I did the lightweight stuff.

When the boys were little, I used to make up stories to tell them at bedtime. One of their favorites was a collection of stories about four snowflakes named Inky, Winky, Pinky, and Splat. They had many adventures in which they barely survived the perils that surely befall the typical snowflake. In each adventure, they went through the entire process of falling from the sky, dealing with what life threw their way, and then melting and heading back up to the sky, only to return once again another night, with a whole new set of adventures. I can still remember Marc's delightful laughter as the scenes played out in his mind. He didn't need a movie or television. I guess I was always fascinated by snowflakes and have always loved wintertime. While the stories were made up for Marc's entertainment, they were also a way for me to indulge myself in an area I loved.

Wintertime was a great time to see the bare bones of mother earth, to admire her amazing structure. Christmastime was the heart of the winter, and my heart would always overflow with the simple joys that time of year brought. Regardless of personal beliefs about Jesus and his birth, I could never imagine how a person could not get swept up in these joys. All my decorations seemed to burst with Christmas joy as soon as they were removed from their storage boxes.

I have an extensive collection of snowmen of all shapes and sizes. The bulk of them sit on the mantle above the fireplace. A garland with wooden decorations hangs across the edge of the mantle. A few years ago, I found snowman lights that I immediately fell in love with. The bodies of the snowmen are made of little white wire spheres, they have tiny black hats, and sparkly metal snowflakes are glued to their sides. The same place where I bought most of my flowers and shrubs always had a wonderful selection of Christmas decorations when the gardening season was over. Being a bargain hunter, I generally waited for the post-holiday sales. I knew the snowman lights would never last that long, so I bit the bullet and paid full price for them.

Arranging the snowmen on the mantel was always one of my favorite parts of holiday decorating. That Christmas, however, I was unable to place most of the snowmen; it involved too much stretching and overhead reaching. These activities seemed to drain my energy within a very short time. So I directed Bill while he strategically placed each of my little friends. Some of the joy was lost, but I still got a rush of pleasure each time I came down the hall in the morning and saw them all sitting there. A few years ago, we had a very wet year, and since we had them stored under the basement stairs, the moisture ruined all but four of my snowmen. I was deeply saddened by this, but I moved through the mourning phase quickly when I realized I'd have to shop and replace them all. Nothing like a good excuse to buy more snowmen! One of the casualties was my favorite, simply named "The Snowman." When he had been mass produced several years earlier, he came in several sizes and even had a book and video of his personal life story. Imagine my surprise and delight when my friend Sandy had found him on eBay and given him to me for my birthday! I had imagined him gone for good, and with this replacement, he became all the more dear to me.

As the holiday season segued into the new year, I desperately tried to find some purpose for my life. About fourteen years ago, I had developed an idea for a book. I was fascinated with it, but I had never done anything to take action on it. Now, I was preoccupied with my life with cancer. Perhaps my first book would have to be about this experience. Slowly, the idea began to grow in my mind.

A WIN—STATISTICALLY SPEAKING

I began to have some strange abdominal pains—strange only because I was unfamiliar with them. It seemed that I had noticed them since I had come home from the hospital, but they were vague. Initially, I thought I was just getting readjusted to eating regularly again. But as time went on, the pains remained, and progressed. I mentioned them when I had my appointment, and I was sent for a scan. It showed no evidence of recurrent or metastatic ovarian cancer. This was welcome news, but it didn't provide an answer to the abdominal pain I was experiencing. We went to my sister Joan's house for Thanksgiving, and I remember that the pain was particularly intense that day. It seemed worse when I moved or got up to walk. By the time we returned home, I had trouble making my way up the sidewalk and into the house.

After that day, the pain seemed to come in cycles, about twice a week, and it would last for around one to three days. It would be safe to say it was there most of the time. At different times during the pain cycle, I noticed a large bulge right above the site of my stoma. Always a stickler for details, I tried to pin down when the bulge was there in relation the pain cycle. I had trouble understanding this. When I went for my appointments, I was told by whichever PA I saw that the bulge was stool. This didn't seem to fit with the timeframe of when I had the bulge.

In my appointment on December 27, 2011, I was very weepy. When Jackie asked me how I was feeling, I told her. I detailed the side effects of the chemo that I was experiencing. I told her I felt crappy all the time. The peripheral neuropathy was getting worse, I had the constant sore in my nose that got worse a few days after I had chemo, I felt weak and achy all the time, and, of course, I was losing my hair. Although I had no sores in my mouth, my gums were sore constantly. I continued to have the dry eyes that required drops multiple times a day. I mentioned once again that the abdominal pain was still there. I asked if that was just something that I was going to have to live with. With her back to me, she nodded, and she asked if I'd ever had irritable bowel syndrome. I told her I hadn't. I was told that if I was constipated I could take Colace or Miralax. My CA-125 was now 102. I had asked some question she didn't know the answer to, so she said she would bring Dr. Sukumvanich in.

When he came in, accompanied by Jackie and Melissa, he asked me if I was upset. I thought this was so funny that it made me laugh out loud.

"I'm sorry if I asked a stupid question," he replied, very seriously. Apparently my affect was inappropriate to the situation.

"Well, yes, I guess I am upset. I guess with each new phase I go through, I feel a little bit lower, and it takes me a while to adjust to the new lower level. Eventually I get there, but it takes a while sometimes. Then, just when I think I'm getting used to things, I drop a little lower again."

In the background, I could hear Jackie saying out loud, but to herself, "It's stress." I imagined that she and Melissa had gone out and relayed to Dr. Sukumvanich my mood and my weepiness. This was what had prompted him to come in and talk with me. He must have commented that I was stressed; perhaps this was an explanation for my pain, my slightly elevated blood pressure, or my mood. While my BP was by then generally in a satisfactory range, it was usually elevated when I had my appointments. The more they commented on it, the longer it took to come down. For sure, my blood pressure elevation in the exam room was due to stress. I tried to figure out what was going through their minds.

"We've talked about this before," he said. I imagined it must be very frustrating for him. "When you have a disease like this, and you can get some level of control over it, it is considered a win. A number in the low one hundreds is not really bad. You're really not that bad off. You're not coming in here in a wheelchair. I'm concerned about your mental state. There is a psychologist, Dr. Susan Stollings, who works with oncology patients. She's very good at what she does, she's a really nice person, and she is very easy to talk to. Maybe it would be helpful for you to talk to her; maybe she can help you deal with what you're feeling."

"I am familiar with how therapy works; I did therapy with people for twenty years." Perhaps I was a little insulted to be told that I needed therapy.

"Oh, good! So you know all about it, then. Do you want to do it?"

"No, I really don't," I replied, feeling very frustrated myself.

Now it was his turn to laugh out loud. I guess he thought he had done such a good job of explaining therapy to me that he had me sold. Clearly, he had not been expecting the answer I gave him.

I was disturbed by this appointment. I wasn't sure exactly why at first, but I went upstairs and had my chemo. It was a rough day, trying to act cheerful with the nurses in the cancer center. That evening, I sent around an e-mail update to my family and friends. When I got a response back from Mary, my tai chi instructor, I understood immediately why I had been upset after my appointment that morning. In her e-mail, Mary commented that she was sorry to hear that I hadn't gotten better news. She stated that a "statistical win" might be nice for the oncology team, but that it would have little meaning for me; that there is a huge difference between being a statistic and feeling good or being happy.

As soon as I read her words, I said out loud, but to myself, "That's it!" She had put words to what I was having so much trouble verbalizing. I knew that Dr. Sukumvanich was telling me that I was in pretty good shape so far and that my reaction to my situation was out of proportion. I think the unspoken message was that it was way too early for me to be getting this upset, that things were still going to be much worse.

The idea that having a number in the low one hundreds was considered a win was clearly designated by someone who did not have cancer. Fitting in that statistical category left no room for consideration of my quality of life at the time. Yes, I could take care of myself; I could bathe and dress myself, feed myself, and still drive myself to appointments. What more did I want? Call me greedy. I wanted a lot more.

It made me think about people who have serious illnesses, and what quality of life they have; how much I have taken for granted all these years. My friend Lynn, whom I have known since college days, had polio when she was nineteen months old. While this surely changed the course of her life, I have always considered her a strong, independent woman. She graduated from college and worked as a speech therapist for thirty-five years. She is married, has a husband she loves, three beautiful and talented daughters, and a grandson whom she is clearly smitten with. I almost don't even notice, when I am with her, that one of her legs is shorter and smaller than the other. She walks with built-up shoes and uses a cane, sometimes two canes. How could I not notice these things? She has lived her entire life this way, but it has never stopped her from making good things happen. Is she a statistical win?

Maybe I'm just being a big baby. Maybe I should just get over it, and be happy with the life I have. Maybe what I have is more than what a lot of people have. For sure, that is true; there are many people who are worse off than I am. That is always true; no matter how bad you think your life is, there is always someone worse off. Somehow, this has never done anything for me. This knowledge has never made me feel better. And it doesn't now. Am I selfish? Do I lack compassion? Is there something wrong with me? I don't know, but I don't feel better when I think of people who are worse off than I am. I want to feel better than I do, plain and simple. Being a statistical win doesn't do anything for me either. Mary is right; I want more.

MY MENTAL STATE

In spite of the fact that I definitely did not want to see a psychologist, I left my appointment on December 27 with her card and a pamphlet about her services. Things were left at "I'll think about it." While I was still talking with Dr. Sukumvanich, Jackie had left the office to get these materials for me. When she came back in and handed them to me, she said, "You can think about it and decide for yourself. I don't think we're dealing with a psychiatric issue here."

Thank you very much! A psychiatric issue! Wow! I had no idea I was coming across that badly. And thank you for letting me decide for myself. I tried to keep myself calm. I tried to think about things from their perspective. I had trouble understanding what they were looking for. Clearly I was not acting the way I should be acting.

After I had my chemo, I had to stop back at the office to ask Melissa a question. While I was there, I decided to see if I could get the information I was looking for.

"Can I ask you a question?" She nodded, so I went on. "What did I do or say when I was with you and Jackie today that made you so concerned that you felt you needed to talk to Dr. Sukumvanich?"

She bent her head at an angle, looking away from me for a few seconds, and then looked back. "Well, we just want you to be happy."

"Ah, I see," I replied, a glint of understanding beginning to sparkle in my dense brain. So this was the problem. This was why the doctor said he was concerned about my mental state. I wasn't acting happy at my appointments. "I just wish I could find a way to help you understand how I feel. In my retirement, I sold baked goods at the farmers market. I was telling someone how I can't do any of the things I used to do, and they said 'Can you bake a pie?' I told them that I could, and they said, 'There you go.' Baking a pie for me has nothing to do with selling baked goods."

"I think I understand how you feel," said Melissa. "I used to do massages, and I had a spinal injury. The doctor told me I better find a new line of work."

"Yes! Now if he had said to you, 'you can't do massages for a living anymore, but you could give your husband a massage at home every once in a while,' what would that do for you? Would you feel contented with that?"

"No," she replied thoughtfully. "That is not the same."

I felt a rush of satisfaction; finally someone was beginning to understand what I was feeling. I was so happy that I wanted to give her a big hug. She went on to say that having cancer is tough, and that she thought all cancer patients should be given antidepressants when they get their diagnosis.

"No," I countered. "You'd have to strap me down and inject it into me. That is the only way you could ever get an antidepressant into me. I want to experience my feelings and decide what to do with them." Still, I was very appreciative that she had taken the time to talk with me. At least I was beginning to understand why this medical team thought I was depressed.

When I came to my appointments, they asked me how I was doing. When I told them, and was upset about it, I was perceived as depressed. Nobody ever asked me if I sat around at home crying all the time, or whether I was constantly focused on feeling bad. The answer would be a resounding "No!" Of course, I have my moments. Yes, sometimes I do think about how bad I feel and how useless I feel. But not all the time. I have made rules for myself. I never allow myself to cancel something I have planned, simply because I don't feel like it or I'm feeling down. Unless I am physically unable, I do it. I am almost always glad I do. Since there are few things I can still do, anything that I can do, I do. It still isn't enough to fill my days; that's one of the reasons I push myself.

After talking with Melissa, I had hope that it was possible for them to see things from my perspective.

In spite of how much I didn't want to see the psychologist, I felt that I should. I understood myself, and my family and friends understood me. I wanted Dr. Sukumvanich and his team to understand me too. So, the next day, I called the psychologist, Dr. Susan Stollings, and scheduled an appointment. Completely unrelated, a few days later, I received an e-mail from the National Ovarian Cancer Coalition, and they offered a website where I could see videos of most of the lectures from their program calendar for 2011. Dr. Stollings was one of the lecturers; she had given a talk on dealing with the uncertainties of having cancer. I watched the video, thinking it would give me a sense of how she worked.

I liked her. She struck me as a little nervous, which told me she was not a woman of pretense. This was very important to me. She came across as down-to-earth, not full of herself. This was a good start. Her job, then, was to listen to me and provide me with feedback, to reflect back to me what she saw, and, where necessary, to help me see things in new ways or to teach me. When I met her for the first time, I found out that I was not wrong about her; she was indeed a down-to-earth person, yet she was very knowledgeable and professional. I saw her once a week for the first three months, and then we gradually cut back to monthly meetings, which is what we continue to do. She has helped me with many things. As she listened to me cry and talk, she never judged me, corrected me, or told me what I should be feeling or thinking. She would plug in new ideas where they fit, and offer suggestions, or ask me questions about what I was saying.

We covered a wide range of topics. We discussed better sleeping techniques and mindfulness. I made a list of things that were important and pleasurable to me, and what kind of things I could still do. In addition, we discussed dying a good death, and this book. I think I was already putting into action many of the ideas around dying a good death. My ideas about this book were in the very early stages when I first started to meet with her. As things progressed, I would give her copies of what I had written. Dr. Stollings would read my work and give me feedback. Although I had already been pondering writing this book as a result of talking with her, I made the actual decision to move forward, and the idea became a serious project. I realized that deciding to write the book was, in a strange way for me, giving up. It meant admitting that I was only capable of doing mental tasks and typing. This seemed to be a failure to me; I was admitting once and for all that I could no longer bake or garden. I realized it was irrational to view this as a failure, and just verbalizing this out loud was freeing. This freedom came at a hefty price, but the step had to be taken.

Since the idea expressed by my medical team that I was, or seemed, depressed bothered me so much I asked Dr. Stollings what my diagnosis was. She was surprised and expressed that most people didn't ask this question. She informed me that my diagnosis was adjustment disorder with depressed mood. This meant that I was having trouble adjusting to having a mostly fatal disease and that I was depressed about it at times. I definitely agreed that I was having trouble adjusting to having cancer, and for sure I had moments of depression. I never believed I was clinically depressed. So I saw this diagnosis as a middle ground.

After reading a few chapters of my book, Dr. Stollings stated that she had gained a better understanding of me and that she did not see me as depressed. I was happy to hear this. Life is in the details, I have always said. Don't make your judgment until you have all the facts. Anything new that impacts your life in a big way requires some level of adjustment, and the bigger the change, the larger the impact and the more time it takes. I think everyone finds his or her own way, and there is no set amount of time this adjustment process takes, or should take. However, if the disruption to your life lingers long enough that it interferes with you being able to live your life, then maybe you need some help, professional or otherwise.

Finding out I had cancer caused a major disruption to my life. My biggest struggle has been my desire to continue to live life to the fullest while being severely limited in what I can actually do. Some of what I do is in tiny doses, in comparison to before, but it is what I can do. In the movie *Fragments*, Dakota Fanning plays a surviving victim of a random shooting in a coffee shop. The movie is about how she and the other survivors pull the fragments of their lives back together afterward. The last scene in the movie portrays her riding in the backseat of a car, reflecting on the process she has just been through: "In the ordinary world, we trust in where things belong. Everything has a place, and believing in that makes us innocent. And through the days under the same sky, we hope, dream, and love. We find and lose our way. Endings are beginnings, and moments, like pieces, fit together again."

When I found out I had stage IV ovarian cancer, I lost my way. I have spent every moment since February 25, 2010, trying to find my way again. That way has been lost and found over and over, and I have yet to find a way to put all the pieces back together again. Somehow, they never quite seem to fit. It helped when I realized I needed to stop trying to fit them back together the way they used to be. But the new frame still eludes me. Will I have time to build a new one? Maybe. But I must go on regardless, fitting pieces as I go.

I even changed a flat tire on the highway a few months ago. I had no choice; I didn't have my phone with me, and nobody stopped to help me. I didn't think I could do it, but with a lot of extra time, I got 'er done! It took me about an hour, and I had to stop and rest every five minutes or so. It was one of those ninety-five-degree days that we had so many of during the summer of 2012. Since my AC wasn't working in my car, I opened all the windows and doors so that when I sat to rest, it was as cool as I could make it—which is to say it was still pretty darn hot! But it was the best I could do. I wouldn't want to do this every day, but it was nice to know I could pull though in a pinch. The sore muscles lasted for several days. All that extra sun on my arms, in combination with driving with the windows down because of a broken air conditioner, led to a rash that lasted for over two months before it gradually began to fade. Just another small consequence of chemotherapy.

I think I do understand why my medical team sees me as sad and depressed. I am not a good pretender. In my appointments, when they ask me questions about how I am doing, I answer them truthfully and with feeling. For me, that means I cry. I guess this is the universal sign of depression. For the first year after I found out I had cancer, whether it was the medical assistant taking my vitals, the PA who saw me at my appointment, or the visiting nurses after my first big surgery, at the first sign of tears, they would immediately ask if I was taking something for depression. Then, when I said no, I was offered something. I always said no to that question. Renetta, the visiting nurse who was a wound care specialist, confirmed this protocol for me. Those drugs may be helpful to some people, but I want to find my own way. I want to experience my feelings, sort them out, and decide what to do with them. My belief is that if I blunt them with pills, I won't know the full scope of what I am feeling.

I think I have always been this way. I was having lunch with a group of women, one of whose mother had died a couple years earlier. She was talking about how she was just beginning to be able to watch sad movies again. I am the opposite. When I am going through something like that, I want to go into it further. It helps me to identify my feelings, and then I can find my way back to a more rational place. Then I feel better. Avoiding anything that stirs up the feelings doesn't work for me.

In our local daily newspaper, The Leader Times, is a puzzle called Celebrity Cypher Cryptogram. I do this puzzle every day; sometimes I even figure it out on my own. The quote one day expressed how I feel exactly. "Crawl into your wounds to discover where your fears are. Once the bleeding starts, the cleansing can begin." This quote was attributed to Tori Amos, who apparently writes songs. She expressed my sentiments beautifully. I think maybe we get too uncomfortable when we see someone doing this. We want to take the pain away quickly, perhaps more to soothe ourselves than the person in pain. Maybe that is what my oncology team is trying to do; they want to take my pain away, especially since they know they can't really fix me. While this is certainly a laudable goal, it is not what I want. I am sorry if my way causes them discomfort or pain, but I must go through the process that works best for me.

These medical people are doing an amazing thing. Not too many years ago, I would have been dead shortly after I found out I had cancer. I know how lucky I am to be alive today. While I may not be happy with the quality of my life, I am still glad I am alive, at least so far. And I know I have them to thank for that. I will be forever grateful. For them, I can imagine the only thing better than keeping someone alive is to see them happy about it. I guess I have deprived them of that. This is what they have missed in treating me. But I can't give them what is not there. They will have to struggle along with me. I just don't fit in the cancer patient box. I felt that seeing Dr. Stollings was a reasonable compromise. While they may not see tremendous changes in me as a result of my therapy, there are changes indeed. You just have to think outside the box sometimes.

WHAT'S LIFE GOT TO DO WITH IT?

OR

THE FUNDAMENTAL DIFFERENCE BETWEEN CANCER AND LIFE

I have already said that since I found out I have cancer, I have been in a world different from the one most people are in. The constant recommendation to "stay positive" is offensive to me, coming from people who generally have no idea what they are asking me to be positive about. Cancer and life are at odds with each other. As I watch myself slide further and further away from life, I try to still the panic that begins to rise within me. Today, two and one half years after I found out I had stage IV ovarian cancer, I am no more settled about leaving this life than I was on that fateful day. I can't bear the thought that I might never see a grandchild from my son Patrick and his wife Carrie. I can't bear the thought that I won't get to teach Molly some of the little wonders of life. I want to die when I think about not seeing Marc and Nikki, and Pat and Carrie, creating wonderful families. I hate that I will not enjoy the company of Nikki and Carrie at our family get-togethers. I love seeing Nikki with Molly. She is a wonderful mother. (No more about Molly until chapter 12!) I love talking with Carrie about her work. I wish I could have had her for a teacher when I was in fifth grade.

I can't even think about not spending my golden years with Bill … all the things we were going to do in our leisure time. We still have so many national parks to see. I used to picture us working outside together; Bill in the vegetable garden, me in the flowers. This year I asked Bill if he wanted to do a vegetable garden. He immediately said yes. But he never really got to it. As he was doing things in my flower gardens, I kept telling him I wanted him to do his vegetable garden first. We decided I would hire someone to do some of the maintenance in my biggest flower garden. Still, the vegetable garden lay empty—or still covered with weeds from last fall and early spring. Bill did get about half of it weeded, and he dug up the soil by hand; our garden tractor would no longer work with the tiller that attached to it. I kept insisting he go and buy his plants before they were all picked over. I even bought a couple for him myself. He said he wanted to wait until the garden was all ready before he bought plants. That time never seemed to come. He finally bought a handful of plants, but I could tell his heart wasn't in it.

When I look out the window over the sink and I see the sad state of the garden, it makes me think of myself. My life is in a sad state too. I feel about as healthy as that garden looks. I can't even see any of the vegetables; the weeds have far outgrown them. The weeds are like my cancer; they have taken over and grown far beyond the life that was once there. It takes some looking to see that life. While people still tell me how great I look when I go out, I know that it has nothing to do with the life that is left inside me. I think what they are really saying is "You look great ... for someone who is dying of cancer!" I suppose there is a stereotypic image of what someone with cancer is supposed to look like. I should look pale, maybe emaciated, and sickly. Nope! Not me! I haven't lost any weight. When I wear my wig, I don't even have the telltale baldness to clue them in.

In the beginning, someone said to me, "Only the people who really don't want to live die of cancer. You'll be all right." I recall at the time thinking, *Wow! That's a pretty hefty prediction to live up to. I guess that means that if I die, people will think that I didn't really want to live.* At that very second, I was already afraid. What if I couldn't pull it off? I mean, I have had plenty of thoughts about dying; does that mean maybe I really want to die? I can't seem to control them. Am I supposed to be able to immediately turn them off as soon as they come into my mind? Maybe if I took that medication for depression, I wouldn't have those thoughts. Maybe the pills would turn them off for me. I still can't go there. It's a risk I'll have to take.

As the date for the 2012 NOCC run/walk approaches, I see the 2012 spokesperson on television with increasing frequency. She is a very attractive twenty-six-year-old woman who had stage IV ovarian cancer at age nineteen. She tells us she has been cancer-free for five years. Wow! That is impressive and wonderful. I am so happy for her. She was in college when she found out! That just isn't right. She should have her life. And, so far, she does. I hope she goes on and on. There is nothing pretentious about her. She still seems like a girl to me. I am so jealous of her—not of her personally, but of the fact that she got through this and it doesn't look like I will.

When I read the inspirational books about cancer, I hear from people who have beaten the odds. Frequently, they tell us how to do it;

they know the right things to do. After all, it's what they did, and here they are. People are quick to want to take the credit when things go well. It must be that Reiki, that natural chi movement, those mushroom capsules containing the dried powder of that rare mushroom from some tiny corner of the earth that nobody ever heard of. It must have been that four tablespoons of canned pureed asparagus eaten daily. It must be the better diet, the elimination of processed foods, the more expensive diet of only organic foods. Yes, they have the answers.

Somehow those things didn't do the trick for me. I wonder what I did wrong. I know I am part of the larger group of cancer patients who don't live very long; I wonder if they feel like I do. So I plod along, trying to feel and act happy to still be here. Never mind the fact that I can't really do anything anymore, that I struggle each day to do things that actually seem worthwhile, to make myself believe my life has some meaning. Of course, I go out, have lunch, run to the store, and pick up my meds, and all these things momentarily make me feel as though I am a part of the world around me. This makes me feel better, as well as the people around me. But, in the end, life as I know it is over. In the end, I wait—and watch—for those little kernels of hope. And life goes on around me.

Acceptance-Winning, Acceptance-Losing

As time went on, I did realize that life as I knew it was over. It was a bitter pill to swallow. The thing that was so odd was that I felt as though by accepting this, I was giving up. As long as I could think that I was going to get better, I had hope. Now, after realizing those chances were slim to none, that thin thread of hope I had been clinging to was gone. Okay, so maybe it wasn't completely gone, but it was so thin it could not even be visualized anymore. In my rational moments, which were fast replacing the irrational hope I had hung on to, there was no more thread. It was what I verbalized to others. In fact, I had been verbalizing it to others all along. I did admit to others in the beginning, though, that I still wanted to be in that small percentage who made it through the first five years. Why not? Somebody had to make up that statistic—why not me?

On the other hand, it was a lot more likely that I would be in the other much larger percent! I was fast finding out I wasn't as special and unique as I'd always thought I was. I was just a regular old person who got cancer, like lots of other people. All the control I thought I had over my life was mostly an illusion. Yes, I had control over what I did on a day-to-day basis, and for sure, putting one foot in front of the other in the direction of my choosing had something to do with where I ended up at the end of each day. But in the overall picture of things, that was like scooping out the ocean with a thimble. There was a lot that I had no control over. At the time, I had no control over whether I lived or died, or whether my cancer would progress or go into remission.

In the beginning, I thought I had some of that control. I did my imagery every day. I even took some of those mushroom capsules. I went to the natural chi movement seminar, and I went to Reiki classes and had friends do Reiki on me both at my home and long distance. And in that first six months, I responded very well to treatment. How could I not think I was doing well? My CA-125 went from 15,820 to 176. This all made it easy for me to maintain the illusion that I was going to be a winner!

Acceptance is always the goal. It's always better to accept reality than to fool yourself. Isn't that one of the critical steps in the grieving process? In fact, it's the last step. Once you've reached acceptance, you've achieved the healing. True, this doesn't mean you have happiness; it means you've stopped trying to fool yourself—no more bargaining, the anger has dissipated, you've begun to accept life without that which you have lost. So that means I've begun to accept life without life. How does that work? If I accept that I'm going to die, what have I accepted? Now how do I live my life? Oh, that's right, I make the most of the time I have left, when I am unable to do any of the things I've spent my life doing. Now that I'm almost out of time, and I've finally accepted that, I can quickly figure out what will make my life meaningful in that little bit of time I have left.

But wait. There is hope connected to the acceptance. Hope for what? One of the things I've had to accept is that there is no more hope. That was the whole struggle. I have no reason to hope that things will get better. So, by accepting that my life as I knew it is over, and that almost certainly life itself is almost over, I have won. But in that acceptance, I have lost everything. Once again, I have to ask: how does that work?

Verbalizing all this to Dr. Stollings makes the irrationality of my hope very clear. It forces me to accept the reality. But I don't feel better; I feel worse. When I see Dr. Sukumvanich for the first time since I have begun to see her, he asks me if I'm still seeing Dr. Stollings. I tell him I am. He asks if it helps. I shrug my shoulders and say, "Yes, but it doesn't really change anything." He tells me that I always seem very sad and depressed. I say I am not sad and depressed. He tells me that he doesn't think people should ask how much longer they have to live; rather, they should focus on enjoying whatever time they do have. He cites his grandparents as examples. I have never asked Dr. Sukumvanich how much time I have left, and he has never given me a time frame. I don't think he can tell me, because he doesn't know. Of course, he can give me a general guideline that adheres to a typical person with my general health status, but I could figure that much out myself. I don't bother to narrow it down. I have that general idea floating around in my mind, but I don't pin it down. I let it float loosely.

I say that I still do everything I can do, but it's hard to get excited about life when you have so little and can do so little. I tell him that's why I'm writing a book—because I don't think people really understand what it's like to have cancer. He agrees with me. I think he is one who doesn't understand. He has said this before, but it is hard for me to grasp how he can't understand when he's been dealing for years with people who have cancer. Maybe he doesn't look into it that deeply. Maybe that's how he survives day in and day out dealing with cancer. How else could you survive seeing people die as often as I'm sure he does? He just focuses on keeping them alive; what they do with the extended life he gives is up to them.

Of course, that isn't his responsibility. That is up to each individual person to figure out. Once, I complained about this to one of the visiting nurses. She told me that Dr. So-and-So said in a training she attended that he just gives quantity of life, not quality. This is right, and I applaud him for being honest enough not only to acknowledge it but also to verbalize it. I don't expect Dr. Sukumvanich to make my life meaningful, but it might help if he better understood *my* struggle to do that.

So here I am. I have finally accepted the cold, hard truth. That should make me a winner. But in winning, I feel that I have lost everything.

FINDING MY NEW GIFT TO THE WORLD

When you graduate from high school, you're supposed to have figured out some general direction you want your life to take. That way, if you go on to more education, you know where to go and what kind of courses to take. If you are going immediately to work, you are supposed to know what you want to do. So, in your first eighteen years of life, you end up with at least some idea of what you want to be when you grow up. We all know that is at best a vague notion, generally speaking. How many kids change their major halfway through college? Lots. But in the end, the idea is that you have chosen a course that fulfills you, and in that fulfillment, you will be doing something you are good at. You will be making a contribution that will be meaningful both to yourself and to the world. It is your gift to the world. It is the best you have to offer. It is your way of, regardless of the size, giving something back.

Since I have accepted that my old life is a thing of the past, I now need to fill it with something else. After I graduated from college (where I changed my major halfway through) and before I settled into my first real job, I took a trip. It was the end of the hippy era, and although I didn't partake of most of the offerings of that time in history (such as drugs, sex, and rock 'n' roll), I liked the idea of "finding yourself." So I took a motorcycle trip, alone, to Maine. Of course, my mother was beside herself, but it was something I had to do. Suffice it to say, it was relatively poorly planned, and I returned home three weeks later with $5.00 in my pocket, a sore ass, and legs that were vibrating like a sewing machine while I walked like a cowboy. I was no closer to finding myself than I had been the day I left. Still, it was a wonderful adventure, and it went a long way toward cementing my independence, both in living and thinking.

It only took me another two and a half years to get my first real job. But it was a good one, and I stayed there for twenty years, working my way from an aide to clinical director at ARC Manor. Following my retirement from ARC Manor, I spent the next ten years doing home baking and gardening. Now, once again, I am on the road to discovery.

The awareness has come in small pieces, and separate stages, but I know I need to write this book. As I go along on this cancer adventure, I find myself learning more about myself and about others. Life is one big learning experience. Thinking about it coming to an end is daunting. Have I made the most of my opportunities? Surely I have wasted some of them. I probably didn't even recognize many when they came my way. I think about people who have been important to me and are gone from my life, having left in one way or another. I wonder if they gave much thought to what kind of mark they may have made in their living, and in their leaving.

While some e-mails should be thrown away for good, others recycle themselves periodically. One of my favorites is the one that talks about people moving in and out of the seasons of a person's life. How long they remain in your life is not the critical factor; it's the impact that matters most. The tiniest thing can have monumental importance. The quietest things can speak boldly and have the loudest message.

One of my favorite movies is *A Christmas Carol*. I think the one starring George C. Scott as Ebeneezer Scrooge is the best one. Indeed, I watch it every year at home while decorating, or wrapping presents. There is no end to the good messages in that story. When Jacob Marley comes back as a ghost to visit Ebenezer Scrooge, he has an ominous task—to awaken Mr. Scrooge to his own good spirit. We all know it is buried deeply. He says, "It is required of every man that the spirit within him should walk abroad among his fellow men, and travel far and wide! And if that spirit go not forth in life, it is condemned to do so after death! It is doomed to wander through the world and witness what it cannot share but might have shared, and turned to happiness!"

Mr. Marley had been in Ebenezer's life for many seasons, and he makes a brief return, in the form of a ghost, in an effort to salvage what is left of Ebenezer's life. While Ebenezer has become quite wealthy in the material world, he has not only kept all that to himself, but he also has yet to share anything of his spirit. He has made no gift to the world. This is what he is lacking, and the three spirits visit him in an effort to teach him how he can still do this. In the end, Mr. Scrooge decides to share not only his money but also, and more importantly, his spirit. And the world is a better place for it.

In the movie aptly named *The Bucket List*, Morgan Freeman and Jack Nicholson play characters, both diagnosed with cancer, who go off on a series of adventures to fulfill their dreams. The list includes things like skydiving, driving race cars, and traveling to visit wonders of the world, with a few more spiritual goals thrown in by Morgan Freeman's character. When I found out I had cancer, I had no bucket list, and I was not inclined to develop one. True, I always wanted to see the Redwood Forest, and I thought it would be amazing to spend time in Alaska. But I could die quite peacefully without ever seeing those places. It was the idea of visiting the national parks with Bill, the love of my life, that was special to me. More importantly, I wanted to make whatever moments I had as meaningful as I could. If I spent time with someone, I wanted it to be meaningful. I couldn't waste time on small talk anymore. Life was serious business to me now. I had to make sure I took advantage of every opportunity that came my way. I had to be sure that my spirit took every chance to walk abroad.

This meant that I would have to do what was best, not what was easiest (either for me or the other person). I had to be willing to go outside my own comfort zone. I had to speak with honesty and conviction. And I had to write this book. As the words flowed from me to the paper, I tried not to think about how the things I was writing sounded. I have written things exactly as they happened, as I remembered them, with my thoughts and feelings attached. Sometimes, in reading over what I have written, I have been shocked and have wondered at my own audacity. I have not allowed myself to change any of it.

It occurred to me that in this cancer journey, I have walked many new paths. I have gone into uncharted territory; I have been without a map. Perhaps what I can do is leave a map for others. Perhaps this can be my gift to the world. Then maybe others can use this map, and their journey will not be so lonely, so fearful. I must make the map as accurate as I can possibly make it, and therefore I can't be worried about how it sounds. Maps, of course, only provide direction. They don't tell you what to do when you arrive at your destination.

Chapter Ten

Taking a Break or Feeling Normal Again

Getting through the holidays was made more difficult with this pain that seemed to be cycling through my body at regular intervals. At one point, one of the PAs suggested it could be a hernia. Aside from that, I had the usual tiredness and dryness in my eyes and nasal passages, and I would get out of breath with minimal exertion. Just walking up the basement stairs would exhaust me. The peripheral neuropathy moved in small increments upward and, combined with the destruction of my fingernails and toenails, left my hands burning with major changes in temperature. From my toes back through the balls of my feet, I had a constant burning and tingling sensation.

I had a regular scan on March 23, 2012. It showed that I had a hernia "left paramedian in location containing nonobstructed portions of the GI tract. The gap at the level of the muscle layer measures about three centimeters." The scan showed no signs of metastatic disease at the level of the chest, abdomen, or pelvis. There was a "small, stable low-density area in the spleen most likely representing epithelial cyst." Since the scan on May 18, 2010, each of five scan reports noted "nonspecific low attenuation lesion in the spleen" that "remained unchanged." On March 28, 2012, my CA-125 was 155.

Once again, I was in the position of having an ever increasing CA-125, while my scan was showing no evidence of cancer. This was dramatically frustrating for me, but the PAs seemed unfazed by these conflicting results. Apparently this was not an unusual situation. All it meant was that there was cancer growing but that it was still too small to be seen on the scans. I, in contrast, was very much fazed by these results. I wanted a clear-cut answer. I wanted something definitive. My post-scan visit was with Nora, and as I expressed my frustration, she remained unfazed. I asked her if my number could be influenced by the hernias. After all, I had been told repeatedly that the CA-125 is not just elevated by cancer; there are a number of things that can cause it to rise.

"Maybe, but it wouldn't be the whole thing. I'd say it might take it down by half, say to seventy-five, but that would be the most."

This was not what I wanted to hear. I was desperate to find a non-cancer explanation for my ever-increasing number. Well, at least now I had the explanation for my pain—a hernia. I needed to focus on that.

"So, then what about this hernia? I guess that explains the pain I've been having." Nora asked me a few questions about my pain.

"That sounds exactly like the way people describe hernia pain."

"So what do we do about it, then? What is the treatment?"

"Well, most likely, you just deal with it. They don't usually do surgery unless the pain is severe."

"How severe is severe? I think it is severe, when it gets bad."

"You could try wearing a girdle."

"Do you know what it's like for a fat person to wear a girdle?" I was quite sure she had no idea. Nora was very tall, probably at least five feet ten inches, if not closer to six feet. Everything about her was long and lean, from her figure to her hair. Melissa was standing to the side, and I saw a quick look of mirth pass over her face at my question to Nora.

Melissa was my size, so she knew exactly what I was talking about. I was already imagining myself like a stuffed sausage, not being able to breathe, with the girdle digging into the creases of my legs.

On rare, more formal occasions, I had worn a girdle—and been dramatically uncomfortable the entire time. Since it was so snug, it pressed everything in. The fat has to go somewhere. If it all stays under the girdle, then you can't breathe. If it gets pushed up, then you still can't breathe. It's like having an inner tube, blown up to the point of explosion, pressing against your ribs and smashed up under your boobs. When you want to really flatten yourself, you also wear control-top panty hose, which causes your thighs to pop out right below the creases in your legs, where they rub all night long. Generally, the next morning, and for the next couple days, you have a pressure/heat rash that burns like crazy. You have to keep trips to the bathroom to a bare minimum, because the amount of time it takes to get the pantyhose/girdle combination down and then back up is long and exhausting, not to mention painful for arthritic fingers. Now someone was suggesting I spend every day like this, all day long! Just shoot me now, and get it over with.

"Just try it!" Nora was saying; not sharply, but still conveying the message that maybe it was going to be my best option.

I could feel myself getting whiny, feeling overwhelmed with the idea that this was one more thing I would just have to suck up because cancer rules all! Nothing else can be dealt with when you have cancer and are doing chemotherapy. Surely, if they knew how much pain I was having from the hernia, they wouldn't be so glib about it.

"You know, the pain is pretty bad. I'm afraid to move sometimes, it feels like something is just going to pop or burst in there. If I am going to sit, or lie down, I have to move very carefully and hold my stomach."

"That's exactly the way people describe having a hernia," she repeated.

"I'm just so tired of all this. My vision is terrible. I saw my eye doctor, and in the last three months it has gotten worse than it did in the whole year of 2011. I don't want to go blind. I just want to feel like a normal person again. "

"Have you ever had a break?"

She had my attention now. "Do people take breaks?"

"Women take breaks all the time, for a variety of different reasons."

Then why were they working so hard to keep *me* from taking one? "No, I've never had one, other than when I had my surgery."

"Aw, we are so hard on you guys. Give me a hug." Nora bent over the table and hugged me. I cried more. She was right; they were hard. But it was what they had to do. I didn't expect anything less from them. "You're not going to go blind; it's the chemo." It was easy for her to say I wasn't going to go blind; I was the one who couldn't see three months after I had gotten new lenses. And besides, saying it's the chemo doesn't change anything. "Would you like to skip your chemo today?"

I hesitated, not sure how to respond. "I'm afraid that if I skip it and my number goes up, it will be because I skipped it."

"It's not going to go up if you skip one week. If it does, it will not be that much, and it will come back down."

"Is there any evidence about how taking a break impacts on cancer overall, and whether or not it shortens your life?"

"It doesn't make any difference in the end."

Well, that decided that. "Okay, then. Maybe I will skip it today."

"Maybe you can have that hernia repaired; maybe it's time for a second-look surgery. Maybe it's time for a different kind of chemo. I can talk with Dr. Sukumvanich about these things. He might say, 'Nora, you're nuts! You've lost it!' but I don't think he will." She was smiling. I felt better already.

I began to feel more hopeful, which should have sent my alert signals flashing and blaring on high. Nope, not me. I had already begun playing out scenes in my mind of a whole new start—a better one. I would turn this thing around.

"We'll schedule you to see Dr. Sukumvanich next week, and you can discuss these things with him."

"That sounds good."

I left the hospital feeling a little weird, as though I had forgotten something important. I had: my chemo treatment for that day. Would it actually make any difference? Would I actually feel better with a whole week off chemo? It didn't matter. It was more of a moral victory. Mentally, I felt better.

Two days later, I had lunch with my cousin, Kathy, at a local Panera. We had finished eating and were sitting there chatting, reminiscing about our younger years. I suddenly began to have some abdominal pain. It was a severe cramping, and I felt too weak to sit in the chair. Fortunately, a booth near us had emptied, so I stretched out as well as I could on the cushioned bench. The pains came in waves, and I felt a cold sweat encompass my body as everything got lighter. I knew I was on the verge of passing out. I wasn't sure what to do. My cousin was beside herself, trying her best to be helpful. She brought me paper towels she had dampened with cold water. She asked if I wanted her to call anyone, or to go to an emergency room. I just kept hoping it would pass. It did—about twenty minutes later. When it was all over, I was spent. I felt so weak I didn't want to get up. I felt chilled and as if I had undergone extensive physical exertion.

I knew I would have to make a trip to the bathroom before we left the restaurant. I could feel that my bag was full. Finally, I made my way to the back of the dining area. My cousin shadowed me, her anxiety level still over the top. Sitting on the toilet, I managed to do the necessary work. It exhausted me further. Kathy insisted on driving me home. I was glad she did; I still felt so weak that I'm not sure I could have been attentive to the road. That night, and the next day, I experienced bloody mucous from my stoma, in addition to blood in and around my stool. The third day, the blood was reduced to trace amounts around the outside of the stool.

The next week, I received a call from Melissa informing me that Dr. Sukumvanich was not available to see me the next day. She stated she would determine the next time he was available and call me back. Within a few minutes my phone rang, and she offered me the option of seeing the doctor who was the head of the entire practice, or I could wait to see Dr. Sukumvanich.

While I definitely preferred to see my regular doctor, I didn't really want to wait. Surely this doctor could answer my questions, though. I accepted the appointment.

When I arrived at the waiting room, I was dismayed to see that it was almost completely full. Bill and I managed to find two seats together and settled in for the inevitable wait. It was about an hour—completely out of character, in our experience. Finally, we were called back to an exam room. After another, briefer, wait, Melissa entered the room, followed by a woman I had never seen. She introduced herself as a PA and assured me that she had read my file and so had all the pertinent information.

I felt that my mental processing abilities had slowed considerably over the previous year or so. Was this what they call "chemo-brain," or was it normal aging? Who knows? At that particular moment, my processing was very slow. I knew (or at least I hoped I hadn't made it up) Melissa had told me I would be seeing a doctor, and I was sure it was a man. So who was this, and why would I be seeing another PA? How would she be able to answer the questions that Nora had not been able to answer the week before? I looked from her to Melissa, trying to find an answer. There was none forthcoming.

The PA was waiting for me to ask her my questions. I felt bad for her; it seemed that somehow she had gotten thrown into the middle of a very confusing situation. Slowly, I pulled myself together and tried my best to focus.

"Yes, my recent scan showed I had a hernia, and I wanted to talk about the options for treatment related to that" I stated—or something like that.

She looked a little confused, and said, "Oh, I looked at your scan report, and I don't recall seeing anything about a hernia."

What? Melissa had called me within an hour of when I had the scan, telling me that no cancer had been found. I had been thrilled, but I then asked her what the heck could be causing all my pain. After a brief pause, she told me that the report stated that I had a hernia.

I felt some degree of satisfaction at the time, because at least I had found out what the problem was. In addition, Nora had spoken about the hernia in my appointment the week before. Now here was someone telling me she had no recollection of any hernia, and this after she had assured me initially that she had reviewed my file and was up to date on my situation. I was beyond confused; I was starting to feel annoyed.

"Well, it is there, I saw it in the report."

"I don't remember seeing anything about a hernia." Was she deaf? We had the same exchange three times. I began to feel that she was trying to make the hernia nonexistent, as though if she said it wasn't there enough times, then I'd drop the whole thing. I looked toward Melissa, who I knew was aware of the hernia. She was silent. Finally, the PA pulled the scan report up on the computer and acknowledged that it did indeed mention a hernia.

She continued to downplay it, recommending I wear a girdle. I would have to maybe cut a part out, to accommodate for the colostomy, but that could be done. Sure, just one more tiny accommodation, one more little thing to add to the list of ways I wasn't normal, another little thing to suck up. Maybe now the colostomy, with attached appliance, would show through my jeans; a little pop-out effect, since all the flab around it would be flattened out by the girdle. How cute! I couldn't wait!

I told the PA about my experience in the restaurant and asked if it could have been a result of my hernia.

"That would be really hard to say. It could have been that or any number of other things. It might happen again. Or it might never happen again." Well, that narrowed it right down.

She went on to talk about the emergency situation that would require surgery. Generally, in a pelvic hernia (which was what they told me I had) or abdominal hernia, a part of the intestine would be pushed through the opening. If that got stuck there, it could become strangulated and begin to die. This would require emergency surgery and was a very serious situation. But people knew when this happened because it was very painful.

"So, then, I can suck it up and wear a girdle, or wait until an emergency situation occurs and hope I can have surgery before I die." I wanted to be clear on what my options were.

"Well, there is a middle-of-the-road course. You could be evaluated by another doctor. We could refer you to Dr. Ramanathan. Dr. Sukumvanich has worked with him before, and he is a very good doctor. But he is the kind of doctor who will tell you if he feels he can't help you."

I would hope so! What else would he do? I was trying to understand why she felt a need to emphasize that point to me. My conclusion was that she was trying to tell me that he would likely tell me the same thing she had told me—that I didn't need surgery.

"I would like that. Thank you."

"But you realize, then, that you would need to take a break from your chemo, and then your number [CA-125] could go up."

"I would still like to have an appointment."

"Okay. We can get that set up for you."

This was already my second week without chemo, and there was no point in starting it again if there was a possibility I might have surgery. It was a Tuesday, and I was scheduled to see Dr. Ramanathan on Thursday of the following week.

I had a lot to think about before that appointment. From everything that had happened so far, it seemed more likely than not that I would not have surgery and that I would just have to deal with this pain for the rest of my life, however long that might be. It made me cry just to think about it. Was I just being a big baby? *I* thought I was in severe pain when it happened. By the reactions of the people I had spoken to thus far, they seemed to think it wasn't that big of a deal. What would this new doctor think? How could I make him understand what it was like for me?

I knew that I had a tendency to get stressed once inside a doctor's office. I decided the best thing to do was write everything down in chronological order. I would just stick with the facts. Then the doctor would have all the information and I would have to accept his recommendation. I felt more relaxed about the whole thing already, just having a plan in my mind. I wrote everything down in detail. I was the queen of details. Nothing slipped by me.

I arrived at my appointment that morning with time to spare. I was seen by a resident first. I gave her my written information, and she reviewed it with me, asking a few questions. Then she left, and about fifteen minutes later, the doctor came in. He was tall and lean, and he looked to be Indian. He spoke with a slight accent, but very clearly. I appreciated that I could easily understand every word he said.

He introduced himself and shook my hand. He seemed very relaxed and calm. His manner was deliberate, and he was clearly not going to hurry through the appointment. He had my written information with him. He sat down at the computer and asked me if I had seen my scan.

"No, I haven't," I replied, surprised that he was offering to show it to me. I liked the way he went about doing things.

He explained what the different shapes and colors on the scan represented, and he pointed out the two hernias I had. I wasn't aware I had two hernias. Only one had been mentioned on the scan report. He studied them intently, going over and over them. One was near my belly button and was very small. The other, much larger, was above and slightly to the left of my stoma.

"What did Dr. Sukumvanich tell you about having your colostomy reversed?"

"He told me I had to be cancer-free for two years, and I have never been declared cancer-free. I take that to mean I will never have the colostomy reversed," I replied, with a slight shrug of my shoulders.

"It would be much easier to repair the hernia if I didn't have to work around the colostomy," he explained. "With the colostomy in place, it is also more likely that the repair may not hold up as well."

He did an exam, intently looking at the areas I complained about. He asked me questions as he went along, taking nothing for granted. I appreciated that he was interested in my perspective on things and wanted all the details of my experiences with the pain. He asked if he could do a rectal exam to evaluate the length of my rectal stump, after finding out that I didn't know what it was. Not a piece of information I had committed to memory. I consented, but it was quite painful, and I was unable to relax enough for the exam to be successful. I apologized, and he assured me that it was okay.

"There are three options," he said. "You can do nothing and just deal with it as it is. I can repair the hernias and work around the colostomy the best I can, or I can reverse the colostomy and then repair the hernias. It also depends on how long you're going to be around. If you're going to be here in about six months, then repairs can be done. But, if you're to the point where chemo isn't really working any more, then there is no point in doing the repairs. I don't mean to be blunt."

"No, that's okay. I don't mind blunt. I prefer it."

"Oh, okay, then." He was looking at me intently. I didn't know what he was thinking, but I wanted to be sure he knew that I knew how precarious my life was. I wasn't afraid to talk about it like it was.

"I can tell you right now I don't like the first option. When you have cancer, there are so very few things you can deal with. Most things you just have to live with. If it's possible, I'd like to have it fixed."

"Okay. You can think about the other two options and let me know what you want to do."

"I don't need to think about them. I know which one I'd like to have done. I'd prefer the third option; I just never thought I'd be able to have it done, since I'm not cancer-free."

"You realize that is a major operation."

"I don't care." There was nothing to think about, as far as I was concerned.

"If there were to be a leak, then you would end up with a permanent colostomy."

"I don't care about that either." Until then, I had already thought I had a permanent colostomy, so this outcome would be no different from the way I had been living.

"Then why don't I see if I can get ahold of Dr. Sukumvanich and see what he thinks about all this?" He made his way out of the exam room.

"Okay." Was this a real possibility? Was I going to actually get rid of the colostomy? I felt light, as if I were floating slightly above the chair. I thought I must be imagining this whole thing. Maybe I was still in bed, in my own bedroom in Kittanning, and I was dreaming. Maybe I hadn't even gotten up yet. Could this all be real?

Within about fifteen minutes, Dr. Ramanathan was back in the office. "I talked with Dr. Sukumvanich, and he is fine with that option."

I assumed he was talking about the second one, but as he began to go into the details of what I would need to do to prep for the surgery, and then what he would be doing, I realized he was discussing option three! I was stunned! I would be getting rid of my colostomy! I couldn't believe it!

He handed me a packet of papers with information and instructions, and he circled some things for me. He gave me a tentative date of April 30 as my surgery date. I was so ecstatic that I had to force myself to listen to him.

"I want you to have a colonoscopy before your surgery, and make sure you tell them that I want an evaluation of the length of your rectal stump." He had written this on the prescription for the colonoscopy, but he wanted that point stressed. He could count on me to do that. I would be sure everything was done to the letter of the law.

"Thank you!" I was shaking his hand, getting ready to leave. This was an appointment that had definitely not gone the way I had expected it to. The words of the consultant from ARC Manor came floating back to me, all those years later: "Prepare for the worst, hope for the best, and stack the deck like hell in your favor." I had certainly been prepared for the worst. I had hoped for the best but was so sure I wouldn't get it.

When I had written everything down, I had assured myself I had done everything I could to convey the information accurately. I told myself I would just have to accept what he told me, knowing his conclusion had been based on the facts as I presented them. And here I was, with results I wouldn't have put a penny on if I were a betting woman.

Clean Teeth

"Your teeth are so strong you could pull a car with them!" My dentist was doing the cursory check of my teeth and mouth after the cleaning had been finished by the dental hygienist.

I had been going to the same dentist for about thirty years. Although occasionally I was a month or so late, I almost always had my teeth cleaned every six months. I had had a few problems over the years: a partial loss of one tooth that resulted in a root canal with a crown, a small cavity here or there, an old filling that needed to be replaced. Even though I had cared for my teeth poorly in my younger years, genetics had saved me. Despite a few lapses here and there, eventually I settled into a routine that resulted in a healthy set of teeth. They looked like they would last me a lifetime.

My habits were set, and even on nights when I would decide I was just too tired to floss, that I might just this once skip that step, before I realized what I was doing, I was sitting on the toilet for that one last pee before bed, flossing my teeth. For the previous several years, I had been complimented by whoever got the lucky job of cleaning my teeth. They would tell me several times what good shape my gums were in. There was usually very little to no bleeding during the process.

I was dismayed to learn, once I started chemotherapy, that I would not be allowed to get my teeth cleaned. This was unbelievable to me; a simple thing like having my teeth cleaned had become too risky of an undertaking. Apparently the risk centered around my blood counts, once again. If my platelets were too low, there would be the issue of bleeding too much. If the white blood cell count was too low, there was the issue of infection. While getting your teeth cleaned is not generally considered a high-risk procedure, all that prodding of the gums and scraping of the teeth right around and under the gum lines could create an open wound and lead to infection.

My last precancer teeth cleaning had been in December 2009. I was able to have them cleaned again right before my surgery in August 2010, so I was only two months behind. After that, I was so sure I was going to get rid of the last vestiges of the cancer with chemo; I knew I'd be able to get my teeth cleaned again before too long. This was a dream that never came to pass.

Shortly after I started chemo, I had consulted with my dentist, and he prescribed me a rinse that was made for people on chemo. It is called Caphasol and came at a hefty price. Fortunately for me, once my deductible was paid, it was completely covered by my insurance. This ready-mix rinse was to be used four times daily, but I varied the frequency, depending on how much the chemo I was on at any given time impacted on my gums. I averaged twice daily, and this was enough to keep me from having any serious issues with my mouth and gums.

Just a little over two years into my cancer adventure, by the time I had my appointment with Dr. Ramanathan, it had been three weeks since my last chemo treatment. After seeing him, it looked like I would be having a much longer break from the chemo. With surgery scheduled for April 30, and a likely four weeks for recovery, I would have a total of nine weeks off chemo—a good time to see the dentist. I wondered how many people became this excited about seeing the dentist.

The dental hygienist was amazed at what good shape my teeth were in, considering it had been nineteen months since my last cleaning and I had been undergoing chemotherapy that entire time. Although my teeth were not a nice white color, they were healthy and strong. They would last me; indeed, they would probably last longer than I would live.

After my big surgery in August 2010, when I still fantasized that I would get my old life back, I told Bill that once this was all over, I wanted to get my teeth whitened, whatever that took. He agreed with me. He would have agreed with anything I wanted at that point. That was one expense we never had to worry about, because there was never a need for me to get my teeth whitened. I never got my old life back. It was a frivolous thing to think about doing anyway.

Colonoscopy

The day my colonoscopy was scheduled, we ran into some serious traffic issues. With the warmer weather just beginning, construction was everywhere. We had left with plenty of time to spare, but it was looking like we might not get to the preop area of the hospital when they wanted us. I made several calls and as soon as I arrived, they ushered me back to get me ready. Within a very short time, the procedure was underway. I didn't have time to think about anything, which was probably a good thing. The doctor had introduced himself, and I had stressed that Dr. Ramanathan wanted him to evaluate the length of my rectal stump. It seemed like I had a lot riding on this figure, so I wanted to be sure the measurement was carefully made.

I had no discomfort from the procedure, and the doctor had assured me that I had a good fifteen centimeters left of my rectal stump and that Dr. Ramanathan should have no problem reversing the colostomy. It's amazing how easy a colonoscopy can be when you don't have cancer squeezing your sigmoid colon shut.

Things moved fast from that point. As I moved further away from my most recent chemo appointment, I felt better and better. While I would not say I felt near normal, I felt significantly better than I had while on chemo, which is to say that I felt better than I had in over two years. I had talked with a friend, Rick, about paying him to do some weeding in my big perennial garden. There was a lot of catch-up work to be done, so he was at my house early several mornings to weed. I took a chair to the front of the yard, where I would eat my breakfast while chatting with Rick. I spent some time each morning weeding—sometimes from the chair, other times bent over. I tried to stay out of the sun, since that was not recommended when chemo was being done. Although it had been a month since my previous chemo treatment, I still wanted to be careful.

Just sitting out in the morning, chatting with a friend, and pulling a few weeds was tremendously healing. I imagined myself getting better, and once again, I allowed the cancer to fade. Yes, the yo-yo was moving again. I was making a slow but deliberate ride to the top of the string. I began to think about life in my garden again. Soon I would be able to do the weeding on my own. Once I had the surgery and got things fixed up, I would mend fast, and life would be mine again. How easy it was to fall into this illusion once more. I wanted it desperately.

HERNIAS

I arrived at the hospital early. I wanted everything to go smoothly. No added stress. It seemed like the steps to get me ready for the surgery went on forever. The number of people who came in and out of my surgery-prep cubicle was endless. Surely, some seemed redundant. But how would I know? So I answered their questions, over and over. For sure, every one asked me to spell my last name and give my date of birth. While this might get annoying, I think it is a great system. It is a way for them to be sure they never get their patients confused. So I didn't really mind.

Closer to the time of my surgery, I learned that Dr. Sagan, the urologist who, in my estimation, saved my life, would be putting stents in my ureters. This was so they would be lit up, and so that when Dr. Ramanathan did the surgery, there would be no mistaking them. I wished that I would be awake to see her so that I could thank her for her thoroughness on February 18, 2010. I would thank her in my heart. I did mention this to the person who told me she would be performing that procedure. I should have asked him to give her the message.

Dr. Ramanathan came in to see me, and he reviewed my file. He asked me if I was still having the pain, and I assured him that I was. *Yes, there is still a reason to perform this procedure; don't worry.*

Eventually, I was wheeled down the hall to get started on my surgery. I think it was around noon. I felt light and free, even aside from the medication that had been started to relax me. This was going to be a turning point for me. It was one of the few things I had been able to get fixed since I found out I had cancer. It was a really big thing I would not have to just suck up. Not only would I be rid of the pain from the hernias, but I would also be able to sit on the pot and poop again! This was such a big bonus; it was almost like a fairy tale. Dr. Ramanathan surely had no idea how significant an event this was. Bring it on!

I woke up in the recovery room somewhere between six and seven that evening. I felt severe pain. The nurse asked me to rate my pain on a one-to-ten scale—surely one of the most annoying systems for medical personnel to evaluate a patient's pain. Still, I can't think of another way, so I guess it's better than nothing. I told her it was a twelve.

"Twelve!" You just told me a little bit ago it was a four!"

"Well, I guess I wasn't really awake when I said that. Or the anesthesia hadn't worn off yet!"

"Okay. Let me see what I can do."

She put something into my IV, and very shortly, I was floating again, the pain fading away. Once it was determined that everything vital was satisfactory, I was taken to a regular room. I think it was after nine, and Bill and Pat were there shortly after to say good night to me. It had been a long day for them, certainly much longer than mine had been. Most of my day had been passed in a state of unconscious bliss. They went home, and I drifted off into a drug-induced sleep. Any time I awakened, I had the button in hand and pushed it without a second thought. I didn't really want to wake up that night. I wanted to sleep until I could bear the pain of being awake.

Anyone who has ever spent time as a patient in a hospital knows that patients never experience anything akin to normal sleep. Medical personnel are constantly checking on you, taking your BP, pulse, and temperature on a regular basis. Blood draws are done at least once a day, in my case around 3:00 a.m. Checking on the bag attached to the catheter, emptying the bag, 1:00 a.m. visits from the respiratory therapist—it seems most convenient for the medical personnel to do these things during normal sleeping hours.

Although it seems that there is no need to get out of bed, just this act alone becomes the goal. Yes, they want you up and moving around right away, even if it is only to sit in a chair. The next morning, bright and early, after a very choppy night's sleep, the doctors are there to see how you are doing. They always come in groups, and they always introduce themselves—not that I would recall any of their names. Only Dr. Ramanathan's name sticks with me. I remember telling my husband in great detail about the appointment after the first time I saw him. I couldn't say enough good things about him. I described him as tall and lean. I was somewhat surprised, when I saw him after that, to see that he wasn't exceptionally tall. It had more to do with my opinion of him as a doctor; that had made him tall in my mind.

He told me on his first postsurgery visit that everything had gone well. He explained that he had stitched the smaller hernia together and had used a biological mesh to cover the other one, located above the beast. He stated time would tell if it would hold, and if it didn't, he would need to replace it with an artificial mesh. He stressed again that being overweight was a factor, and that gaining any weight would not help matters. I asked him if he had gotten the biopsy results yet.

Shaking his head, he replied, "We didn't do a biopsy."

I guess maybe I knew that. But he had told Bill they had cut a grayish piece of tissue from the end of the stump. Other than that, there had been no signs of tumor or cancer. I was thrilled about this. My surgery had been laparoscopic and had taken about five and one-half hours. That was a long time to be looking and poking, cutting and sewing through those tiny little openings.

"We know your number is going up, so something must be going on. You'll have to talk with Dr. Sukumvanich about that." I got it. He was dealing with hernias and colostomy reversals; Dr. Sukumvanich was dealing with cancer. The two would not cross over. That was okay. I could deal with that.

Since I hadn't eaten any solid food since Friday evening before the Monday of my surgery, there was nothing to pass through my bowels. I was definitely feeling some anxiety about what that first bowel movement was going to be like. I mean, I was out of practice. Would my body remember what to do? Would it be painful? I knew that rectal exams had become quite painful. When I had an appointment at the oncology office, the PA always did an internal exam and a rectal exam. This was not something I looked forward to. I had concluded that lack of use had left the muscles somewhat atrophied. Funny, it had never occurred to me to ask the doctor about this issue prior to my surgery.

I was slowly started back on food; first it was clear liquids, then soft liquids, then soft solids, and then solids. Although I ate very slowly, and small amounts per meal, I tolerated them all well and looked forward to adding more variety to my diet. Each day, sometimes more than once, I was asked if I'd had any bowel movement, and each time, I had to say no. That came gradually too. First I began to feel some gurgling in my stomach. Then I passed gas. A fart never felt so good!

One of the residents working with Dr. Ramanathan explained to me that they had chosen to leave my wound open, as this method generally leads to fewer problems with infection as it heals. The first time the nurse removed the dressing to change it, I was appalled at what I saw. There was a huge crater where my colostomy had been.

"That looks disgusting!" I said to her.

"Aw!" she replied, not at all shaken at the sight.

Still, I looked intently at the crater, taking in all the details. I estimated its dimensions to be 3½" × 2½" × 3". All that exposed "stuff" was gross. What was it? The nurse answered my questions, identifying the various things I saw exposed, and then at the end she added, "Well, some of it's just fat." Ah! That was the biggest part of what I saw. So that's what fat looks like underneath your skin. Gross!

Each day, this large sterile pad had to be removed. Two smaller sterile pads were dipped in a sterile solution, wrung out slightly, stuffed into the crater, and then covered with a new dry sterile pad. I couldn't imagine how this crater was supposed to fill in when it was stuffed with wet gauze. Apparently they wanted it to heal from the bottom up so the sides would not touch each other until the bottom had healed. It was still a hard concept for me to grasp. I had my doubts about this method, but I had to trust that they were the experts. I was sure I wasn't the first patient they had used this method on. Sometimes you just have to let go of the control.

My healing went well, and with a little extra urging from the doctors, I forced myself up and out of bed to begin walking around the halls, dragging my IV post along with me. What a sight I must have been—with the little white patches of stubble here and there on my head (what now passed for hair)—the beautiful double-gowned figure dragging her big, old sorry ass up and down the halls. I like to think that maybe the nurses were so used to seeing sights like this that I blended into the woodwork.

I went home on Friday afternoon. I had a last visit with the doctor earlier that day, and it was decided I could go home. Shortly before I left, I had my first bowel movement. It was not really painful, so I was quite happy about that. What a celebration of life!

Things went well after I went home. The visiting nurse came the next day to change the dressing on my wound, and she continued to come every few days until I was discharged from their care on June 1, 2012. By that time, I was cutting a tiny corner from a gauze pad to fill my wound. What had once seemed to be a crater the size of the Grand Canyon now had just the slightest of indentations. I was amazed. I had survived this process with minimal pain, and just a slash remained as a reminder of my days with the beast. The fact that I had no feeling in the tissue below where the beast had resided probably helped.

No More Colostomy

I adjusted quickly to sitting on the pot again. I have always said it's the little things in life that really make a difference. The first day the visiting nurse came, Bill packed up all my colostomy supplies, and I donated them to the visiting nurses. I was sure some poor soul could make good use of them now that I no longer had any need for them. The nurse told me she knew just the person who would be thrilled to have all these supplies. I was so happy to be able to perform this charitable act.

I had my postsurgical appointment with Dr. Ramanathan three weeks later. By then, everything was running smoothly. He asked if I was having any trouble with diarrhea or constipation. I was happy to report that things seemed to have equalized. I was pleasantly surprised that there was no pain to speak of, only a mild discomfort initially, as I resumed my old bowel habits.

My wound was well on its way to being healed, and I could tell when he examined it that he was pleased with how it looked. He suggested that I wear a girdle, and perhaps in response to the look I tried to keep off my face, he added that I needn't wear it all the time, but only when I was up and about. To myself, I commented that one of the reasons I had wanted the surgery was to avoid that very thing. I would be so extra cautious and careful about everything I did that there would be no need for a girdle. He also stressed once again that my being overweight was not a point in my favor, and that any added weight would only serve to put more stress on the hernias he had just repaired. He told me I could go back to Dr. Sukumvanich anytime. I was released from his care and was to see him again only if I ran into difficulties with the hernias. He left his helpers to complete the task of redressing the wound.

After he left, the PA finished redressing my wound, and I told her what I thought of Dr. Ramanathan. I suggested to her that he likely didn't really grasp the scope of what he had done for me. I explained to her how little control I had over my life since I was diagnosed with cancer, and that this was the first health issue I had really been able to do something about. It made a huge difference in my life, for once in a positive direction.

As I left his office, I felt wonderful. I had worn a brightly flowered skirt with a leafy green sleeveless top covered with a bright pink sweater.

It made me feel as though I were walking through a flower garden with everything blooming at one time. It felt like one of those midspring days when the air has warmed enough to feel as though winter is definitely over. The air was light, and crisp, with just a touch of heat from the early afternoon sunshine. As I walked down the hallway from his office, I felt a tinge of "old life" satisfaction. Life was as it should be.

While I still had a fairly large sterile gauze pad covering my wound, it could not be noticed through my skirt. I still had a tendency to lay my hand over it, as I had learned to do when I was wearing the colostomy appliance. This habit would take some time to break. Every time I walked down the hallway to our bathroom, I still lay my hand over that spot. Even when I moved to a smaller dressing, and then to none at all, I still found myself checking that spot. I didn't mind. What a pleasure to remember that I no longer needed to do that. And what a pleasure to not have to move carefully, to not feel like something in my gut was ready to pop if I moved slightly in the wrong direction.

The evening after I'd seen Dr. Ramanathan for the last time, I decided to go back to line dancing. I knew I wouldn't do much, but I was ready. I was feeling like a normal person who had just recovered from an operation that had improved her life dramatically. Everyone was happy to see me back, and I was thrilled to report that everything had gone well and I was on the fast track to recovery. Unfortunately, I learned that one of my fellow dancers had experienced a recurrence of her breast cancer. She had been well for about six years, but her last mammogram had revealed a new lump. I thought about what might lie ahead for her, and I knew it would be a stressful time. I was sad to learn her bad news, but I felt too good about myself to be pulled down too far.

Life without a colostomy was wonderful. When circumstances permitted (and even when they weren't ideal), I showed people my wound. I was still in awe of what I had left behind, of that small slash that would forever remind me of where I had been. The American Indians were right—scars should be borne with honor when they represent brave deeds and difficult times. We should never forget what we had to go through to get them. Still, I was glad mine was covered, unless I chose to show it off.

Paying the Price

Most of the time, my tendency has been to take care of things right away. When I know something needs attention, I usually dive right in. At least, if it's familiar territory, that's true. As I got off the elevator on the first floor, I walked deliberately down the hallway to Dr. Sukumvanich's office to schedule my first appointment there since March 23. Dr. Ramanathan had told me I could go back anytime, so I figured I might as well get it over with. As I rounded the corner, my pace slowed. With the doorway directly in front of me, I hesitated, turned on my heel, and took the elevator to the parking garage.

I felt so good, and I decided that one more week surely would not make any difference. Besides, I wanted that wound to be completely healed before I started back on chemotherapy, when all the natural healing processes would be slowed down. It was Thursday, and I would call the following Tuesday, hoping it would be another week before they could get me an appointment.

I had big plans for the coming weekend. Bill and I had met at Michael Bros. Nursery one evening when he was on his way home from work, and there we had purchased the annuals I would need to put in the first level of our retaining wall. This year, I wanted multicolor flowers. I also wanted to see if I could fill the wall at a lower price, so I bought only cell packs. The cost of a three-to-six-cell flower pack averaged under $2.00, while the cost of a single four-inch pot was around $4.00. I generally used around one hundred four-inch pots, so this would be quite a savings. In the past I had always figured that as long as I spent around the same amount on flowers as my husband spent on golf, I was okay. This year, I was on a mission. I wanted to see if it was possible to just do cell packs.

I knew I couldn't do a lot of the hard work, but I could do some planting along the lower part of the wall. This was the third spring since I found out I had cancer, and during the first two years, I had been unable to do any of the work involved in planting this area. I was excited.

Bill had already cleaned out the debris from the 2011 plantings and turned the soil over. While leaving this preplanting work to their husbands was common practice for some of my gardening friends, it was an integral part of the gardening process for me. This was what made it *my* garden. This year I would have to content myself with the minimal bit of work I could do and still think of it as mine. Or maybe I would just have to feel good about the shared effort.

Early on Saturday morning, Bill and I were at the wall, ready to work. I had my gardening hat on, and a long-sleeved shirt. Even though it had been eight weeks since my last chemo, I didn't want to risk too much sun exposure. Bill and I strategically arranged the back row of flowers—that is, the tall ones. I wouldn't be able to plant any of them. It was about two feet from the edge where I would be standing to where the tall flowers would be planted—too far for me to reach. I was already sweating just standing there. Bill brought one of our plastic chairs down for me to sit on while he planted. Even with this, I had to go inside a few times, as the heat left me feeling weak and light-headed. As the morning wore on, we finally got to the middle row, and I was able to plant some of those flowers. It felt so good to have my hands in dirt. The only thing better than the smell of freshly turned soil in the spring is the feeling of putting your hands into it. I was connected to the earth. We finished the plantings by Sunday evening, and I loved the exhausted feeling I had as I relaxed in the air conditioning later on.

When I called the oncology office the following Tuesday morning to schedule an appointment, Melissa seemed surprised that I was ready to come back. Since the following Monday was a holiday, Memorial Day, and the schedule was already jammed tightly, she suggested we wait until the following week. Adding that extra week made me a little nervous. Just a few days earlier, I had made a conscious choice to delay my return to chemo treatments, but now I didn't want the additional week I was being given. In the end, the difference between nine weeks and ten weeks couldn't make that much difference. Still, it brought the reality back to me. Yes, I did have cancer. After skirting the edges of that world I longed to be living in again with the little jaunt I had just taken, the cancer was right there waiting for me. I felt myself resisting its pull. I never thought I could feel that good again. It was reassuring to me that I still could. It told me that, yes, it was the chemo that was making me feel so bad. If I could only get rid of that last little bit of cancer once and for all, and stop the chemo treatments, I might really have a normal life.

Melissa left me an order for blood work, to be completed before my appointment. That way they would have my CA-125 by the time I returned for treatments. I had the labs drawn on Monday, and my appointment was two days later, on Wednesday. As I sat at home, I debated whether to call Melissa to find out what my new number was. If it was bad, I reasoned, at least I could prepare myself better before my appointment. My anxiety level rode high that day, and by early afternoon on Tuesday, I picked up the phone and dialed her number.

"Hi, Melissa, this is Jamie Schneider. I thought I'd call to get my CA-125 so in case it's not good, I could prepare myself."

"Well, it's up there."

"Oh, really?"

"Yes," she went on. "It's in the seven hundreds."

"Oh, well that is bad, then."

"Yes. Don't worry. We'll get it down."

"Okay. Thank you." I wanted to get off the phone as quickly as possible. Seven hundred! On March 23, it had been 155, and I thought that was terrible. How could this be? I felt so good! When Dr. Ramanathan had done my surgery, he hadn't seen any signs of cancer, outside of the questionable tissue he had removed. I somehow managed to keep a little gate shut so that the panic in my brain couldn't reach my heart. I began searching for explanations for that high number that didn't include large amounts of cancer roaming around through my body. I knew the yo-yo had once again plummeted to the depths, but I refused to acknowledge that I even noticed it.

I had been told repeatedly that any kind of abdominal irritation could make the number go up. Surely the five to six hours of surgery I had recently undergone could be considered a strong irritant. I knew, though, that after my big surgery in August 2010, there was no such similar spike in my number. Four weeks after that surgery, my number had been only slightly increased. And that surgery was much more involved than my latest one. There really was no way around it. The only reasonable explanation was that the chemo had been keeping the cancer under some degree of control, and ten weeks without it had left the cancer free to begin roaming. Could it possibly be brought back under control? I had my doubts, but I couldn't think any further about it.

The first thing to go through my mind was how I would tell my family and friends. They had seen me coming back to life in the last two and one half months; how could I tell them what had been going on during that time? It was too soon to panic. That evening, when

Bill came home from work, I knew I had to tell him. I was no good at hiding things.

"Well, I called Melissa today to get my number."

"Oh, yeah?"

"Yeah, and it's not good. It's in the seven hundreds."

"Tsk!" He stopped in his tracks, trying to absorb this piece of information that seemed so counter to everything that had occurred in the last ten weeks. He had a slight frown on his brow. Neither of us said anything else; we let the elephant just plunk there, in the middle of the room.

In my appointment the next day, I met with the doctor. He explained that he wanted to continue the same chemo treatments I had been receiving. Since I'd had the ten-week break, it was almost like I was starting it again, and he liked to do at least three cycles to see how it would impact my numbers. If they stayed relatively stable or went down, then I would stay on it, but if they went up, then he would get another scan and evaluate things from there. There wasn't much else to say.

Melissa came in to see me before I left. She seemed as surprised as anyone at the climb my number had taken. She referred to the postsurgery impact. I commented that I'd had no similar spike after my big surgery. She just shook her head.

"We'll get it down. You're not going anywhere fast." I felt great, and she thought I looked great. Jackie, whom I hadn't seen for several months, popped her head in the doorway to say hello and comment that I looked great. While they always said this when they saw me, her and Melissa's comments seemed quite heartfelt. Maybe I just thought that because of how good I felt, and for once *I* thought I looked okay. Once again, I marveled at the disease cancer; at how sneaky it is, and how it can be in there destroying your body while you go on with life, oblivious to the fact that you're dying.

After returning to chemo treatments postsurgery, my number stabilized somewhat. From March 20 to May 31, it had gone from 155 to 768. From there to July 30, it went to 964. Certainly, it had slowed down in its increase. But when it went from 908 on July 30 to 964 on August 20, I got a call from Melissa. Since it had gone up again, Dr. Sukumvanich had decided he wanted to get a new scan. If there were new findings on the scan, he would change my chemo. Melissa explained that since I had been off, it seemed likely my platelets had recovered, and that might lead to the use of one of the chemicals I had quit previously because of a low platelet count. This sounded reasonable to me. I had the scan on August 22.

Recently, I had been receiving copies of my medical testing on my Healthtrack account generally before I got the results from whoever ordered them. This was an online account available to patients using UPMC services. For whatever reason, by the time of my oncology appointment the following Wednesday, I had not received the report. Melissa had called me the Monday before and given me a very general description of the scan results, and then she called me Tuesday to tell me that I would be going back to a previous chemo treatment I had received from November 9, 2010 to June 21, 2011.

I arrived on August 29 at 10:40 a.m. for my appointment with Rachel, a new PA that I had begun to be scheduled with. I met first with Melissa so she could review the side effects and I could sign the new contract for that treatment. I had already reviewed the information myself at home the night before, so I was familiar with the information. She reminded me that I would need to do at least about four cycles before they would really know if it was going to work. I did remember this.

Rachel came in next and did my internal exam followed shortly by Dr. Sukumvanich. He entered the room in his blue scrubs and was not his usual friendly self. He gave me a cursory report on my scan and reiterated what I already knew—that I would be starting a different chemo that day. He told me again that the side effects were mild, and I made no comment to this. I knew how it had affected me before, and I would never describe it as mild. I told him I was glad to see him and that I wanted to apologize to him for something I said the last time I had seen him.

He shook his head in perplexity as he said, "You don't ever have to apologize for anything."

"Yes, I do. The last time I saw you, when you asked me how I was doing with side effects, I said, 'It is what it is.' While that was true, it wasn't very helpful to you. I don't want to be that way with you." I just wanted him to know that I had thought about what I said and knew it was the wrong way to respond to him. Of course, in the overall picture of things, I guess it might not be something that would really stick with him. But it bothered me.

"I just want you to feel good, and be happy," he said. I assured him that I was aware of this and that I appreciated it. "So make sure you don't wear tight shoes. Get yourself some Birkenstocks. They say they are very comfortable. And don't wear shoes that go in between your toes ... like those." He pointed to the shoes I had on. I knew I wasn't supposed to wear them when I was on this chemo. I thought I would just sneak one more wear in.

"Melissa already told me that. But they matched so well that I just had to wear them."

"Yes, I see that. You have the little bit of red in your shirt. That looks nice."

"That's pretty good for a man," I responded, and we both laughed. I felt good that the appointment ended on a positive note. I guess I wanted to make him happy too. I knew that in the end, it was likely that I would cause him sadness, so this little bit of laughter was a small gift—maybe for both of us.

Somehow, I was still keeping that little gate shut. It seemed to me that I was the more cheerful one in that appointment. I asked for a copy of the scan report. I wanted to read it for myself. I knew I would eventually get the report on my Healthtrack account, but I couldn't wait any longer.

I went upstairs to the cancer center and checked in, and I then sat down and pulled the scan report from my bag. As I read it, I was careful to keep it on an intellectual level. After I was done, I just looked around the room, somewhat in a daze. There had been six changes since my last scan, two months earlier. I ticked them off in my mind. None were definitively labeled as cancer, but they were nodules, or small growths, that had increased in size. It didn't take a genius to do the math. With my number moving ever upward and a scan reporting various places with nodules growing—gee, I wonder what they were?

Since I had subdued my emotions, I had no problems greeting the nurses with a smile pasted on my face. Barb, the chemo nurse who most often treated me, was in her usual pleasant mode, and I tried to let myself be drawn in by her well-meaning demeanor. I tried to ignore how long I had waited and how long it had taken her to get the chemo from the pharmacy. After all, none of this was her doing. It worked, too, until she informed me that "they" wanted me to have a bag of fluids because my creatinine level was elevated. This had to be given separately from the chemo, so it would add an extra hour onto my already long day. This was the straw that broke the camel's back. I became upset and complained about how long I would end up being there today. Barb tried to calm me, but it was too late; the gate had been opened. I spent the next hour crying off and on, feeling sorry for myself.

Eventually, I fell asleep, and when I awoke, I was spent, emotionally and physically. I had nothing left, either for whining or smiling. I had returned to a neutral zone. I knew Barb didn't deserve for me to unload on her, so I did my best to be at least mildly pleasant, and I returned the hug she offered me when I was done. I gave her a weak smile, the best I could muster. As I walked down the hall to get my parking voucher, I wondered what the nurses did after a patient like me left. Did they just go to some private corner and cry? It's what I would have done. But maybe they were beyond that. Maybe after one does work like this for years, it just rolls off like water off a duck's back. That is not to say they were cold and callous; I never felt like that. They all seemed conscientious and compassionate, and they seemed to put heartfelt effort into their work.

In my curiosity about this kind of thing, about a month or so earlier, I had asked Melissa if she would talk with me about her work as an oncology nurse. I wanted to know what motivated a person to choose this kind of work, in which nurses and doctors had to deal frequently with people dying. It seemed it would be so much safer to just be a nurse in a private practice, where one would deal with colds and the aches and pains of everyday life. I imagined that occasionally there would be a patient with issues outside the box of ordinary health issues; but that would be the exception, not the rule. Being an oncology nurse seemed like it would put suffering and death front and center.

To my surprise, Melissa readily agreed to talk with me, and we met the very next week. She explained that she felt good helping people with a disease they had done nothing to bring on themselves, in comparison to people who refused to make lifestyle changes that could lead to them being much healthier. She referred to things like smoking and eating poorly, which can lead to heart and lung issues. In addition, she saw herself as an advocate for cancer patients. I imagined her as a soldier on the front line. While the doctors, like the officers who strategically outlined the battle plans, had the big picture and used their knowledge and expertise to decide the next steps, depending on which direction things went, she was down in the trenches. She could see the lights of the enemies' eyes—in this case, cancer. She knew what was happening on a more primeval level. She could alert the doctor to what she was seeing.

Melissa also told me that most people in her position had dealt with loved ones having cancer, so they had seen its devastation firsthand. Perhaps they had watched and admired a nurse who worked with cancer patients, trying his or her best to make life better and more bearable. Perhaps they had been thus inspired to choose a similar career path.

I left the meeting with Melissa with a greater degree of understanding, and more appreciation for her perspective and her contribution to my struggle with cancer. I extrapolated this to all the medical personnel I encountered; I applied what Melissa had told me about her role, and it usually helped me to understand them better. Although I may not always have shown it, I have a deep sense of gratitude for these people, the ones who wage the daily war against cancer. Surely their contribution to saving lives and adding some measure of significance and dignity to these lives is no less than the contributions of the men and women who literally fight for our freedom in the traditional sense. Perhaps they should be recognized with a greater degree of appreciation and gratitude than they currently receive.

The Friday before my next appointment at the oncology office, and my next chemo treatment, I had blood work. In less than a week, I would find out if this chemo was going to be of any help to me. While I wasn't expecting any giant leaps, surely there would be some indication of whether it would work. I refused to call Melissa early for the results. For some reason, I had a feeling the news would not be good. Although it had taken a while before the chemo started to catch up to me post-surgery, I still felt better for the first couple months. Now I was back to the old familiar weakness and the bone and joint pain. It was always a crap shoot to figure out whether I felt bad from the chemo or the cancer. But I had to believe, since I had felt so good during the ten weeks off chemo, that a significant amount of my feeling bad *was* due to the chemo. That was, of course, as long as my number wasn't so high as to indicate that a significant amount of cancer was growing.

My appointment was again with Rachel, and she came in trailed by a new PA that she was apparently helping to train. I know she came in with a smile on her face, and I gave a friendly handshake to both her and her sidekick. I remember what Rachel looks like, but I recall only a vague outline of her trainee. I know Rachel spoke clearly and slowly, seeming to have a desire to be precise about everything. I think she started out by asking me how I was and how the side effects had been, and as I sat there trying to come up with something clear and original to say about them, I heard her ask me something like, "Are there any side effects … constipation, body pain … that are not under control with what we have given you?"

Ah! This was a much better way to ask the question. I could give a simple answer to that question: "No." Under control was vague enough to cover a wide territory, and I could safely say no and not have to worry about whether I had given her an accurate reflection of the truth. Under control means the problem isn't gone but has managed to stay under some nebulous line and I can still manage my day-to-day living well enough to get up and get going every day. Under control means I still have enough quality of life to take care of my own basic needs. Yes, I liked this format. Much better than when I had to try to put my experience into words without sounding too pathetic, yet making sure they had all the pertinent information.

"And what about your quality of life …?" This question trailed off, as though she knew it was silly to ask. Or maybe as though she wished she had a better way to ask that. *What does this really mean?* I wondered. She got an A+ on the first question, but this second one needed a little work.

I found myself giving an involuntary chuckle. "What does that really mean? I mean, yes, I can take care of myself, I can clean and dress myself, I can feed myself, I can even still drive myself to these appointments. But I can't do much else. So I don't think I even know what that means anymore."

Rachel just looked at me and nodded her head slowly in a way that wasn't a resounding "Yes, I understand." It was more like a "Well, okay, then … moving right along …"

"Do you have any questions?"

"Yes, what's my number?"

She turned to look toward my file and opened it up briefly, a motion I felt sure wasn't really necessary, but just something to do to deflect away from what she had to say next.

"Well, it's pretty high."

She still hadn't said the number. I felt like I should say something.

"Oh, really?"

"Yes, it's in the sixteen hundreds."

It's funny how clear some memories are, while others live in some sort of hazy place and are always fuzzy around the edges when I go to retrieve them. In those instances, what seems clearest is the way I felt when I experienced them. I can go into great detail about my feeling state regarding those situations, but I have difficulty being accurate on who said or did what.

I might have mumbled a response, and I think I gave a half of a head shake to indicate I got it. This is where things began to get hazy. My husband was in the room, but momentarily, I seemed to have forgotten that. I worked hard to keep that little gate up; I wanted to finish this appointment without completely falling apart. I finally glanced his way, and I thought I could see his little gate too. His face looked as though it were about to burst, like when you're outside in the summer and—all of a sudden, seemingly from out of nowhere—one of those crazy little rain showers just pops up and you wonder where the heck it came from. Or maybe his face was a mirror image of my own.

Maybe I tried to take charge. "Well, I know Melissa said that I had to do three or four cycles before we would really know if it was going to work, but I guess this isn't a very good sign, huh?"

Maybe she shook her head in agreement with what I had said. I could feel the panic trying to push its way through that little gate. By that point, it was like that little gate in *The Wizard of Oz* when Dorothy reconsiders her plan to run away and returns to the farm just as the twister is about to hit. She struggles to open the gate, and then, in a burst of Mother nature's fury, it just lifts from its hinges and flies away like a small, insignificant pile of twigs someone collected from around the yard with plans to burn it later on. My little gate was on the verge of flying away too.

As I listened to Rachel, I realized she was asking me what I wanted to do. This seemed like an odd question to me, and in my haze, I struggled with it, trying to make some sense of it.

"I guess I thought you were going to tell me about my options. How would I know what to do?"

I think Rachel was trying to bring something sensible to the discussion too. She was trying to find some way to pull all of this together. I recall things like "No idea what you must be feeling right now," "... seeing the doctor sooner than four weeks ...," "This is something I can do for you," "... expedite matters ... find out what your options are ..."

Later that day, Bill told me that he thought Rachel had done a good job of dealing with the situation. She hadn't tried to candy coat anything or pretend things were better than they were, but she had laid things out without embellishment. He felt that she wanted to be able to do something for me, and realizing there was nothing she could do to change things, she wanted to at least make things the most bearable for us. He did a good job of summarizing the appointment, and I agreed with him wholeheartedly. I had to ask him if I had done anything to convey otherwise to her, and he reassured me that I hadn't.

We walked out of the office, still struggling to hold our gates, now in tatters, but still clinging to their hinges, in place.

"Do you want me to stay with you for a while?" Bill asked. I still had to go upstairs to my chemo appointment.

"Sure," I said. It was just a thing to say, without thought or realization of what meaning it might have. I couldn't even process this simple question to know what I wanted. We entered the waiting room of the cancer center and took our seats, still in shock. There was no reason for us to be surprised. Maybe some things can never be prepared for. Maybe they have nothing to do with rationality and awareness. Maybe it's when they hit you in the heart that all your ammunition becomes useless. All your knowledge and preparation is in another place. And I had already been here. Two and one-half years ago, I'd walked into this world. I'd never really left, but somehow, through the passage of time, the windows had become opaque. Now the light was blinding. Everything was amazingly clear.

Bill and I sat side by side with a small table between us. Neither of us spoke. We were both in danger of bursting, and it wouldn't take much. Little sobs and bursts of tears escaped here and there.

Finally I looked at Bill and said, "You might as well go. There is no point in this." I didn't need to say any more. He knew I was right.

"We'll talk later," one of us said to the other. We hugged and kissed, and Bill left. He had to visit an account in West Virginia that afternoon. After all, life goes on.

"Drive carefully," I called after him.

"You too." We both knew what that meant. I knew I was in danger of not being as attentive in my driving as I would need to be. It was difficult to focus on anything.

I sat back down and tried to decide whether to attempt reading my book. I knew the chances I could concentrate on what I was reading were slim to none. In a short time, a nurse called my name. She was very cute, and all smiles. *Oh, God!* I thought. *Can I really get through this?* As I got up and walked to the door she was holding open for me, I tried to pull myself together. *Fuck it!* I decided I wasn't going to worry about it.

"Hi! How are you?" the nurse said as she smiled brightly.

"Just peachy," I mumbled, more to myself than to her. I mumbled something about not being used to the area we were in. I almost always went in the other doorway to another set of chemo treatment rooms. This was a good way to shift the focus from my lame greeting to something more neutral. As I sat down in my treatment chair, I looked around and didn't see the usual little box that contained about twenty half-sized Kleenex. I decided I might as well get the necessary supplies right off the bat. "I'll need some tissues," I said. She had to leave and go to a storage area, and she came back with several boxes. That was good; I might need them all.

"Do you have a cold?" she asked pleasantly. I looked at her, rolling my eyes fiercely in my mind.

"No, I've been crying," I said as if any idiot could determine the difference between a person who has a cold and one who's been crying because she just found out her cancer had taken a giant leap from getting worse to being bad.

"Anything I can do to help?"

"No, thank you, though."

"Do you want to talk with someone?"

"No." I had just seen Dr. Stollings the day before. I hate when I'm right. I told her I was pretty sure I wasn't going to get good news the next day. You'd think I would have been more prepared to receive it.

The nurse went on about the business of getting my treatment started. A few minutes later, she was back with the form I had filled out downstairs before my appointment there. I had filled one of these forms out prior to every chemo treatment I had undergone for the past two years and eight months, and this was the first time anyone had ever made a comment on what I had written. This nurse was desperate to find a way she could do something for me.

"I noticed on your form here that you said you're having shortness of breath."

"Well, not now. That's only with exertion, like if I walk up a flight of stairs, or something like that."

"Would you like me to check your oxygen level?"

"Sure." I knew there was no need for this, and I wondered how much my insurance would get billed for the use of that little machine. She wheeled it over and clipped the little device to the tip of my finger. In a couple seconds, the results flashed on the screen.

"Oh, it's ninety-nine," she said, clearly disappointed. She unclipped it from my finger and wheeled it a few feet away from where I was sitting. "Well, I feel better" she said as she giggled. "It's all about me today."

I smiled at her and then looked away. Well, at least one of us was better now. It made me laugh to myself, in spite of how bad I felt. It also was a classic demonstration of the helplessness people feel when they are around someone who has cancer. The desire to have a way to make things better, even if only for a second, and in a very trivial way, must be overwhelming. I decided it was worth it for my insurance to pay for this. This nurse would have to get through the rest of her day dealing with people more or less like me. She would be providing treatment that, in many cases, perhaps gave but a tiny bit of respite in that never-ending downward spiral. At the very least, she would be aware of how miserable it made her patients feel physically. She deserved that tiny moment of reinforcement, checking my oxygen level. Good for her.

As I sat there with the chemo coursing through my veins, I experienced a momentary sensation of something strange happening to my body. I'd had similar sensations before, but not with every chemo treatment. When it happens, I can feel a sort of heat coming up my throat, which is weird, because the chemo is being given through an IV inserted into my PowerPort, which has a catheter that is inserted into my superior vena cava. A chemical-tasting heat pours up my throat and then swishes and bounces around in my mouth. My mind drifted to the Indiana Jones movie *Raiders of the Lost Ark*. At the very end, when Indiana and Marion are tied to the pole in the cave and their German captor decides to open the ark, all the spirits within are released. You see them swirling and wafting in every direction throughout the cave.

During these episodes, it seems that when I open my mouth, surely, I will see those spirits, in miniature form, exiting through my lips and bouncing around the room. I take a quick peek downward, but there is nothing there. I look around to be sure nobody is watching, partly to be sure nobody thinks I'm crazy and partly to see if they notice anything weird emanating from my cubicle. Everything looks like business as usual. I am compelled to keep my mouth open a crack. It just seems to make more sense to release this foul-smelling and foul-feeling sensation into the air. Surely, if it is trapped in my mouth, it will do some dastardly things to me.

That day, in addition to the spirits rushing around in my mouth, I could feel them seeping through every part of my body. My head, which had already been traumatized by a morning of crying and the pressure I'd had to exert to keep that little gate closed, feels as though it is about to explode. I feel pressure from the inside and on the outside. My legs have begun to feel as if they are on fire, as though millions of tiny particles of electricity are jumping and wiggling through them, mostly in my thighs. My gut feels the pressure too. It hurts and just plain feels like there is too much in there. I try to ignore this. One of the symptoms that was probably the most pronounced in the month or so before I found out I had cancer was the bloated feeling. I tell myself it is the chemo. I don't even want to consider that the cancer is now at the same point as it was when I started.

A couple months ago, my friend Lisa made me a graph of my CA-125 numbers. As I studied the almost perfectly inverted bell-shaped curve, it slowly dawned on me what it represented. I began to cry. I think it took me a week to quit crying, and during that time, I couldn't write. I lived on the verge of tears every waking moment. The graph showed the number two months after my diagnosis was virtually the same as my number when Lisa made the graph, in October 2012. That meant I had spent over two years traveling the cancer journey, only to end up pretty much where I had started. Now *that* was depressing. The visual image of the graph made it impossible to deny the facts.

When I am confronted with the frailty of my life I believe I've earned the right to weep. Yes, the light is blinding, but I have no doubts about what is happening to me. These moments of intense sadness show me in no uncertain terms where I am. Yet, they give me such clarity. The sadness becomes overwhelming, yet I can go from there into a moment with someone special and experience the joy and pleasure they bring, only it is multiplied exponentially. I cling fiercely to these moments, be they high or low. They let me know that I am still alive, that life still means much to me, and that weeping is a sign of living intensely.

In his book, *Tragic Sense of Life*, Miguel De Unamuno has much to say about weeping. Indeed, this book was written exactly one hundred years ago. How ironic that it speaks so plainly to my soul today.

"A pedant who beheld Solon weeping for the death of a son said to him, 'Why do you weep thus, if weeping avails nothing?' And the sage answered him, 'Precisely for that reason—because it does not avail.' It is manifest that weeping avails something, even if only the alleviation of distress; but the deep sense of Solon's reply to the impertinent questioner is plainly seen. And I am convinced that we should solve many things if we all went out in the streets and uncovered our griefs, which perhaps would prove to be but one sole common grief, and joined together in beweeping them and crying aloud to the heavens and calling upon God. And this, even though God should hear us not; but He would hear us. ... It is not enough to cure the plague; we must learn to weep for it. Yes, we must learn to weep!"

For those who find it unbearable to allow someone to weep, take comfort, weeping has availed me much. The act of not weeping does not equate with happiness. I would rather weep than sit stone-faced with my soul in a fog. For those who believe that weeping equates with depression, I want to reassure you that it is not so. Weeping has allowed me the opportunity to see my life and be grateful for all the wondrous things I have had the good fortune to experience. In turn, it has allowed me to see the depths to which I have plunged as a part of that process. Weeping has kept bitterness from taking root. When I wept with a friend, I was not alone.

I woke up in the chemo chair to the sound of the beeping that signaled my chemo bag was empty. Someone came over, readjusted the dispensing mechanism, and went away. I heard her telling my nurse that there was still a little bit left. I waited impatiently to wrap this session up. I wanted to get out of there.

As I drove home, I cried almost the entire trip. Images kept flashing through my mind. I saw our backyard from the past weekend, when we had held our annual pig roast. I knew that was likely the last pig roast I would attend. I wept to think about the friends I might have seen there, only five days ago, for the last time. I wept that I would never be getting all my little vases out again and filling them with flowers to decorate the tables, so our friends could enjoy them as they visited each other and caught up on the previous year. Even though my sister, Joan, had done virtually all the work the last two years, I did what I could. I wept that my granddaughter had been sick this year and she and her mother hadn't been able to come. At almost fifteen months, Molly would have had a blast.

Bill and I had planned to take a trip to Utah in the spring to visit some national parks. Now I wept to think I might not be here long enough to go. It didn't matter what came into my mind. It all made me weep. It was like finding out all over again that I had cancer. I was back at the beginning again, with that heightened sense of awareness of everything.

I managed to get home, munching on grapes to keep myself awake and reasonably focused. I couldn't get in the house soon enough. After changing into comfortable clothing, I settled into my chair and fell asleep. I awoke a couple hours later, my eyes burning and scratching, my body still feeling trashed. I struggled to keep myself from crying. I didn't think my eyes could tolerate any more. I stayed in the chair until Bill called me, telling me he'd be about an hour late getting home from West Virginia. After he came home, we just sat in front of the TV.

"If you don't mind, I don't want to talk anymore about this tonight. My eyes can't take any more crying." I just didn't have the energy. "I'm supposed to have lunch with Betty and Lisa tomorrow. I already sent them an e-mail about today's appointment. I didn't think it was fair for them to get all that by surprise over lunch. They both said they'd still like to get together. I'll see how I feel tomorrow. I might still cancel."

Bill gave me a tip of the head to say that he heard and understood. Neither of us even had the energy for unnecessary words. I decided not to send an update around to family and friends. How could I? I'd wait until after I met with the doctor. I couldn't even think about telling people.

We both crashed early. I was tired but unable to rest. Images of people's faces and scenes of the small joys of living bounced off of each other, skittering through my mind. These were interspersed with flickers of sadness: Bill coming home from work to spend the evening alone, family Christmases without me, flowers blooming happily in the spring without me to inspect them or smile down upon them. I had no way to turn it off. Even the sleeping pill I took every night seemed somehow impotent. Sleep would be slow in coming this night.

Chapter Eleven

———•———

DOING WHAT I CAN

In my search for some way to get rid of my cancer, I had begun exploring multiple perspectives. As a person who had always believed in taking charge of life, I struggled with acknowledging I had no control over the cancer that was roaming around in my body. I read about chakras, Reiki, power animals, and healing light. I attended a natural chi movement class and Reiki classes, and I had acupuncture done. I gave up many processed foods, started buying organic food when I could, and bought bath and body products that were free of potentially cancer-causing agents. I used guided imagery, did relaxation exercises, and attended a cancer hypnosis seminar. I even took supplements for a while. All these things made me feel like I at least had some control over what was happening to me. Did they make a difference? Who knows. At least I *felt* like I had some impact on the cancer.

As I closed in on my first year with cancer, I seemed to be living in that legendary land of limbo. While I didn't achieve the sought-after designation of "cancer-free," I was so close I could feel it. For a little over a year my CA-125 bounced around just above the number I longed to hear, before it started its gradual climb back into triple, then quadruple digits. I never achieved the normal feeling that lingered just out of my reach. I walked on another plane, parallel to the one where the rest of the world resided.

Despite all of this, I forced myself to participate in that world. I visited it when I could. Although I had been forced to give up the activities I loved so much, I clung to whatever tiny piece still held some meaning. It wasn't much, and I felt far from contented, but it was what I could do. Spaced throughout my days from February 25, 2010 to present (or at least the end of this book) were some events that might be considered highlights by people living life in some normal fashion. Vacations and parties always have a little more emphasis than the day-to-day living we do in whatever version of the nine-to-five, Monday-through-Friday lifestyle most ascribe to. So, I've saved them up here, thinking by their sheer number they perhaps lend more authenticity to my lonely world. I want to show that I made every effort to make my life as normal as possible.

May Party

Browsing through Half Price Books one day, I came upon a book about Beltane. Beltane literally means "bright fire" and refers to bonfires lit during the season of May Day celebrations, a time to acknowledge the return of growth and the end of decline within the cycle of life. I found the history fascinating, and it appealed to my pagan sense of spirituality. In February 2011, I still had hopes of getting below that magic number of 35. Ticking off the numbers in my brain, I calculated what I thought was a reasonable amount of time to reach my goal. I decided May 2011 would be a wonderful time to celebrate. A May party was just the ticket. In addition, it took on the theme of the kind of party Bill and I had discussed for my funeral party. It celebrated flowers as renewal of life at the time of year when they did just that.

I loved having parties. I loved using all my beautiful dishes, getting out my colorful tablecloths, arranging flowers in my tiny vases. I loved making good food. This would be a great time to do all of this—in a small way. Yes, we had been having an annual pig roast for about twenty years, but it was a much bigger event, with generally about one hundred attendees. I wasn't ready for that. Maybe I could do a May party—something small, with just women. Only women would appreciate the significance of Beltane. I invited about sixty women, knowing that not all of them would come. I did everything in small stages, as I was unable to work for long periods.

I decided to have the party on my front porch, unless I received many affirmative responses to my invitations. If that happened, I would rent round tables and put them in the front yard. Our porch ran the full length of our house, with a room-sized section at one end measuring 16' × 20'. I could fit three card tables at the narrower end (8' × 20') and at least four in the larger section. I could squeeze in one or two more if I had to, including tables for food and drinks. I'd get it figured out. I knew Bill would do all the physical labor of setting up tables and carrying things.

I bought several small organic pork loins, planning half to be seasoned with five-spice and the other half with an island seasoning. In addition, I had salmon. Bill actually prepared these dishes. I made a couple side dishes and appetizers, as well as a May Day cake from a recipe I found in a Beltane book. Each person who came was to bring a dish designed around flowers—that is, decorated with flowers or made to look like a flower. In addition, each person was to bring a single annual flower plant, which we would trade. I used a recipe from my Beltane book to make a May wine, since I was unable to purchase it already made in any of the area liquor stores. This simply involved putting fresh strawberries into bottles of Riesling wine.

Within a few days of the party, I had only gotten affirmative responses from about twelve invitees. This would be easy to do on my front porch. However, by that Saturday morning, I knew I would be having thirty women. Yikes! I scrambled around to borrow tables and chairs from friends. Fortunately, I was able to get enough of each and squeeze them all onto my porch. My sister Joan and my friend Jackie came early to help.

It was a wonderful evening, with more than enough food. All of the women who attended outdid themselves, bringing their best dishes. Some had clearly worked hard to incorporate the flower theme, while others felt more challenged. We had lots of fun. Everyone voted on the best flower dish, and my sister Janice won by a landslide. She had created a simple but very clever dish, pan frying baby red potatoes and then smashing one end so they would stand, and putting a chive flower into the top of each one—simple, but very cute. The dish looked like little families of rock people with their best bonnets on, out for a Sunday stroll.

My friend Elaine brought me a few sprigs of hawthorn, which in Irish lore is purported to have magical qualities. It was said to protect homes from evil. It was put into bonfires as an act of purification and protection. While I didn't follow the ancient ceremonies to the letter of the law, I honored the spirit of the celebration. Bill built a nice fire before he left so that we could have the ceremonial May wine toast.

Shortly after twilight, we all walked to the backyard, and everyone had a small glass of the May wine. I read the toast with a full spirit, feeling the goodwill and friendship of my friends and family. All present would benefit from this. A positive spiritual connection is a powerful thing.

Blessing for May Wine
Blessings be upon this wine, which is the essence of
the secret of transformation. The blood of life flows
again back into Nature and summer approaches
with the promise of fullness. May all who drink this
wine be filled to the brim with all that is good in life.

As soon as I finished reading this, I threw the sprigs of hawthorn into the fire. We all held up our glasses, wished each other well, and drank the small sip of May wine. I felt giddy with the positive energy. We all stood around the fire and chatted for several minutes. Gradually, everyone made her way back to the front porch and the party began to break up. Several friends stayed to help put things away and clean up. They just took charge, and in no time, the work was done.

While I knew there was nothing magical about the fire, the hawthorn, or the May wine, there is something magical about the gathering of friends of the same spirit. There is a feeling of goodness that can't be produced any other way. This is what I think of as praying. Surely the strength of the prayers made that night had as much power as the traditional recitation of verse memorized in the young life of someone raised in a more structured religious setting.

Visiting Longwood Gardens

While I love flowers, and have spent innumerable hours digging, pulling, planting, and rearranging in my own gardens, I have never mastered the art of landscaping. I just never could figure out what goes where. I understood considerations for sun/shade, dry/moist soil, acidic levels of soil, etc. I recognized the qualities of texture, growing habit, height, color, and blooming time. I was just never good at putting everything together into an overall plan for a particular plot of land.

As a result, all my gardens would be classified as informal. When I saw a plant I liked, I bought it and planted it where I thought it might look best. Generally, this resulted in frequent rearrangement. This random arrangement was a good reflection of my personality. I marveled at gardens that seemed to be so precise, with everything in just the right place. Longwood Gardens was just such a place, on a large scale. I wanted to see it. I had heard stories about it and had looked at photographs, and now I wanted to see the real thing. Something built and maintained purely for its beauty has to be something special.

After numerous e-mail exchanges with my sister-in-law Mary Ann, my cousin Kathy and I made plans for a four-day visit. We would stay with Mary Ann and my brother Jerome, who lived in Lawrenceville, New Jersey. Mary Ann belonged to the Grounds for Sculpture near her home, so we included that in our plans.

It was a wonderful adventure. Kathy and I took turns driving, and we never seemed to run out of things to talk about. We felt comfortable and relaxed with Jerome and Mary Ann, and they made us feel at home. The gardens surpassed my expectations. It was a warm summer day, and the sun shone brightly, sharpening the colors of the flowers. The pathways were lined with lengthy stretches of flowers. The blooms were color coordinated and arranged for maximum impact of size, shape, and texture. How do they do that? Fortunately for me, since I needed frequent periods of rest, there were park benches interspersed with the flowers. I had purchased a long skirt and a big, floppy hat to keep the sun off my skin. Even here, wandering amid all this beauty, I couldn't get away from the cancer. Traveling with the beast, I had to make frequent use of the bathrooms. Luckily, these were also generously apportioned.

The trip was a success. A tiny little spot in my soul filled up. I had seen Longwood Gardens, spent the day in good company, and had a delightful lunch. What more could a person want? The next day at the sculpture gardens was equally delightful. While I had been anticipating natural sculptures, I wasn't disappointed by the sculptures of people doing all sorts of things, some more suited to adults than the general population. We laughed and inserted ourselves within the scenes, memorializing ourselves forever with photos of us doing things we would never do in real life. My favorite was the circle of naked people doing what looked like ring-around-the-rosy on the hillside. It reminded me of a scene from a Beltane fertility celebration. No, I didn't strip, but I stood among that group of not-quite-anatomically-correct figures! They were quite large compared to me; still, I was one with them in spirit.

The Pig Roast

When we moved to our present location in 1988, Bill and I were immediately in love with not only our log home but the land surrounding it as well. Marc and Pat had one adventure after another there. We moved into the house in April 1988, shortly before Marc's fifth birthday, when Patrick was just over one and one-half years old. It was the perfect spot. Situated on just over a half acre of land, there was a nice distance between us and the homes on either side of us, with a wooded area behind as far as the eye could see. We had pleasant neighbors, and one of our favorite activities in those early years was to sit around a fire on a summer evening, enjoying a few beers and pleasant company. One neighbor had a daughter Marc's age and a son Patrick's age, so they became fast friends. While we "old folks" sat around the fire having a few beers and eating hot dogs blackened on the tip of a sapling freshly cut for that purpose, or enjoying a s'more, the kids spent hours playing nighttime outdoor games. Their gleeful shouts echoed into the darkness, and we only saw them when they came for a snack, or to catch their breath.

On any given weekend, it was not uncommon for us and our neighbors on one or both sides of us to spend two entire days working outside in our yards. On some of these occasions, we would loosely put together plans for a cookout at the end of the day. Each family would contribute so that none was overburdened. As the day began to fade, we would speed up our work as we ran out of energy and anticipated the good meal that awaited us. Then we would all shower, and arrive at the same time at one of our houses, food in hand. Our meal together would be spent discussing our various yard projects and their current levels of completion, along with long-term dreams for our yards.

It was likely on one such neighborly occasion with Mike and Icel that the idea of a pig roast first came up. They were our neighbors to our right, and we were all equally infatuated with the idea. Discussion went on at some length, and we left not being sure how serious each of us was. At the end of that third year, we found ourselves planning the first of what would become an annual event. It was a glorious affair, considering it was planned and executed by people who had no idea what they were doing. One way or another, the pig was done, and there was lots of good food, plenty of beer, and scores of wonderful desserts. Most people were gone by around 10:00 p.m., but there was a crew that lingered into the wee hours of the morning. Not bad for our first time out.

There couldn't have been two better people with whom to plan such a large event. We all worked hard and shared in not only the expense but also all the work that went along with the event. Each year thereafter, we modified our strategies, and small improvements here and there made the whole thing easier to plan and execute. We even enjoyed the cleanup, which was generally done sometime the next day. The fact that I got pleasure out of cleaning up was quite a testament to the success of this event.

Although the date varied, it was held mostly toward the fall, so pumpkin carving was a natural activity. With Pumpkin Masters carving tools, the "kids," young and old, enjoyed producing fun faces from the patterns provided, or striking out on their own to deliver devilish designs. As soon as it was dark, we would line up all the pumpkins on the edge of the deck, put tea lights inside them, and light them up. All the guests would file past to inspect the clever creations, while a steady stream of oohs and aahs mixed with gay laughter.

In the earlier years, for the younger kids my sister Joan provided a piñata filled with toys and candy. One year she filled it with Beanie Babies, much to the dismay of my friend Sandy. Sandy is a collector of all things collectible, and she couldn't bear to see the popular Beanie Babies being knocked to the ground and strewn about, only to be rescued by the grubby little hands of the excited kids.

We had something for everyone; volleyball, horseshoes and croquet kept the big kids happy. Regardless of age, everyone was happy to spend an inordinate amount of time just sitting around eating and visiting with each other. The first year we had to deal with all-day rain, it left us all the wiser. We were completely unprepared, and the day ended up being split between our two houses. Things happened so fast that there wasn't even time to worry about it. We don't have a large house, so it was jammed to the smallest nooks and crannies with everyone inside. Mike and Icel, much neater people than Bill and I, had a clean garage, and they set up tables and chairs there. By 10:00 p.m., the rain had stopped, so we visited each other's food tables, and it was like a whole new event. After that, if there was a hint we might have rain, we set up tents. The best way to keep the rain away, we found, was to be prepared for it.

As the summer of 2010 drew to a close, I was just recovering from my big surgery. My sister Joan had been talking since earlier in the summer about having the pig roast. She knew how I felt about this event, and she wanted to make it possible for us to have it, regardless of my cancer. She promised to come to my house and do all the work, both in preparation and for cleanup, and just let me visit with my friends. While this was appealing to me, I just didn't have the energy even to think about the possibility. It was the only year we have missed having a pig roast since 1991.

At the end of summer 2011, Joan began once more talking about our pig roast. She told me she would come to our house Friday and do all the preparation—and do it however I wanted it done. We laughed about this because we had differing ideas about having parties. She has had an annual picnic celebrating the Fourth of July at her home for many years. Being much more practical than I, she has purchased things like warming trays for her food. I liked to use my pretty dishes. One year, she headed out my back door with the potato salad in a big aluminum bowl. I caught her just in time. I would have no aluminum bowls on *my* food tables! She rolled her eyes, brought the food back in, and transferred it to my huge pottery bowl with blue lines around the rim and flowers on the bottom. I had a matching smaller bowl, and a huge platter I used for the pork and stuffing. These were clearance purchases from my favorite store—well, one of them: Marshalls or TJ Maxx.

Joan and I met for lunch and planned everything—who would do what and when. I was not allowed to add anything to the list unless I also added the person who would perform that task. This required delegating, and delegating requires organization. You have to know what needs to be done before you can ask someone to do it for you. Of course, I knew everything that needed to be done; I'd been doing it for twenty years. But breaking the setup down into individual tasks that someone else could do was another matter. Reality has a way of making its demands. I was forced to learn to delegate.

The list I made with Joan's help made all the difference. She showed up that Friday with her daughter, Cassie, and we got to work. A group of lady friends came over that evening and helped fill the vases; cut up bread, celery, and onions for stuffing; put candy in dishes; etc. When I was in charge of a Little League concession stand, my motto had been, "If everyone does a little bit, nobody has to do a lot." It was definitely true in this case. I was appreciative of my friends' willingness to jump in and help, all without being asked. Times like this are when you learn what kind of friends you have. They all laughed and chatted as they worked, creating a wonderful atmosphere.

While I relished the feeling of friendship and camaraderie, I still felt sadness because I was not able to do these things myself. It wasn't just the visiting with friends that made the pig roast such a special event; it was also enjoying the work of putting it together. It took constant reminders to myself for me to stay focused on the good feelings of friends gathered together, and to keep from feeling sad that I couldn't do it myself. Those feelings hung just out of sight, and it would take only a quick peek to bring them front and center. I knew that once that happened, it would take more than a small amount of effort to tuck them away again. So I kept them safely out of my emotional field of vision.

Bill worked nonstop on his part of the pig roast. This included cutting the grass, cleaning up the yard, bringing all the pop and coolers up from the garage, getting the beer and ice, setting up the tents, tables, and chairs (to my specifications, of course), stuffing and cooking the pig, plating the pig and stuffing when the time came, etc.—just a few "small" tasks! He added a few of my jobs without batting an eye. We had learned not to pay any attention to how tired we were—at least not until the middle of the next day.

While there was always enough food to feed everyone all over again, there were a few things that I felt a need to supply myself. I always made six pies: blueberry, black raspberry, cherry, peach, apple, and pumpkin. These I did in stages that year, making the dough Thursday evening and then the actual pies Friday. My niece Cassie helped me with the pies. After years of summer visits with her cousins, during which baking was a major activity, she was happy to put her skills to work. She put together some beautiful pies. In addition to the pies, I always made potato salad and a huge pot of fresh green and yellow beans. That year Joan made the potato salad, and her husband, Albert, was kind enough to pick the beans from their garden and have them in a pot, ready to cook, when he arrived. You can't get much fresher and faster than that!

The pig roast went off without a hitch, thanks to Joan. She never stopped, and any time she saw me doing something, I got yelled at and was told to sit down. Still, I managed to sneak a few small jobs under the radar. The weather cooperated, and we had a beautiful early-fall day, with the usual crowd. I took extra pain pills that day, and by the evening, I was completely played out, but it was all worth it. As a result of the chemotherapy treatments I was receiving at the time, I was having severe joint/bone pain. I had trouble getting up the steps and into the house to go to the bathroom, but seeing so many friends and family members together made it all worthwhile.

There was a small, special group of people who took it upon themselves to clean up as the day went on. By the time everyone left, there was very little left to be done. Joan came back the next day, but there was little for her to do. Bill already had the tables and chairs collected and stacked, the tablecloths started in the washing machine, and the yard cleaned up. I spent the day relaxing and napping. What a wonderful thing it is, to have people who care so much about you that they make it possible for you to maintain such a huge tradition, when so much work is involved. Just thinking about it fills me with a sense of gratitude that goes a long way toward replacing the sense of fulfillment I would have gotten doing all the work myself.

As we prepared in the same way for the pig roast this past year (2012), I was ambivalent. In my last appointment at the gynecology/oncology office, my CA-125 was 954, and my doctor had decided to switch to a different chemo. My next appointment would be the week after the pig roast, and I had a bad feeling that I would not receive good news. As the day of the pig roast approached, I pushed myself to use the mindfulness concepts I had learned from Dr. Stollings. Not only did I feel sad that I could not get things ready on my own for the pig roast, but I also kept having the idea that this would likely be my last pig roast. Fortunately, there was enough stimulation that day to keep me busy. It seemed like a larger-than-usual crowd.

After raining off and on all morning, the weather cleared and we had a beautiful afternoon. Although I had ordered the usual 150-pound pig, this year's honoree weighed in at 182 pounds! For some reason, the meat was exceptionally succulent, the dishes were more tasty, everything looked more colorful, and the sun shone brighter. It was a busy day. I moved from one person or group to another, not finishing any of my visits. While I wanted to spend more time with each person, I was happy I had the chance to see and speak with the next one. There was very little time to think about the idea that this might be my last pig roast. There would be plenty of time later for that.

Christmas at Our House

As a child, Christmas with my family was always chaotic. When we were kids, we rarely had visitors over the Christmas holidays, but with just the eleven of us, it was enough for a party atmosphere. Since my birthday is the day before Christmas, perhaps that ramped it up a bit for me personally. It was always exciting, nevertheless. We never went without the necessities, but we didn't have much extra either. That didn't seem to matter. It was the feeling of excitement that I loved.

As we grew up and went our separate ways, we developed the tradition of always celebrating the Bentley Christmas the Saturday after; that way there were no conflicts with in-laws and such. As the families expanded, if everyone attended, there could be upward of thirty-five people present. We never did anything formal; rather, it was every man for himself. Food was set out, and you grabbed a plate and found a spot to sit, even if it was only on the steps.

After my mother sold her house and moved into a one-bedroom apartment, we had to design a whole new program. We settled into a new routine of taking turns hosting Christmas, still on the Saturday after. I loved hosting Christmas. I never seemed to have enough holiday goodies, shopping until the very last moment to add more treats to the menu. I would have happily hosted Christmas every year at our house. But I controlled myself, waiting to see if someone else would offer first. If a few years had gone by since my last turn, I would jump in. Or I would put the word out that I could be considered a backup, in case nobody else was interested in hosting or able to host Christmas that year.

The Christmas of 2011 was just such a year. As time closed in on that magical moment, nobody had volunteered. My last turn had been Christmas of 2009, the one before I found out I had cancer, so I thought it unlikely I would have another turn so soon. I was running low on energy and dealing with the abdominal pain, so I wasn't sure I was up to the task. However, I didn't hesitate to take on the job. As I planned and got things ready, I could feel the old Christmas excitement returning.

We have a relatively small home, but I never think about that when planning a family get-together. All rooms are open, and we have space in a semi-finished basement for game playing and just hanging out. In 2009, the weather was actually balmy, and several people congregated on the front porch, enjoying the unseasonable warmth. One way or another, people find a spot. Christmas with the Bentleys is not for the faint of heart. If you're not used to it, you can easily become over-stimulated, and perhaps uncomfortable. Over the years, I just learned to tune out what I considered, at any given moment, to be extraneous. My filters had become fine-tuned; there was always a thin line between what was labeled extraneous and what might actually be important. My filters steered me toward more pleasant conversations. I couldn't be bothered with petty grievances at a time like Christmas.

So, as Christmas 2011 approached, I looked forward to another— perhaps my last—Christmas with my siblings, et al. It was a pleasant day, with plenty to eat, more than enough presents to be opened and fun times all the way around. Around the major holidays, our local drugstore sells chocolate-covered red raspberries and strawberries, some of my favorite treats. I always buy two boxes of each. At $20.95 per box, they make up a significant portion of my candy budget. I always supported my nieces when they sold candy as a school fundraiser, and I bought scads more chocolate on multiple occasions when shopping at Marshalls and TJ Maxx throughout the holidays. There was never a shortage of chocolate when the holidays were held at my house. In addition, there were multiple other snacks and appetizers.

The host always supplied the ham and drinks, while other guests filled in around the edges. Bill and I decided to add a salmon dish in 2011, and it was well received. Suffice it to say that after everyone has eaten his or her fill at a Bentley Christmas, there is still enough food to go around a few more times. Desserts are in a class of their own. Generally, more than one person signs up to bring dessert, while others just "happen to have" an extra pie, cake, or plate of cookies lying around. It is a time of plenty, for sure, and a time of good cheer, when going overboard is more socially acceptable than at any other time of year.

As the candy, snack, food, and dessert platters overflowed, so did my heart. I wished I had enough money to buy lots of gifts for everyone. Through the years, Bill just learned to turn a blind eye toward my extravagances. As it got closer to Christmas, I would tell him that I thought we should get some particular gift for one of the kids. That meant we had to get something else for all the others, because it was important to keep everything even. Not that any of them ever gave any indication they paid any attention to this sort of thing; if I made any comment about it, they would just roll their eyes telling me they weren't worried about that. I knew they weren't, and I wasn't really worried either. Still, it was important to me. Regardless of the source of my sensitivity to this issue, I wanted to be sure my kids (including Nikki and Carrie) got equal treatment.

Although I bought lots and lots of gifts each Christmas, it was never about material things. It has always been about the feelings. It is the specialness of the time that sets it apart from the rest of the year. It is common to hear people say we should hold Christmas in our hearts throughout the whole year. While this is true, I see it as a time to take stock, to honor those people and relationships that have some extra significance. The gifts are a way to pay homage. As the wise men brought their best offerings to mark the birth of Jesus, we can give of our best to mark those who are important to us. This is what fills my spirit at Christmastime.

The Christmas of 2011 seemed to be even bigger than usual just because of the thought that it might very well be my last. Perhaps these family traditions are the hardest to let go of. My mother's last Christmas was 2006. It was hard to deal with the holidays of 2007 without her. Regardless of her role in the family gatherings, when she was not there to fill it anymore, the whole configuration changed. I can't picture the events going on without me. How will the configuration change once I'm gone? I can only hope there will be some fun stories to be told, and a few laughs shared at my expense.

A Quick Trip to Florida

Bill never could plan anything in a small way. Once, when the vinyl flooring in our kitchen was in desperate need of replacement, I told Bill I'd go scout out the remnants at our local floor covering store, to find a cheap substitute. I didn't care how cheap it was, just so long as we got *something*. After I had narrowed the choices down, I took Bill to show him my selections. He looked at them briefly and then said, "I'm not buying some cheap piece of flooring like this. If we're getting a new floor, we might as well get a good one." And we did. And he laid it himself, following the instructions to the letter of the law. Twelve years later, it is as good as new.

When he began talking about taking a trip to Florida in the spring of 2012, he did the same thing. Although I hated to fly, I knew that if we were going to take a quick trip, there was no other way to get there. So we selected our six days, and Bill bought the airline tickets. Then he set about the task of planning our activities. He wanted to be sure we had fun. That was his whole plan—for me to have fun. After thirty-four years of marriage, Bill knew what I enjoyed. He took deep pleasure in finding just the right gift for me, whether for my birthday or Christmas. While I can't give him a 100 percent success rate, he has definitely scored in the high nineties. I could always tell he had been paying attention throughout the year, gathering possibilities, so that when the time came, he could have the pleasure of seeing me excited, if not overwhelmed, by his thoughtful selection.

Bill spent many evenings exploring the Internet to see what fun things might be available for us on this trip. We solidified plans to stay with my brother Judson, and his wife, Peggy. They were always willing to accommodate visitors from the north. We would rent a car from the airport and be able to come and go on our own. In the past, we generally would spend any good weather days at the beach. Since

I wasn't allowed to be in the sun, we would no longer have those lazy afternoons where we read, dozed, and played in the water, or walked the beach looking for shells. We kept the plans loose but had in mind a visit to Butterfly World. Bill had scoped this out and knew it was something I would take great pleasure in exploring.

Our plane arrived at the Miami airport at 12:30 a.m. By the time we arrived at Judson and Peggy's house in our rental car, it was about 2:00 a.m. They had left the door unlocked for us, and we quietly settled into the guest bedroom and fell quickly asleep. By the time I got up, they had already left for work, and Bill had walked to a local grocery store to get our breakfast supplies.

I wanted this to be a fun, relaxing time, but I was a little nervous. I had talked with Dr. Stollings the week before, explaining that it would be hard for me to focus on having fun without getting caught up in mourning the loss of my old fun-in-the-sun vacations. I would give it my best shot.

The visit to Butterfly World was amazing. I have always been fascinated by butterflies. For about three summers in a row, I had put parsley in the planters on our deck. I was delighted to have attracted the swallowtail butterfly caterpillar to feed upon those curly green leaves. I took many photos, and I marveled at how well they could clean off an entire stem of parsley, leaving little green balls of parsley poop behind in the soil. I was also amazed at how big they became through the process. More recently, I had planted milkweed at the back of our yard, for the monarch butterflies. The first year, I was rewarded by being able to watch a caterpillar move to the chrysalis stage. The chrysalis looked like a beautiful piece of jade dotted with flecks of gold. What a lovely pendant it would have made. This eventually turned brown as it moved to its last stage of development, the monarch butterfly. Mother nature at her best!

As we entered the first room full of butterflies, we looked around in amazement. It took a minute to adjust to the constant motion. There was a group of young girls around age six, perhaps on a school outing. As they entered the room Bill and I were in, one of them started shrieking. Somehow, she seemed terrified. I found myself wondering if she had some sort of inner ear problem or a balance issue. That would have been a very unpleasant experience. The motion was constant, and it did indeed take a moment of adjustment.

I never knew how many different varieties of butterflies there actually are. They come in all shapes, sizes, and colors, measuring anywhere from an inch to about four inches, and in every color combination. There were tiny moths of earthen browns and tans, as well as exotic large-winged butterflies of neon blues and greens. My favorite butterfly was the piano key butterfly. It came in unlimited combinations of reddish-orange and black and white, and it did indeed look like the keys of a piano. No two looked alike. We spent the afternoon there. Once again, I had to take several breaks on the plentiful supply of park benches.

We visited the room with the lories and lorikeets, where we purchased a cup of nectar for $1.00. I no sooner had the nectar cupped in my hands than about six of the brightly colored, parrot-like, six- to fifteen-inch birds swarmed me. One tried unsuccessfully to settle on my big, floppy-brimmed hat. There were two that held the front positions, never willing to relinquish their spots to the less assertive of the bunch. These birds have special tongues with brush tips that are made to soak up nectar. When they had licked every last drop of the nectar, my blouse was spattered with tiny peach-colored dots. How many cups of nectar do they go through in a day? What pigs! I guess they never get enough!

The next day, we decided that even though we couldn't sit on the beach, we could eat at one of our favorite beachside luncheon spots. Unfortunately we forgot we were just in time for spring break. When we got to within a mile of the beach, there was bumper-to-bumper traffic, and what normally took about five minutes to travel took forty-five minutes. At the same time, I began to have flashes of past trips to Fort Lauderdale Beach. I kept my face diverted to the passenger-side window, not wanting to dampen our plans to have a pleasant afternoon. How do you let something like this go? Our family vacations had tended to alternate between the mountains and the ocean. Each seemed to have an equal amount of power, and I always came home feeling regenerated and renewed.

After the kids were grown, and it was just Bill and me, or even just me, there was an even greater sense of peace. Gone were the childhood distractions of wave-hopping with the boys, building drip castles in the sand, and traipsing the boardwalk in search of some novel way to spend money. Our vacation destinations became places to forget about self-importance along with the minor but plentiful stresses of everyday life.

I was but a tiny piece of stone, perhaps broken from a huge rock formation jutting into the sky, or a drop of water in the ocean. Although insignificant by size, these tiny specimens were part of the whole and, therefore, contained the whole within them. Their life coursed through my veins. I didn't have to worry about what important things I thought I had to do, or what significance I thought I had in the overall scheme of things. When I sat on the beach, drowsing in the heat and smelling the ocean on the breeze, I blended into the sand and sun. I could let myself drift away, the salty odor tingling in my nose, while my soul flitted around like a seagull scavenging from tourists like myself. All my senses seemed to blend together; the smells, sounds, feelings, and sights of the beach were in union, and I was one with them.

As we crawled toward the shopping area that day in Florida, the sense of loss was unbearable to me. I wept for that peace I would never feel again, the delight in the purest feelings of relaxation that were gone forever. Now I was an observer on the sidelines. Yes, as Alfred, Lord Tennyson said,

> 'Tis better to have loved and lost
> Than never to have loved at all.

I was lucky to have had the pleasure of loving all things beach, and had I known this would one day be denied me, I would happily have chosen to lose it rather than never experience it. Yet this sense of loss was profound; it engulfed me. I felt weak with sorrow.

I turned in time to see our favorite restaurant pass on our left, while the beach stretched before and aft on the right. With no place within walking distance to park, we turned left, and left again, heading back to my brother's house. Once we were out of the backed-up traffic, we stopped at a chain restaurant for lunch. With the chemo I was receiving at the time, I had little ability to taste, so it didn't really matter what I ate.

We spent the rest of our visit going out to eat with Judson and Peggy, and it was their company more than the food that was so enjoyable. We went to one of our favorites, Big Daddy's, and I tried to enjoy the food from memory rather than actual taste. I got up late, napped every day, and sat on the patio in the shade, reading "beach books." I made every effort to maintain the spirit of the visit, even if I couldn't participate in the old activities. As with other activities I was no longer able to do in the manner I had become accustomed to, I did what part I was able, and I knew I was filling my days with what I could, and getting as much pleasure as I could from them. They were scraps of my former life, yet they were all I had, and I had to make the best of them. A quick trip to Florida on which I would have no fun in the sun, eat food I couldn't taste, and spend more time in a day resting than being active was the best I could do. I would have to make it be enough.

Enjoying the Fall Foliage

Nothing touts the glory of nature like colored leaves in the fall. The combinations are endless, and each one creates a segment of beauty all by itself. Clusters of trees painted a deep gold next to a grove of pine trees is a classic color combo. Driving in the crease between hillsides and taking in the multicolored carpeting spread about can be breathtaking. I am partial to the short stuff—stands of small trees, with shrubs and bushes running along the edge of a road or at the top of a small hill. Therein I see every fall color represented. Rich orange-reds, bright yellows, and lemon yellow, still tinged with lime green. Here it is easy to see the details, the outlines of the trees, and the darkness of the trunks displayed against the bright colors of autumn.

The day after my appointment on September 26, 2012 when I found out my CA-125 had risen to 1,664, Bill suggested we take a weekend in October to get away and enjoy the fall foliage. We had momentarily "fallen asleep at the wheel," but with the knowledge of this number, we were jerked back awake, grimly reminded that I had cancer, and that it was gaining on me. In the summer, we had begun discussing plans to go to Utah in the spring for a shared journey through Arches and Canyonlands National Parks. Knowing my cancer was taking a turn for the worse, although we didn't verbalize it, we both wondered if I would be around long enough to make that trip happen. It wasn't encouraging. Bill suggested we take a trip soon, as it was supposed to be a banner year for leaf color. All he needed was the nod from me, and he was perusing the Internet once again, looking for just the right place.

We settled on the Homestead in Hot Springs, Virginia. It was a fairly pricy resort with many outdoor activities to offer. We decided I could manage a carriage ride, so we scheduled the sixty-minute version. While the day was very chilly and overcast, we enjoyed a quiet ride along a trail that led through the woods. Blankets were provided, so I managed to keep warm enough to enjoy the ride. Otherwise, we ate, read, napped, and ate some more. The food was above average, and the atmosphere was quite pleasant. Since the chemo I was on at the time didn't affect my taste buds, I was able to enjoy the meals. However, I did have to avoid heat, so I was unable to relax in the hot springs. The entire resort was built around the hot springs, but I would have to leave that part out. Our room seemed to be at the very farthest end of the main building. Each time we had to go to the body of the hotel for our activities, I would have to stop once or twice to rest before I could travel the full distance. My body would feel weak; I would get shaky and find myself out of breath and dripping with sweat. I felt pathetic at this point, being unable to even walk at a slow pace to get from one place to another. But I took my time, slowed down, and managed to get there.

Our formal dinner was quite pleasant. We reminisced about the places we'd been, which places we liked best, and what things we'd done at each place. I was happy to have had the chance to spend time not only in exclusive places but also in beautiful and enjoyable places. Who would have ever thought I'd go to Hawaii—what a glorious place. When Bill was able to go as a top-selling agent for a major insurance company, his aunt Jane offered to pay my way. She was a generous person with wealthy means and a willingness to share them at unexpected times. Silently, I thanked her often, not only for her sharing of her wealth but also for her generosity of spirit. A brief few months after she found out she had a cancerous brain tumor at the age of eighty-three, she passed away in July 2010. The beginning of my cancer journey paralleled her entire trip, and I was sad to see her go. In addition, through Bill's work as an insurance agent (when he was a top seller and when he served on boards of directors), I got opportunities to spend time in places like the Phoenician in Scottsdale, Arizona; the Bahamas; Cancun; and Naples. Not only were they extravagant places to stay, but they had multiple activities planned for each day so maximum enjoyment could be had by all. We thanked our lucky stars for these good experiences, as we knew they were things many people would never have the opportunity to do. During dinner, we relived the high points of these trips, and we added this last trip to the Homestead to our list of fine places we'd visited.

MAKING LIFE FROM A SCRAP

Although I wasn't in the peak of health when I found out I had cancer, I still had a life. I walked in one day a whole person, and I walked out a few hours later with a tiny scrap, like a little piece of lint, barely discernible in the palm of my hand. It was as if someone had made a trade for me: "In return for your old life, here's what you get." Not much of a trade.

I got up one morning and decided I needed to get rid of some of the hundreds of old e-mails that were still hanging out in my inbox. I started at the bottom. I saved all the photos Nikki sent me of Molly; how could I ever delete them? I found one from last October of Molly in a Halloween sleeper. She was stretched out in her crib, sleeping in the position she seemed to enjoy the most at that time, with her arms tucked behind her head. I sent it to Nikki so that as she got Molly ready to go trick-or-treating, she could remember how much difference a year had made. We exchanged a few humorous/sentimental e-mails about this.

As I looked at the old photos of Molly, I could feel my heart getting warm. I was smiling inside, happy that I had been around long enough to see this tiny part of her life unfold. I was thrilled that Nikki takes the time to send me photos of Molly all the time, knowing that I don't do Facebook. I didn't get up feeling grateful to be alive, but within the first hour of my being up, I experienced a little fleck of joy. It didn't last long, though, because it quickly segued into sadness for all the parts of Molly's life I will not be able to share. I began to weep for those times I will never know. Have I obliterated those few moments of happiness and wiped the slate clean again? Is someone up there somewhere shaking his or her head, saying, "Tsk. There she goes again, being negative. I saved her life, and she can't even be thankful that I let her see a grandchild, already for over a year, without feeling sorry for herself and focusing on what she won't get to experience! How ungrateful!"

And so the yo-yo goes up and down, spinning round and round, sometimes seemingly in slow motion, sometimes so fast and so wildly I think I might fall off. I am happy for these little moments of joy, no matter how tiny they are or how long they last. I drink them down like someone who has been in the desert too long and must take her water in tiny sips, lest that which could save her becomes her undoing. I take them all, regardless of their size.

When I was the clinical director at ARC Manor, one of the counselors was struggling with her sessions. I could easily see the problem, but I needed to find a way for her to see it. In staff meetings, as she recounted the events of a particular session, I would see her roll her eyes as if to say of her client's disclosures, "Can you believe she said something that dumb?" Her sessions made me think of someone walking along a stream, seeing all the little pebbles lining the banks. Among the thousands of stones are strewn little diamond chips. The person isn't really paying attention, and so she is missing the diamonds. Well, this counselor was definitely not seeing the diamonds, and as a result, she was missing out on rare opportunities to take her clients to new places. Now I am walking that streambank, ever watchful for those diamond chips. When I find them, I cherish them and make them last as long as I can.

If I were Harry Potter after a year at Hogwarts, I would wave my magic wand, and—*Poof!*—my life would be restored to its former glory. Since I'm not, I plod along, struggling to find some treasure, some way to see the pleasure and wonder of each day. My friend Donna gave me a little book of daily inspirational sayings. I get e-mails from people who have little tags at the end about getting up each day thankful to be alive and showing gratitude for life. I wonder how these people would do in my situation. Perhaps they are better than I am. Perhaps they would be able to put aside the fact that, from out of nowhere, their lives have been snatched from them, and in return for all their years of investment, they have been handed a little piece of lint.

Perhaps.

Chapter Twelve

GRANDDAUGHTERS AND WEDDINGS

Tony was a small, wiry Italian man with a thick accent, sun-darkened skin, and the body of a man who had spent many years bent over working in a garden. He reminded me of the fig trees in his backyard, which he brought with him as a teenager when he made the journey to Kittanning from Italy. Tony was very intense, and it seemed he was incapable of speaking to anyone in his family without raising his voice. Yet he had a playful side and never failed to catch some quirky bit of humor in what others said or did.

When I started at the Kittanning Campus of IUP in January 1970, I became friends with his daughter Rose Ann. She worked in one of the local stores that I frequented on a regular basis. I have no recollection of how or why we actually connected, but we became fast friends, and she welcomed me into her home. Visiting her family stirred memories of my mother's family. My grandmother had come from Poland when she was thirteen. No sooner had you walked in than you were ushered into the kitchen and plied with food and drink.

Even after I graduated from college in December 1973, we stayed in touch. In 1977, I once again found myself living in Kittanning, after I took my job at ARC Manor, the drug and alcohol rehab clinic where I worked for twenty and one-half years. On May 6, 1978, Bill and I were married, and we settled down in Kittanning. On a summer evening, when we lived in town, we might walk through the neighborhood, and at times would find ourselves stopping to visit Tony, Rose Ann, and the rest of their family. Tony was entertaining, and to this day, we recall some of his quips and can recite them verbatim.

It is one such quote that comes to mind now. It was perhaps on a day after we found out I was pregnant, and Tony was congratulating us. He likely had taken Bill down to his basement to give him a glass of his homemade wine, to toast the occasion. As we sat in the living room, Tony talked with us about how important kids are. "Two people who are married without any kids are like two logs lying in the corner," he said. This was a powerful statement. We knew what he meant. Children bring a couple to life. Without them, they are like dead wood.

This would have been true for Bill and me. While people certainly have a wide variety of reasons for the choices they make regarding family, having kids undoubtedly has been the single most significant event in our lives. It gave us the opportunity to learn about ourselves, each other, our children, and life in general. I can remember thinking about how I might explain to my child why he had to wear a seatbelt though I wasn't doing the same. At that moment, I began to wear a seatbelt, and I have never gone without one since. Yes, having kids forced us to think about our ideas, values, and behaviors.

Marc and Pat are two souls we have had the extreme honor of being a part of, the most delightful pleasure in knowing, and the deepest sense of responsibility for teaching about life. I remember the day each of them was born, and the look on each of their faces as they made their entrance into this world. Their expressions at that time are forever embedded into my soul. They spoke to me, as if with words.

The next big thing that comes close to matching the feeling of having children is seeing each child married—married to a kindred spirit. When I found out I had cancer, the very first moment of profound sadness was the thought that I had never held a grandchild. Marc and

Nikki had been together for six years, and married for four after that, by the time I had cancer. Pat and Carrie had been together for six years, and although they were not married, I knew that for them it would be a mere formality. Both of my sons were deeply in love, and committed to their women. So my first and deepest sadness was for the grandchild I had never held.

As time has gone on for me, more than I imagined I would have—more than would have been possible but for the fact that it was 2010 when I was diagnosed and I have a wonderfully brilliant doctor—I have been able to enjoy these two biggest of experiences in the life of a parent. I have a grandchild, and Pat and Carrie are married!

MOLLY

It's a Friday evening. Bill has just gotten home from work, and he is quickly changing his clothes, slipping into something more casual. We are meeting friends at St. Jude Golf Club for dinner. I have spent the last hour getting a shower, changing the colostomy appliance, and getting dressed. To be there on time, we need to leave in a few minutes. Bill's cell phone rings. It's Marc, asking if I am home too. He tells Bill he will call us back in a few minutes. I think this is strange, but we are rushing, so I don't give it much more thought.

We are in the car, headed down the road. Within five minutes, Bill's cell phone rings, and since he has the hands-free version, he lets it go to the speaker in the car.

"Well, we just wanted you to be the first ones to know that Nikki is pregnant."

There is a moment of silence.

"Wow! That's pretty exciting news," one of us says, or maybe both.

We chat for a minute or two, getting the details: when she's due, whether everything is going all right, and how Nikki is feeling. Bill hangs up. I feel strangely still and silent. I can't seem to process this information. Somehow, it doesn't sink in, and the emptiness doesn't seem to be filling up, as I would expect it to with this news. Of course, I am very excited, but it doesn't seem to be penetrating into my heart. Maybe I am afraid to allow myself to believe I will be around long enough to be a grandma. It is October, and I have to still be here at the end of June next year. Can I make it that long?

Time slowly moves along. By amazing coincidence, I find myself at Magee-Womens Hospital, having a scan, while Nikki is in labor a few floors up. I am sitting in a waiting area on the first floor, anticipating the phone call that will make me a grandma. How can I go home? In a little over an hour, my phone rings. Marc tells me Molly is here. I go upstairs, and after a brief wait, Marc comes out of the room to greet me. We hug, and I weep. Marc wears the exhausted, satisfied, preoccupied expression of a first-time father; everything is over, and all is well.

"I don't know why anyone who knows what to expect would ever *want* to go through natural childbirth!" he says. He is feeling Nikki's pain, and I can see that he aches for her.

I can't help him with that. It is a thing only time, and watching your baby grow up, seems to impact. It's a very personal experience, and I know Nikki's isn't the same as mine. The good thing is that the labor, in the overall scheme of things, is short-lived. Once you heal, most of the time, it fades.

I walk tentatively into the room, and there is Nikki, sitting up in bed, finishing her lunch. She has the exhausted, pink-cheeked, but somehow happy look of a brand-new mother. I glance to the left, and there, tightly wrapped in a pink blanket, is Molly Elizabeth Schneider. She has a good amount of dark hair peeking from beneath her little stocking cap. Like her mother's, her eyes are deep and dark. They are wide open, and they stay open for the entire visit. She looks directly into my eyes with a thoughtful expression. This was my first impression, and it continues every time I see Molly. She is very thoughtful.

Molly is the apple of her father's eye, the joy of her mother's spirit, and the new love of her grandma's and grandpa's lives! She is already one year and four months old. Of course, she is beautiful, clever, funny, smart, and on and on and on. Early on, she demonstrated an amazing sense of balance. She will be like her mother, with an exceptional talent for dance and physical agility. Like her father, she won't miss a single detail of what's going on in the world around her.

I remember how my kids, when they were little, gave me a whole new appreciation for the world, especially small things and things that were going on below my knees—things in their field of vision. Molly has given me a refresher course. I see in her expressions her mind beginning to work as she interprets the world around her. I remember noticing these things in Marc and Pat, and it is still just as fascinating. I know she is surrounded by so much love from her mother and father that she has a wonderful security base from which to go out and explore and learn.

I run into trouble when I have to think about all the things I would want to do with Molly but will likely not have the chance to do. How can it be enough to just know her for a year or so? What about a sleepover at Grandma and Grandpa's? What about going into the backyard and picking blueberries, and then coming into the kitchen and making them into a pie or putting them in pancakes? What about walking out in the field to see the butterflies and pick wildflowers? What about bird watching, reading books, talking about the past? I bought a book designed to help a grandma to tell some of her stories to her grandchild. I have to get working on that. How can that be enough? It will have to be, along with stories from her mom and dad, from her grandpa, and from her uncle Pat and aunt Carrie. I hope they can make me come to life for her. I want her to think of me as a fun person, and to know how much I love her.

Molly is coming to visit in two days. I am already excited. I bought her a new toy: colored wires with wooden beads, between two round wooden plates. I think she will like it. Bill and I had bought her a giant stuffed dog for Christmas last year, to keep here for when she visits. She is as big as one of his legs, and she has only shown interest in him in the last couple visits. When she is coming, I set him on the floor in front of the fireplace and put her toys around him. Maybe someday she'll take a nap on him. Maybe she'll never be attracted to him. That's okay. It's up to her. I can't wait to see her.

When I go for chemo, if I look sad or am crying, some of the nurses right away ask me, "How's Molly?" I guess they think that will cheer me up. Sometimes it does; other times it makes me feel worse because it reminds me of how little time I will have with her.

PAT AND CARRIE

At the last two weddings we attended as a family, many people, including the bride and groom in each case, commented that Pat and Carrie would/should be next. They both just laughed, and nothing more was said. In December 2011, when Pat and Carrie came home for a weekend visit, Bill and I immediately knew something was different. Not always quick on the uptake, I didn't notice at first that Carrie had her left hand out in front of her. Finally, we both got it. She had a beautiful diamond ring on her finger.

Still delighted, and with high energy, she related details of the proposal, while Pat stood to the side, just grinning. Patrick had planned a romantic series of events that culminated in Dexter, their dog, delivering Carrie her diamond engagement ring. They were engaged! How exciting! After eight years, they had decided to formalize their relationship. They spent the evening visiting friends and family, spreading the good news. The next evening, Carrie was sitting in the living room with her computer, checking out places to have their wedding and reception. No moss grew under that girl's feet! She is a teacher—a planner and organizer. Her skills came in quite handy for planning this biggest of events in her life. And plan she did! Within a short month or two, they had chosen the place for their wedding and reception. Carrie had her dress ordered, bridesmaids outfitted, and colors chosen; everything was in the works.

While I am always happy to help, I would never want to intrude on such a personal and intimate occasion, so I offered my services as a drone. I got to address the wedding invitations since I have some limited skill in calligraphy, and I helped glue flowers to little trees for centerpieces. I was delighted to be of some use. Watching Pat and Carrie orchestrate this occasion brought back memories of their move to Colorado a few years earlier. They seemed to cover all the bases. The wedding went off without a hitch.

I wanted desperately to look like a "normal" mother of the groom. Using mostly the Internet for browsing and getting ideas, I managed to put together the necessities for that day. I ordered a dress and even a new wig for the occasion, and I spent an obscene amount of money on shoes I was not likely to wear many more times. I even splurged on a bra fitting! What a ridiculous extravagance!

On the day of their wedding, I carefully scheduled taking my pain pills, so I could maximize their effectiveness. It was a long day, and I would be much more active than I would on a typical day. As soon as we stepped out of the car, I put my little gate up and left it there for the rest of the day. Mindfulness. I didn't want my cancer to have any place that day; this was about Pat and Carrie's wedding. I pretended I didn't notice the looks I got that said, "You look pretty good for someone who has cancer." I quickly cut off the two people who had the audacity to attempt to strike up a conversation with me about my cancer treatment. I would take nothing away from Pat and Carrie. This was their day.

It was an event to remember. Most of the guests stayed until closing time, and the dance floor was full all night long. Young and old alike had a wonderful time. Weeks after that wonderful day, I was still receiving compliments about what a great wedding it was. I think the sparks of love between Pat and Carrie made it so. During the reception, one of their high school friends wandered around making a video for the happy couple. She would stop people and ask them to say something about Pat and Carrie. Even after so many years together, Pat and Carrie look at each other with stars in their eyes! Sorry guys. Perhaps that sounds very tacky, but it is still true. That was my comment for them, something for them to remember their wedding day by: "May you be starry-eyed for each other as long as you live."

Once again, this is only the beginning. How is it enough? What a bittersweet occasion. To think about all the thrills of their lives I won't be here to share is a sadness beyond measure. To watch them build a family, to hold their first child … it's too much to think about. They are coming tonight, and they will be bringing our grandpuppy! I'll just think about that. I haven't seen Dexter for over a month; maybe I had better go out and buy him a new toy. I still have the "flat cat" I bought him a couple months ago. I think it has lasted longer than any other toy I've bought him, but that's because it had no stuffing to begin with—hence the name. He loves it. We've spent much time playing with it—throw fetch, or "Just try to get this away from me!" Yes, tonight will be a good night.

Chapter Thirteen

THE GIFT

Go in search of your Gift. The more you understand
yourself, the more you will understand the world.
—Paulo Coelho, *Life*

It is Tuesday, January 15, 2013. It has been one week since my manuscript was returned from the line editor. I know I need a new title and a new ending, but my writing seems to have run dry. Concentrate as I might nothing comes to me. My body feels heavy, the sadness in my soul hanging there like a piece of lead. Maybe I resist ending this book because it makes me feel like I am ending my newly discovered purpose in living. I only just found that purpose such a short time ago. Will I have to start again then, searching once again for some sense of fulfillment? Will I go back full time to sitting in my chair, watching as this now all-too-familiar shadow of my former self fades even further?

I am getting ready to have lunch with Patrick and this makes me happy. I concentrate on this, knowing it will be a pleasure to see him. I look forward to his company. It doesn't matter what we talk about; I know I will leave him with my spirit rejuvenated.

The phone rings. I look at the clock, seeing that it is 12:10 p.m. I feel a slight reaction of annoyance, since I need to leave by 12:30 p.m. to be on time for our luncheon.

Who is calling me now? I ask myself in irritation.

I answer the phone completely surprised to find out that it is someone I haven't had a conversation with in fifteen years. It is someone I had no interest in having a conversation with. When we parted ways all that time ago it was not on the best of terms. She lived in a part of my life that I put behind me. She has no place in my current journey. Yet here she is seeking entrance. By the end of our conversation we have scheduled a time to get together and talk.

I hang up the phone and continue to get ready. I can feel my body shaking. I almost feel giddy, with a sort of buzzing sensation fluttering through my body. I come out to the kitchen and decide to take my blood pressure. When I took it at 10:30 a.m. it was 100/64, and my heart rate was seventy-eight. Now it is 134/81 and my heart rate is ninety-three. For some reason this makes me laugh. I write it down because I want to be sure to tell this person what kind of effect she still has on me.

Last week, in a conversation with a friend I made the comment that I would not refuse to talk with someone who has asked to speak with me. I have a friend whom I've all but begged to talk with me so we can resolve a conflict. She has been unwilling. It is almost impossible to think of a time or situation where I would refuse to honor such a request.

Sometimes coincidences seem to be much more than just that. When they pack that extra punch I always think of them as opportunities. My friend Lynn and I have discussed this concept many times. If something stands out, or maybe seems to be an omen of sorts, it should not be ignored. Could an opportunity ever be more clear than this one I have just become aware of? This person from my past has told me that after a friend's death it set her to thinking about her own life, perhaps her own mortality, and somehow, our old relationship came to her mind. Maybe this is a way for her to sort some things out. Maybe she has some things to look at, and maybe I can help her. Yes, this is an opportunity I dare not ignore. Here is about the biggest chance I could ever get to be a woman of my word.

Harry Chapin was a wonderful storyteller who had a knack for putting his tales to music. His songs bring to life the complicated relationships between people and the dilemmas of everyday living. In his album *Greatest Stories Live,* Harry entertains the audience with that epic tale of "Thirty Thousand Pounds of Bananas." Unable to come up with a good ending, he goes through four possibilities, much to the enjoyment of those in attendance. In his final ending, Harry conveys the message that even though there was a horrific crash, a man died, and the thirty thousand pounds of bananas were destroyed, life in that small town goes on.

Maybe I'm like Harry Chapin. Maybe my book is like his song and I can't find a good ending because although it's the end of my book, it's not the end of my journey. Maybe when I got that call today it was a reminder that I still live, and therefore I still have things to do. Maybe it's not about the accomplishment of some fantastic feat; it's about making the most of those opportunities I do get. I may feel like I'm living a scrap of a life, but that doesn't measure the level of meaning attached to what I do. Maybe this woman who was once my great friend needs me to help her with her journey.

We don't always get to choose the way life teaches us lessons, or the way we learn what we need to know. If we open ourselves, opportunities present themselves in many ways, sometimes when we least expect them and sometimes in barely discernible ways.

I chose to write this book because it was an opportunity. It was an opportunity for me to use what I learned to help others understand some important things. Although this part of my journey has been related to cancer, life has presented me the opportunity to learn about many things beyond cancer. It is about finding a way to make life meaningful in its day-to-day passage. It's about not turning away regardless of how happy or sad I might become. In this journey, I have experienced a depth of sadness I could never have imagined and I think I had to experience that. If having cancer came with an instruction manual, I think it would say something like: "Do not change the volume. Do not adjust the color. Best when traveled 'as is,' and experienced with your heart and soul open. No additives included."

Having cancer ended my life as I knew it, but it took me a while to realize and accept that. In some moments it feels like I've had cancer forever, yet at other times it seems I've just begun. Here I am now, though, closing in on three years of this shadowy life. When it all started I would never have believed I could achieve the sense of fulfillment I've gotten from writing this book. It is an awesome feeling. Yet a heartbeat away, just a fraction of an inch from my emotional field of vision, hide the never-ending moments of intense sadness that have become the stock-in-trade of my life. I don't know if the yo-yo has stopped moving, or if I have become so accustomed to the ups and downs that it just feels still. Maybe it doesn't really matter. In the end it is my life.

While the writing of this book is almost over, I still live and I still have things to do. I have this former friend to talk with. I have so many more lunches to have. I bought my husband an online cooking class for Christmas, so I have many more new meals to sample. He and I have to make a trip to Utah to see Arches National Park together. I have two new ideas for books I want to write. And while I do these things, I still have so much more I need to learn about life.

Endnotes

1. Paulo Coelho, *Life: Selected Quotations* (London: Harper Collins Publishers, 2004).
2. Ted Andrews, *Animal-Speak: The Spiritual & Magical Powers of Creatures Great & Small* (Woodbury, Minnesota: Llewellyn Publications, 2009).
3. "Ovarian Cancer," American Cancer Society, accessed November 28, 2012, http://www.cancer.org/cancer/ovariancancer/detailedguide/index.
4. Foundation for Women's Cancer, *Understanding CA 125 Levels: A Guide for Ovarian Cancer Patients*, accessed November 27, 2012, http://www.wcn.org/downloads/CA125levels.pdf.
5. "Master Gardener Program," Penn State College of Agricultural Sciences, accessed November 28, 2012, from http://extension.psu.edu/master-gardener.
6. A. Tresca, *Inflammatory Bowel Disease (IBD): What to Expect Before, During, and After Colostomy Surgery*, accessed November 28, 2012, http://ibdcrohns.about.com/cs/ostomyinformation/a/colostomysurg.htm
7. Lois Almadrones, Anne Marie Flaherty, and Catherine Hydzik, *Your Guide to Intraperitoneal Therapy*, published 2005, http://www.gog.org/ipchemoed/iptherapyguide.pdf.
8. Steven Vasilev, "Ovarian Cancer: Optimal Cytoreduction or Debulking," last modified February 18, 2008, http://ovariancancer.about.com/od/surgery/a/ovca_debulking.htm.
9. "Implantable Port Devices," C. R. Bard, Inc., accessed November 27, 2012, http://www.bardaccess.com/port-powerport.php.
10. David Servan-Schreiber, *Anticancer, A New Way of Life* (New York: Viking, 2009).
11. Miguel De Unamuno, *Tragic Sense of Life*, trans. J. E. Crawford Fitch (New York: Dover Publications, 1954).
12. Raven Grimassi, *Beltane: Springtime Rituals, Lore & Celebration* (St. Paul, Minnesota: Llewellyn Publications, 2001).

Acknowledgments

What started out as a five-hundred-word paper for an online writing class turned into a book. I thank the teacher who, unbeknownst to him, inspired me to even think about something like this. When I've read acknowledgments in other books, it has been difficult for me to understand the level of gratitude I've often found expressed. Now I get it.

I could never have done this without the help, support, and editing efforts of my friends. Lisa, you have been my guide. You helped me to think like a writer. You asked me the questions so I knew what answers to search for. And, more importantly, you walked with me on my journey, on so many levels. Darlene, you kept the larger objective in mind and considered everything in that light. Rick, you pushed me to continually reveal deeper levels of my soul. Cassie, I have been amazed by your astute editing skills. Betty, you helped me stay attuned to what were the key elements of my book. You have all been my lifeline. Each of you has been able to provide me with invaluable insight, emotional support, and never-ending encouragement. Marc, Pat, Nikki, and Carrie, your willingness to respond has filled me with love and reminded me that I still have things to live for. Marilyn, Sandy, Elaine, Lynn, Terry, Donna, Mary, Jackie, Diane, Susan, and Mary Ann, you have all helped me to remember the reader's perspective.

You have all come into my world without question, with love and a willingness to learn with me and to walk this journey with me. Because of you, I have not been alone.

Bill, in your willingness to read as I've written, you have taken the journey twice. I am sad to think of the pain you have experienced, but I am happy that it is you who has been with me throughout.

CPSIA information can be obtained at www.ICGtesting.com
Printed in the USA
BVOW080745270313

316532BV00002B/4/P